Trading Fixed Income and FX in Emerging Markets: A Practitioner's Guide

Trading Fixed Income and FX in Emerging Markets: A Practitioner's Guide

DIRK WILLER

RAM BALA CHANDRAN
KENNETH LAM

WILEY

Library of Congress Cataloging-in-Publication Data

Names: Willer, D. (Dirk), author. | Chandran, Ram Bala, author. | Lam,
   Kenneth (Emerging Market Strategist), author.
Title: Trading fixed income and fx in emerging markets : a practitioner's
   guide / Dirk Willer, Ram Bala Chandran, Kenneth Lam.
Description: Hoboken, New Jersey : John Wiley & Sons, Inc., [2020] |
   Includes bibliographical references and index.
Identifiers: LCCN 2020029294 (print) | LCCN 2020029295 (ebook) | ISBN
   9781119598992 (hardback) | ISBN 9781119599029 (adobe pdf) | ISBN
   9781119599050 (epub)
Subjects: LCSH: Fixed-income securities—China. | Foreign exchange
   futures—China.
Classification: LCC HG5782 .W55 2020 (print) | LCC HG5782 (ebook) | DDC
   332.63/2044—dc23
LC record available at https://lccn.loc.gov/2020029294
LC ebook record available at https://lccn.loc.gov/2020029295

Cover Design: Wiley
Cover Image: © metamorworks/Getty Images

Printed in the United States of America.

SKY10076511_060324

Contents

List of Figures

List of Tables

Introduction

This book will make you a better portfolio manager and risk-taker. The key to succeeding in markets is twofold. First, a solid methodology is crucial. And second, conviction to press the bets when the stars align may be even more important. The two issues are obviously linked. A solid methodology is, after all, what creates conviction. Such a methodology can come from participating in markets for a long time and internalizing what "works" along the way. The gut feeling of an experienced portfolio manager may be what gives conviction. But there is a shortcut: data can substitute for hands-on experience and is likely superior. After all, backtesting trading rules and analysing what works across many countries, instruments, and time periods is more reliable than just using data subconsciously collected during an individual trading career, which is necessarily more limited in terms of instruments traded and timespans covered. This book does the data analysis for our readers to generate a robust trading methodology for emerging markets. The result is a set of empirically validated rules of thumb that we find helpful to generate alpha. The rules are valuable for benchmarked long-only investment funds as well as for hedge funds. We establish both what works and what does not work (even though many think it does). Often, it is of equal value to understand what does not work, as noise reduction is important to generate conviction.

This book will make you a better policy maker. While the book is written from the perspective of making money in markets, some chapters are also relevant for policy makers. In particular, it is very important for policy makers to understand how markets will react to their various measures, whether they are FX interventions, IMF programmes, or interest rate policies. The actions of policy makers generate many of the opportunities for markets. But at the same time, understanding markets creates opportunities for policy makers.

This book will make you a better academic and quantitative researcher. This book is not written with an academic mindset. And although writing the book involved a significant amount of coding, we also do not do the work of hardcore quants. We are willing to live with small sample sizes and simplifying assumptions in our backtests. In order to bring the ideas across, we typically assume zero transaction costs, and we don't worry about risk-management overlays. But the book is about systematic ideas and figuring out how markets work. We trust that academics and quantitative researchers will find many of the ideas interesting and worthy of further study. This book will make academics' output more relevant to the real world.

Combined, the authors have more than 40 years of experience in emerging fixed-income and FX markets. Having interacted with thousands of investors across real money funds, hedge funds, pension funds, sovereign wealth funds, corporates, and policy makers, we have learned a lot from our clients over the years. Dirk and Ken have been ranked the first team in the institutional investor (II) survey for Latin America fixed income for the last four years. The global EM strategy team, headed by Dirk, is ranked the first team for Asia, CEEMEA, and Latam for both FX and interest rates, and the second team for Latam sovereign credit in the first global II survey in 2018. The long-term performance of Dirk's and Ken's published investment recommendations has been very strong throughout bull and bear markets.[1] As such, the methodology that we are proposing in this book has stood the test of time. One reason for the resilience of our framework is that we care mostly about "deep" fundamentals of human psychology and behavioural patterns that are unlikely to change, rather than just economic fundamentals. We therefore expect and certainly hope that our framework will add value in the future. But the future is the future. There are no guarantees, and keeping an open mind is the key to succeeding in trading.

So why did we write this book? Either our framework is helpful to make money, and then why tell anyone, given that it may deteriorate if more traders apply it; or our framework is not helpful, and then why waste the time writing a book about it?

The answer is that we do not think that publishing the book will impact our strategies much. After all, we have produced research on the sell side for many years, and this has not led to a noticeable deterioration of our trading strategies. While markets always change, we think they change fairly slowly. Constant research is necessary to keep on top of markets, and we are excited to keep working to constantly update our framework.

On a related topic, we also note that the bulk of this book was written during 2018 and 2019 in a process that was admittedly slow, mostly due to the demands of our day jobs. While it is always tempting to keep updating the chapters, especially in light of the momentous developments in early 2020, we have resisted this temptation. The vast majority of our trading rules would have worked well since the completion of the relevant chapters, and we think not updating gives readers a good sense of a true out-of-sample performance of our framework.

The book is organized as follows:

Chapter 1: EMFX and Fixed Income: Where the Opportunities Lie. The chapter illustrates the importance of EMFX and fixed-income markets, why continued future growth is likely, and why EM are a key source of alpha. For readers who are familiar with the EM universe, the main topic of interest will be our analysis of the strategies the EM investment funds currently employ to outperform and how much herding behaviour this generates.

Chapter 2: Global Macro Rules. EM is 65% global macro and 35% local, at least in EMFX and credit. EM rates have a higher local component. The chapter explains how views on global macro assets can be implemented in EM to outperform the EM

---

[1]Footnote: For performance attribution of the EM local market (paper) model portfolio, see Willer et al. (2020).

benchmarks and trade EM assets. At times, there are important lags between those macro assets and the EM assets, and lags generate opportunities.

Chapter 3: China: The Only Emerging Market That Counts. China is the only EM that deserves its own chapter. We explain how to trade the Chinese fixed-income and FX markets. We also highlight how China impacts the rest of the emerging world and how to position for that.

Chapter 4: How to Trade EMFX. The meat of the book starts with Chapter 4. Here we investigate which systematic strategies work for EMFX trading and which do not. Many factors have much weaker performance these days: in particular, *carry*, in its simplest form, has broken down. We propose alternative strategies to earn carry. We also highlight growth as a profitable factor. We introduce some technicals that work well.

Chapter 5: How to Trade EMFX: Event Guide. We explain how to generate alpha from recurring events in the FX market, such as intervention, emergency rate hikes, IMF packages, elections, and certain economic data releases. All event-related trading strategies are thoroughly backtested.

Chapter 6: How to Trade Emerging Market Rates: The Cycle. We analyse in depth the reaction function of EM central banks and explain how to trade the typical interest rate cycle in both the US and EM. We show how to use valuation measures like term premia to generate alpha.

Chapter 7: Real Rates: Simply Superior. We explain the important market for linkers in EM and propose some backtested rules of thumb on how to add alpha by switching between linkers and nominal bonds.

Chapter 8: How to Trade EM Rates: Event Guide. We investigate and backtest how to trade recurring events in rates space: economic data, curve inversion, index inclusion, and natural disasters.

Chapter 9: How to Trade EM Credit. We explore how to trade the EM credit cycle, and we explain what Warren Buffett and Ray Dalio would do. We also explain how to trade recurring events like IMF packages, defaults, and credit up- and downgrades, and we analyse when to overweight external debt versus local debt and vice versa.

Chapter 10: Portfolio Construction. This chapter investigates smart fixed-income indexes, frontier markets, and portfolio allocation across EM asset classes and explains the importance of derivatives for alpha generation. We also offer a proposal to make ESG more EM-friendly.

Chapter 11: The (Near) Future: Big Data, Machine Learning, and What If There Are No Emerging Markets Left. We discuss the application of big data to EM, and we propose what to focus on first in terms of implementation. We also suggest some machine learning techniques to use for EMFX trading. Finally, we investigate whether it is plausible that we will run out of EM. We very much doubt it.

Thanks for reading this book. And good luck trading.

New York
March 2020

Acknowledgements

I owe deep gratitude to my parents, who supported me through thick and thin. My father worked extensively in Russia and China in the 1980s and 1990s and conveyed to me his vision of a successful economic future for both countries. Crucially, my mother imparted to me a deep interest in politics. Thanks, Mom and Dad.

I am indebted to Sir Richard Layard for inviting me to join his team in Moscow in the early 1990s to work with the Russian government during one of the seminal moments in post-war history. I am also grateful to Professor David Webb for being an inspiring teacher, and for giving an awesome wedding speech. Throughout my life, I have been consistently blessed with great mentors. In particular, I would like to thank Jose Luis Yepez, Thomas Glaessner, Guillermo Mondino, and Rob Rowe for all their support. I owe Rob Rowe and Andrew Pitt a special thank you for wholeheartedly supporting this book project. It is not obvious for a preeminent research organization to share intellectual property with the world, and Andrew's and Rob's leadership is exemplary. I would also like to thank all my clients/friends as well as my research, trading, and sales colleagues/friends at Citi, who with their feedback constantly improve our research effort.

I also want to thank Gemma Valler at Wiley for believing in the project and Elisha Benjamin, Purvi Patel, Gladys Ganaden, and Tiffany Taylor for countless improvements. Jessica James deserves a shout out for the introduction to Wiley. While all mistakes are the sole responsibility of the authors, I want to thank the friends and colleagues who tried hard to minimize them. Special thanks to Tobias Adrian, Amer Bisat, Gaurav Garg, James Keefe, Luis Loera, Ayoti Mittra, Eric Ollom, Ernesto Revilla, Lu Sun and Bruno Vander Cruyssen. I would also like to thank Willem Buiter, Mike Corbat, Pramol Dhawan, Sam Finkelstein, Rob Gibbins, Hari Hariharan, Antti Ilmanen, Paul Tudor Jones, Andrew Lo, Guillermo Ortiz and Nouriel Roubini for looking at early versions of the draft.

Finally, I want to wholeheartedly thank my incredible wife and soul mate for more than 25 years, who has been very supportive of this project, even with four young(ish) children to entertain, while pursuing a very demanding career of her own. Speaking of kids: thank you very much to Charlotte, Caroline, Sophie, and Anna for always reminding me how fascinating life is.

D.W.

I would not have gotten into finance without the Quant Trading and Analysis programme at Citi. Special thanks to Shelli Faber and Andy Feigenberg for running one of the most unique analyst programmes on the street. Special thanks to all my former and current colleagues for their time and counsel. In particular, I would like thank Dirk Willer, Luis Loera, Pere Sole, Gabriel Infante, Vivek Kapoor, Rupak Chatterjee, Raoul Luttik, Vera Kartseva, Sukhjeet Reehal, and Rob Drijkoningen.

Special thanks to my Mom and Dad for being supportive and always going the extra distance for me. My Mom would probably have been happier if I had thanked her in a PhD thesis, but a book is at least a consolation prize. I am grateful for all the support my sister Rohini has given over the years. I hope she will thank me in all the books that she is set to write in the future.

Finally, I am grateful to my wife Swetha for putting up with me in general, and for being supportive and picking up the slack for me regarding everything in life during this book project.

R.B.C.

I would like to thank my colleagues and friends at Citi for their support: in particular, Dirk, who has taught me so much over the years. A grateful thank you to my parents, without whom nothing is possible.

K.L.

Acronyms

ADR	American Depository Receipt
AMLO	López Obrador, President of Mexico
AUM	Assets under management
BOJ	Bank of Japan
bp	Basis point
CA(D)	current account (deficit)
CDS	credit default swap
CEEMEA	Central and Eastern Europe, Middle East, and Africa
CEMBI	Corporate Emerging Market Bond Index (credit)
CGB	Chinese Government Bond
CIBM Direct	China Interbank Bond Market Direct
CTA	commodity trading advisor
CTOT	commodities terms of trade
DM	Developed markets
DV01	Dollar variation in a bond's value for a 1 bp change in yield
DXY	USD index
ECB	European Central Bank
EM	Emerging markets
EMBI	Emerging Market Bond Index (credit)
EMFX	Emerging markets foreign exchange
ETF	Exchange-traded fund
FOMC	Federal Open Market Committee
FX	Foreign exchange
G10	Group of Ten (developed countries)
GBI-EM	Government Bond Index-Emerging Markets (local currency)
HRP	Hierarchical risk parity
HY	High yield
IG	Investment grade
IMF	International Monetary Fund
ISM	Institute for Supply Management PMI

IR	Information ratio
IRS	Interest rate swap
JGB	Japanese Government Bond
Latam	Latin America
LTCM	Long Term Capital Management (a hedge fund)
MA	Moving average
MCap	Market capitalization
Momo	Momentum
NDF	Non-deliverable forward in FX
ND-IRS	Non-deliverable interest rate swap
NFP	US nonfarm payrolls
PBOC	People's Bank of China
PCA	Principle components analysis
PMI	Purchasing Manager Index
PPP	Purchasing power parity
QE	Quantitative easing
QFII	Qualified Foreign Institutional Investor
R^2	A statistical measure of fit
REER	Real effective exchange rate
RQFII	Renminbi Qualified Foreign Institutional Investor
RRR	Required reserves ratio
SDR	Special drawing right
SHCOMP	Shanghai Composite Equity Index
ToT	Terms of trade
TSF	Total social financing
US AGG	US Aggregate Bond Index
US HY	US High Yield Corporate Bond Index
UST	US Treasuries
VIX	Implied volatility index for the S&P
Vol	Volatility
WGBI	World Government Bond Index (local currency)
yoy	Year over year

Trading Fixed Income and FX in Emerging Markets: A Practitioner's Guide

CHAPTER 1

EMFX and Fixed Income: Where the Opportunities Lie

1.1 EM DEBT – GROWING TOO FAST TO IGNORE

Two main growth stories in the emerging market fixed-income space offer major opportunities and lead to increased investor interest and participation: local markets and external debt.

Ever since the emerging markets (EM) crisis of the late 1990s and 2000s, EM countries have tried to unwind the *original sin* of previously having issued large stocks of USD-denominated debt.[1] The reason is that it was the USD debt that caused, or at the very least intensified, the EM crisis in the 1990s. Back then, the USD was in a strong bull market, making USD-denominated debt more expensive to carry and eventually causing mayhem in EM. The main way to reduce this vulnerability stemming from USD debt has been to develop markets for local currency sovereign debt and to substitute external debt for local debt. Many countries have been successful in this undertaking, and as a result, local sovereign debt markets have grown with a 15% compound annual growth rate (CAGR) between 2003 and Q3 2019, compared to about 7% annual growth for USD-denominated sovereign debt. Amazingly, the 2008–2009 global financial crisis made only a shallow and short-lived dent in the high growth of local debt, even when translated into USD terms, as can be seen in Figure 1.1. This is surprising, as EM currencies depreciated sharply during the crisis, impacting the USD value of these markets very negatively. This strong growth in adverse circumstances demonstrates that local emerging market debt has become a major investible asset class and is here to stay.

At the end of the third quarter of 2019, EM sovereign local currency debt markets were capitalized at USD 10.5 trillion. Around USD 5.1 trillion in local government bonds sit in China (roughly evenly split between Chinese Government Bonds (CGBs)

---

[1]Initially, EM were forced to borrow in USD because local currency debt was seen as too risky for most international lenders. This has been referred to as *original sin* (Eichengreen et al. 2007).

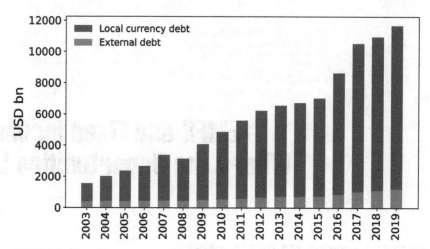

FIGURE 1.1   EM Sovereign Debt Grew Even Through the Great Recession.
Source: Bank for International Settlements.

and policy bank notes).[2] The share of Chinese local government debt as a percentage of EM local debt continues to grow (Figure 1.2).

Another USD 1 trillion of local sovereign debt sits in India. Chinese and Indian local fixed-income markets are not widely owned by foreigners, but this is changing rapidly, partly as China's weight in the global fixed-income indexes grows. China is clearly too large to be ignored by global debt managers, and so is India. China and India are the single biggest sources of growth potential for emerging market debt trading.

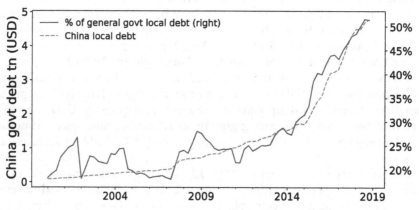

FIGURE 1.2   China is 50% of Local Currency Government Debt – and Rising.
Source: Bank for International Settlements.

---

[2]Adding China's corporate debt and sub-national government debt results in a total market capitalization of around USD 12 trillion.

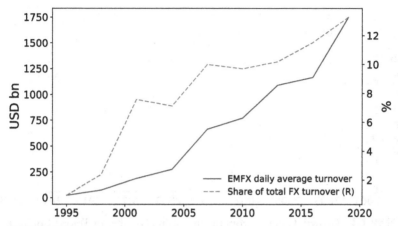

FIGURE 1.3 EMFX Gaining Market Share From G10 FX.
Source: BIS triennial survey.

Furthermore, China entering various developed market fixed-income indexes at a time when it is arguably still an emerging market will force global investors to engage more actively with investing in emerging market local currency denominated bond markets. This is why we dedicate a full chapter of this book to China.

To invest in local currency debt, there is also a need to trade emerging market currencies. Rising EMFX trading volumes are therefore logically going hand in hand with the rise in outstanding local currency debt. As of the last data point (2019) from the Bank for International Settlements, the turnover in EMFX reached USD 1.7 trillion per day, or 13% of the total FX volume, rising from close to zero in 1995 (see Figure 1.3).

External debt is also growing quickly. As of Q3 2019, USD 2.3 trillion of bonds are outstanding. But the shift by sovereign issuers to local markets has muted the growth from existing sovereign issuers. Instead, EM corporate debt issuers are growing rapidly, happily filling this gap. The market has welcomed such corporate issues, in particular from exporters that are considered naturally currency hedged given their USD export revenues. While external corporate issuance has moderated from its earlier breakneck pace, we think it will accelerate again whenever global growth, and therefore corporate capital expenditures (capex), pick up. At the end of 2019, corporate external debt stood at around USD 1.1 trillion. But there also is a growth driver for sovereign external debt, a market that has increased from USD 394 billion in 2003 to USD 1.2 trillion at the end of 2019. Here, the growth story is mostly the increasing number of issuers. Figure 1.4 shows the number of effective country members[3] included in the EM local currency bond index (JPMorgan Government Bond Index-Emerging Markets, or GBI-EM), as well as the EM sovereign bond index (JPMorgan Emerging Market Bond Index, or

---

[3]Effective country members are calculated as $e = \frac{1}{\sum_{i=1}^{n} w_i^2}$, where w_i is the percentage weight of each country in the benchmark. This formula helps to mitigate the impact of countries with a very small weight, as those do not tend to sufficiently diversify the index.

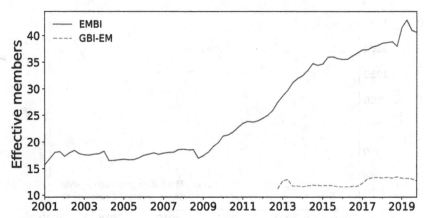

FIGURE 1.4   Growth Coming From the Increasing Number of Traded Countries. *Source:* Bloomberg. Index data courtesy of JPMorgan Chase & Co., copyright 2020, as of 31 December 2019.

EMBI). As can be seen in the chart, post crisis, the number of external sovereign issuers in the index has soared, while the much smaller number of index constituents in the local bond index has barely budged. With new issuers finding it easier to tap the seemingly safer external markets first, this growth of external issuers will eventually spill over into local market issuance and increase the number of countries where local market debt will be actively traded, too.

These EM fixed-income markets are already very substantial and will continue to outgrow their G10 equivalents. In our opinion, EM are currently in a sweet spot. They are large, liquid, and volatile enough to make meaningful investments possible even for large investors, but not so liquid that all the alpha has been arbitraged away.

1.2   RETURNS TOO ATTRACTIVE TO IGNORE

Figure 1.5 shows the historical returns of the most widely followed EM benchmarks for external (EMBI), local (GBI-EM), and (external) corporate debt (Corporate Emerging Market Bond Index, or CEMBI), all produced by JP Morgan. EM sovereign external debt has performed the best since 2003. This is followed by the CEMBI, which in turn has slightly outperformed local markets. Local markets have experienced the highest volatility across the three asset classes, leading to lower information ratios than those achieved by EM credit investors.

To illustrate why this is happening, we take a closer look at the local market index and split the performance into FX and rates, where the rates performances is measured as the EM bond index with FX hedges. As can be seen in Figure 1.6, it turns out that almost all the volatility comes from FX. On a FX-hedged basis, local market bonds display even less volatility than credit indexes. If investors have no edge to forecast FX, the bias has to be to lever up local markets on a FX-hedged basis, rather than to keep EM risk unhedged.

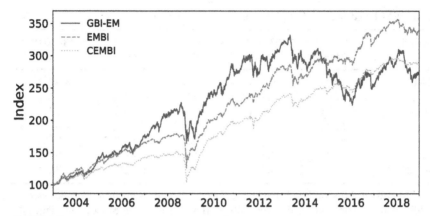

FIGURE 1.5 EM Credit with More Attractive Returns than EM Local.
Source: Bloomberg. Index data courtesy of JPMorgan Chase & Co., copyright 2020, as of 31 December 2018.

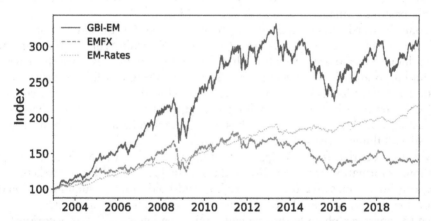

FIGURE 1.6 Most of the Volatility in Local Currency Debt Comes from FX.
Source: Bloomberg. Index data courtesy of JPMorgan Chase & Co., copyright 2020, as of 31 December 2019.

How do those returns compare to global fixed-income indexes? Table 1.1 illustrates the return characteristics of EM versus global fixed-income benchmarks from 2003 to 2019. The table also sheds light on how returns are impacted by the USD. While the early 2000s were characterized by a USD bear market in the aftermath of the bursting Nasdaq bubble, the USD started to rise significantly from 2013 onward. By the end of 2019, this USD bull market has not yet come to an end. Table 1.1 suggests that EM benchmarks have a better return profile than their comparable global fixed-income peers over the full USD cycle. In particular, the EMBI outperforms the broad US credit index (US AGG) over the full cycle and even during the USD bull market (which went hand in hand with an EMFX bear market). Similarly, the GBI-EM outperformed the

TABLE 1.1   EM Fixed Income Outperformed Developed Markets.

Full period	2003–2019			2013–2019		
	Mean	Vol	IR	Mean	Vol	IR
GBI-EM	7.0%	9.5%	0.73	0.17%	8.80%	0.02
EMBI	7.9%	5.5%	1.44	4.52%	4.41%	1.03
EM rates	4.5%	2.6%	1.74	2.13%	2.53%	0.84
CEMBI	6.9%	4.1%	1.67	4.66%	2.67%	1.74
US HY	6.7%	5.1%	1.32	4.94%	3.95%	1.25
US AGG	4.0%	3.5%	1.14	2.64%	3.09%	0.85
WGBI exUSD	4.0%	8.2%	0.49	0.52%	7.28%	0.07

Source: Bloomberg, London Stock Exchange Group plc and its group undertakings (collectively the "LSE Group"), copyright LSE Group 2019, JPMorgan Chase & Co, copyright 2020, as of 31 December 2019.

non-USD portion of the FTSE Russell World Government Bond Index (WGBI) during the full cycle, even though it underperformed during the EM bear market after 2012. Overall, past performance has broadly favoured EM.

Going forward, these trends are likely to continue. On the external market side, this is the case because ratings-adjusted, EM sovereign credits typically trade at a higher spread than US corporates, even though default ratios are usually lower for sovereigns than for corporates; recovery values are also on average higher for sovereigns than for corporates. On the local currency side, rates in developed markets (DM) are so low that EM local rates on a hedged basis will likely continue to outperform. Furthermore, the long-lasting USD bull market, which has undermined unhedged local bond exposure, must, like all things, eventually come to an end.

We also note that from an alpha generation point of view, EMFX deserves special attention. Information ratios in EM credit and in FX hedged local markets may be sufficiently high to bias investors toward a buy-and-hold strategy. But information ratios are too low to buy and hold EM currencies. A more active trading style is therefore needed to generate alpha. On the one hand, this is bad news, as FX is notoriously hard to predict with accuracy and alpha generation is difficult. On the other hand, a focus on FX is a boon for investors, who have an edge as transaction costs for FX are much lower than they are for bonds and leverage is easier to obtain.

There have also been significant differences in performance by region, as can be seen in Table 1.2. In both local and external markets, the highest returns came from Latin America. Luckily for the asset class, Latam also has the highest weight in both local and external debt indexes. In external markets, the Middle East's performance comes close, but on a much smaller index weight. The lowest returns have occurred in Asia for both asset classes. As Latam is famously high carry, while Asia is mostly low carry, returns are in line with the carry on offer. This would suggest that the regional pattern is going to persist, as carry differentials still favour Latam over Asia. Asia also has the lowest volatility in both asset classes. This results in information ratios in Asia that are quite competitive and actually higher than they are for Latam in local markets. In external markets, the Middle East has the lowest volatility, leading to a superior information ratio. For investors with access to leverage, lower-yielding and safer regions outperform.

TABLE 1.2 Latam as a Key Contributor to Index Returns.

	Mean	Vol	IR	Weight
Local markets				
Africa	8.1%	20.5%	0.4	8%
Latam	8.7%	11.6%	0.75	35%
Europe	6%	12.9%	0.47	32%
Asia	5.9%	6.7%	0.88	24%
External markets				
Middle East	5.1%	7.2%	0.70	12%
Africa	4.9%	7.8%	0.62	13%
Europe	4.9%	8.2%	0.59	21%
Latam	5.2%	9.2%	0.57	35%
Asia	4.1%	7.5%	0.54	19%

Note: 2003 to 2019.
Source: Bloomberg, authors' calculations. Index data courtesy of JPMorgan Chase & Co., copyright 2020, as of 31 December 2019.

We address this topic more thoroughly later in the book. But if there is one region that deserves most of the focus, at least for cash-constrained investors, it is Latam, due to its high index weight and strong returns.

1.3 EM AS AN ALPHA OPPORTUNITY

As EM investors understand, and as we will illustrate in Chapter 2, the global macro environment is of paramount importance for EM performance. This poses the question of whether, in the period under study, EM credit investors simply got lucky because US credit did so well. Similarly, EM local investors first benefited from a weak USD environment in the early years, especially in conjunction with broadly falling yields in the US, before getting unlucky with a stronger USD environment in the latter years. If the outperformance of EM was really only about the global environment, it might be better for investors to just trade DM bonds, credit, and currencies, rather than wading into less-liquid EM. To see if EM truly justify the investment of time and resources, we try to replicate the GBI-EM with US rates and the big USD Index (DXY). We first calculate one-year rolling betas of the GBI-EM to those two global factors. We then use the betas to determine the size of the position in US Treasuries and DXY to replicate GBI-EM. Figure 1.7 shows that the GBI-EM strongly outperforms this simple replication strategy. We conclude that there are substantial alpha opportunities in EM and that EM cannot be easily replicated by the equivalent DM assets. At the same time, we also note that the correlation between EM indexes and their G10 replication strategy is high enough to make the applicable G10 assets good hedges for an EM portfolio.

In addition to the alpha that comes from correct global macro or specific EM asset class calls, there is significant scope to generate alpha within the asset class. Figure 1.8

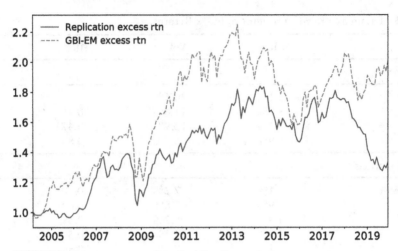

FIGURE 1.7   EM Returns are Hard to Replicate.
Source: Bloomberg, authors' calculations. Index data courtesy of
JPMorgan Chase & Co., copyright 2020, as of 31 December 2019.

shows the dispersion of returns for EMFX, EM rates, and EM sovereign credit, defined as the return of the top 10th percentile minus the return of the lowest 10th percentile of the countries in the index. All three asset classes offer significant alpha opportunities from country selection, as dispersion is often greater than 10%, and rises even higher during crisis episodes. Interestingly, dispersion in EMFX is the highest. Dispersion in credit is very similar to EMFX, while dispersion in EM rates is much lower. To be precise, the median dispersion from 2004 to 2018 was 6.9% in FX and 6.3% in EMBI, but only 4.0% in local rates. The high EMBI dispersion is likely the result of a wide variety of countries being included in that index as compared to the local currency version. It is an interesting observation that dispersion of EMFX returns is high, in spite of the fact that the DXY sets the tone for trading in most EM currencies. One reason for this is the presence of highly managed currencies, which offer attractive hiding places during downturns. Low dispersion in EM rates is likely due to an important US Treasury component, especially in the long end of the curve, which is the key driver for generating local currency bond performance. Our conclusion is that the emphasis for the country selection effort should lie with FX and credit markets, rather than rates, at least for cash-constrained investors who are unable to take leveraged positions in rates.

While inflows into local markets have been slow due to challenging returns, EM credit has seen many years of strong inflows. But the living for EM credit managers has not been as easy as the strong returns would suggest. Not unlike what is happening in other asset classes, passive investment vehicles are gaining share. The good news for active fund managers in EM is that the speed of this development is not as fast as it is for DM. The switch to passive funds is slower because EM indexes are both more difficult and also costlier to replicate. This is reflected in the fact that exchange-traded funds (ETFs) in EM fixed income tend to underperform their benchmarks. In spite of these handicaps, EM ETFs have grown significantly. In the end, such growth may be

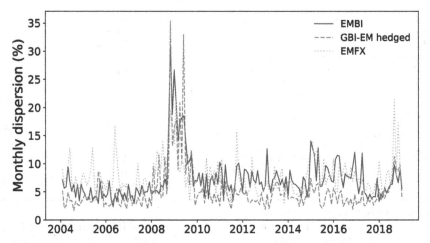

FIGURE 1.8 Dispersion of Returns is Highest in FX and Credit.
Source: Bloomberg, authors' calculations. Index data courtesy of JPMorgan Chase & Co., copyright 2020, as of 31 December 2018.

self-limiting, as an overwhelming share of monies managed by ETFs may well lead to arbitrage opportunities for active managers. But for now, the market share of EM ETFs is still quite limited, especially for local markets. For EM credit, the ETFs are more relevant and can be market moving, though their volumes so far don't offer sufficient arbitrage opportunities to add meaningfully to the returns of active managers.

1.4 SCOPE FOR EVEN MORE ALPHA

When investigating fund performance in the EM space, it has to be taken into account that trading and clearing costs are high, and some countries levy taxes on portfolio investments by foreign investors. For example, Indonesia and Colombia have withholding taxes, as does Brazil, depending on the jurisdiction of the investors. In the past, Brazil also charged a significant financial transaction tax that had to be paid to gain access to local bonds (the *IOF tax*, which is still on the books, even though the rate is currently set to 0%). Such costs are not taken into account by index providers and, ceteris paribus, lead to underperformance for active managers (as well as the ETFs). On the other hand, meaningful outperformance of the new issue market helps active managers offset some of the trading costs mentioned. Furthermore, EM fixed income is still a relatively inefficient asset class. This allows for pockets of alpha, which are harder to find in the developed world. Given all these diverging factors, it is not clear whether EM funds should ex ante be expected to outperform or underperform their benchmarks.

To shed some light on this issue, we summarize the performance of the EM funds in Table 1.3. Here we show the excess returns of EM credit and local currency funds over their corresponding benchmarks. Overall, the excess returns for EMBI benchmarked funds have been relatively solid in the long run but have suffered since the *taper tantrum*

TABLE 1.3   EM Funds Add Alpha in Credit But Not Much in Local.

Periods		EMBI	GBI-EM
2003–2018	Active return	0.63%	−0.14%
	Tracking Error	1.70%	2.64%
	IR	0.37	(0.05)
2008–2018	Active return	0.39%	−0.23%
	Tracking Error	4.0%	4.2%
	IR	0.10	(0.06)
2013–2018	Active return	−0.22%	−0.02%
	Tracking Error	1.16%	1.26%
	IR	(0.19)	(0.02)

Note: Excludes Neuberger Berman funds.
Source: Bloomberg, authors' calculations. Index data courtesy of JPMorgan Chase & Co., copyright 2020, as of 31 December 2018.

in 2013. For local currency funds, excess returns of actively managed funds have been slightly negative over the full sample, though returns have become slightly less negative since 2013. One reason for the superior performance by EM credit managers is likely that trading costs and taxes are more relevant for local bonds than they are for credit. Furthermore, investors generally find it easier to generate alpha in bull markets (for example, by increasing market beta) than in markets that require considerable timing skills, such as FX.

The next question to answer is how the alpha is currently being generated. In EM credit, this is illustrated in Figure 1.9, which charts the beta of the excess returns to

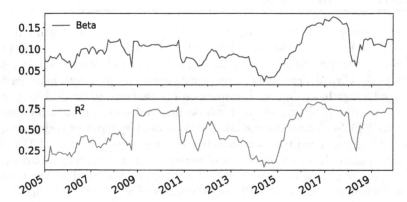

FIGURE 1.9   Alpha in EM Credit from High Yielders.
Note: Beta and R^2 regressing EM credit funds' excess returns on the HY component of the EM credit benchmark.
Source: Bloomberg, authors' calculations. Index data courtesy of JPMorgan Chase & Co., copyright 2020, as of 31 December 2019.

the high-yielding EMBI components (first panel), as well as the R^2 (second panel). This illustrates how much of the excess return is explained by being overweight the high yielders (i.e. HY credits as opposed to IG rated credits). We can see that the average beta of the excess returns to the high-yield subindex is 10%, i.e. quite large. This high beta was only briefly reduced during the commodity sell-off in 2014 and 2015. Furthermore, the R^2 is high and usually fluctuates between 25 and 75%. This suggests that one of the key ways fund managers currently generate alpha in credit is to consistently go overweight high-yielding index components. On average, 37% of outperformance is explained by this strategy.

The same exercise for local bonds is shown in Figure 1.10. Excess returns were close to zero for a long time, starting in 2011. Only in 2018 were funds able to outperform their benchmark. Just like in EM credit, this was largely due to overweights in the high yielders.

While this analysis focuses on the average return of EM funds, we are also interested in seeing whether most funds follow the same strategy of adding exposure to high yielders or whether more differentiated strategies are employed. To answer this question, we run a principle components analysis (PCA) on fund excess returns to see how unique each fund's strategy is with respect to its peers. Figure 1.11 shows the results of our analysis. The first principal component explains about 90% of the variance in EM hard currency fund returns. This suggests that many EM credit funds engage in similar strategies. Of course, there is nothing wrong with this approach, given that EM credit funds in aggregate generate positive alpha. But the heavy use of more volatile high yielders to outperform is obviously a bull market strategy. While managers would surely switch strategies in an adverse market environment, it is still important to realize that a bear market would upend what has traditionally been the main source of alpha in EM credit.

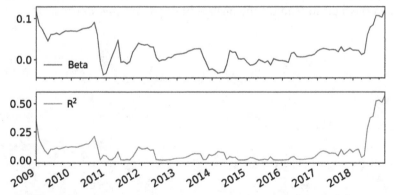

FIGURE 1.10　(Smaller) Alpha in GBI-EM Funds, Also from High Yielders.
Note: Beta and R^2 regressing EM local funds' excess returns on the high yielding component of the EM local benchmark.
Source: Bloomberg, authors' calculations. Index data courtesy of JPMorgan Chase & Co., copyright 2020, as of 31 December 2019.

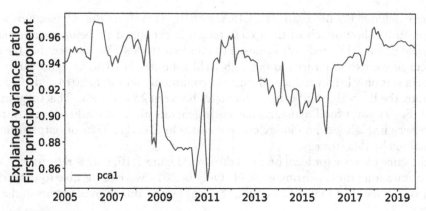

FIGURE 1.11   Herding Behaviour At Work.
Source: Bloomberg, authors' calculations.

1.5   SUMMARY

EM fixed income is a large and fast-growing asset class. It offers important sources of alpha that cannot be ignored. This alpha isn't something that can be easily replicated with G10 assets. Currently, the EM fund industry is focused on adding alpha by over-weighting high yielders. We think that many typical strategies employed in EM investing can be improved upon. More systematic strategies are going to be part of the solution. Part of the problem with this solution may be that the history of EM is still relatively short, and therefore many of the lessons on how to trade EM have not been fully quantified. This book aims to offer the tools necessary to EM fund managers and analysts. The alpha from a more systematic trading effort will be a crucial weapon for EM active managers in the fight to fend off the onslaught of passive investments.

CHAPTER 2

Global Macro Rules

Emerging market trading was aggressively utilized by global macro funds long before dedicated emerging market funds existed. The reason is that global macro funds focus first and foremost on the global business cycle to generate alpha. The global business cycle is driven largely by the US, the EU (rarely), Japan (in the golden days), and, more recently, China. EM are highly dependent on the global business cycle. They tend to have weaker balance sheets, which result in a higher beta to the business cycle than their G10 counterparts display. This fact makes EM a natural hunting ground for global macro funds. This chapter outlines how global macro can be applied to EM. We do this by assuming that investors have an edge in global macro and then suggesting how to trade EM based on this edge. The reason for this approach is that otherwise, we would need to focus on how to generate an edge in global macro, which is a separate book in itself. For readers who feel that trying to get global macro right is a fool's errand, this chapter is still useful to understand what forces they are up against. We also suggest some trading rules that rely on unsustainable divergences between EM and developed markets (DM).

2.1 WHAT YOU NEED TO GET RIGHT: 65% GLOBAL, 35% LOCAL

One important debate in EM investing is the merit of a top-down versus bottom-up approach. Essentially, the question is to what extent local factors matter for EM and to what extent even the best set of local fundamentals is in the end overwhelmed by a challenging global macro environment. To our mind, it is mostly the global macro environment that determines the direction of EM asset prices. Local fundamentals are relevant for relative value decisions but not so much for directional trades. Local conditions are rarely powerful enough to offset global macro forces.

But the explanatory power of global macro for EM asset returns varies depending on which asset class and which time period we analyse. This is shown in Table 2.1. Here we regress EMFX, EM local rates, and EM credit returns on the major macro assets. We also include EM equities in some of our analysis, given the importance of equities in global macro discussions. We think that at this stage, US assets are (still) the dominant drivers for the world. Therefore, we select as the global variables the USD Index (DXY), 10-year US Treasuries (UST), US HY credit, the S&P 500, and the

TABLE 2.1 Think Global, Unless You Trade EM Rates.

Asset class	Current R^2	Average R^2
EMFX	54%	66%
EM rates	36%	36%
EMBI spreads	69%	62%
EM equity	62%	63%

Note: Current R^2 is at end of 2018; average is from 2002 to 2018.
Source: Bloomberg, authors' calculations. Index data courtesy of JPMorgan Chase & Co., copyright 2020, as of 31 December 2018.

Bloomberg Commodity Index (BCOM). We start the exercise in 2002. The fraction of total returns explained by macro factors is high but differs meaningfully across asset classes. EMFX is mostly macro: 66% of the variation in EMFX returns is explained by global macro forces. This is followed by EM equities and external debt. At the other end of the spectrum are EM rates, where only 36% of the variation is explained by global macro factors. This makes intuitive sense, given how important local central banks are for local interest rates. Central bankers presumably place primary consideration on local fundamentals.

THE RISE AND FALL OF DILMA ROUSSEFF – JUST A YAWN

For a stark illustration of the extent to which EMFX is driven by global macro as opposed to local forces, it is helpful to analyse the case of Brazil between 2014 and 2016. On 26 October 2014, President Dilma Rousseff was narrowly re-elected, winning 51% of the votes versus 48% for Aécio Neves, the centre-right candidate. Given that investors had blamed Rousseff during her first term for fiscal profligacy that pushed Brazil onto an unsustainable fiscal track, the market was clearly unhappy, and BRL weakened aggressively both into and out of the election. In 2015, the *Lava Jato* corruption scandal gained momentum.[1] The scandal not only helped push the country into a deep recession but also undermined trust in the government in general, and in Rousseff in particular. Eventually, Eduardo Cunha, president of the Chamber of Deputies, accepted a petition for Rousseff's impeachment on 2 December 2015. This started the long and winding road to impeachment, which ended on 31 August 2016 when the Senate reached its guilty verdict. Markets had begun to celebrate when impeachment became likely, and investors continued to ramp BRL stronger after the fact. This is about as

(Continued)

---

[1]For fascinating in-depth coverage of the story, read Netto (2019) or watch *The Mechanism* on Netflix.

idiosyncratic a story as any in EM during that time. However, in spite of that, the chart of USD-BRL looks almost identical to the overall EMFX chart, as can be seen in Figure 2.1. There was not a single week where BRL sold off meaningfully at a time when EMFX did well. The BRL remained hostage to the global USD even during the most bearish parts of the Rousseff episode. The main discrepancy is a short but sharp period of BRL *out*performace when investors celebrated Rousseff's ouster; but even there, the directionality between BRL and EMFX was largely the same. It therefore pays to follow the global macro much more than the local story when trading FX. Local stories have to be traded purely in relative value terms by choosing a similarly volatile EM currency as a funding currency.

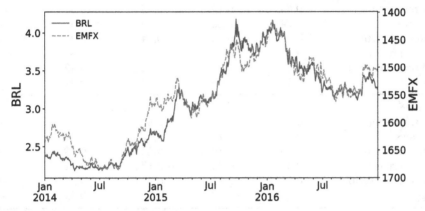

FIGURE 2.1 During the Troubled Times in Brazil, BRL and EM FX Were the Same Chart! *Source:* Bloomberg.

Table 2.2 investigates the impact of global drivers in greater detail. In particular, we show how a one standard deviation move in the global factors impacts the returns of each of the EM asset classes. We split the period under study into two sub-periods: 2003 to 2012 and 2013 to 2018, to illustrate how the importance of global macro factors changes over time. A few observations are noteworthy. First, across asset classes, the S&P 500 has the largest impact. The USD (DXY), commodities, and US HY are also very relevant. Somewhat surprisingly, US rates are not very important. The signs of the coefficients are what one would expect: a higher S&P and commodity prices boost EM returns, as do tighter HY spreads and a weaker USD. US rates are mostly relevant for EMBI spread returns, as higher yields tend to compress spreads. Another important observation is that for most EM assets, the DM counterpart is the most or second most important driver. For example, the USD is the most important driver for EM FX. So is the S&P, for EM equities. The S&P 500 is also the most important driver for EMBI, followed by US HY. For EMBI spread returns, both US equities and HY exert almost

TABLE 2.2   Which Global Macro Factor Matters Can Change.

	SPX	UST	DXY	BCOM	US HY
2003–2018					
EMFX total return	0.56	0.05	−0.71	0.55	−0.39
EM equities	0.72	0.22	−0.30	0.48	−0.55
EM rates total return	0.33	−0.25	−0.30	0.21	−0.20
EMBI total return	0.49	−0.15	−0.34	0.34	−0.37
(EMBI spread return)	0.66	0.41	−0.23	0.40	−0.64
Average	0.52	−0.03	−0.41	0.39	−0.38
2003–2012					
EMFX total return	0.63	0.19	−0.75	0.57	−0.44
EM equities	0.74	0.28	−0.39	0.50	−0.56
EM rates total return	0.39	−0.16	−0.34	0.22	−0.23
EMBI total return	0.52	−0.07	−0.40	0.37	−0.37
(EMBI spread return)	0.69	0.44	−0.32	0.42	−0.63
Average	0.57	0.06	−0.47	0.42	−0.40
2013–2018					
EMFX total return	0.35	−0.19	−0.62	0.46	−0.26
EM equities	0.64	0.12	−0.02	0.37	−0.53
EM rates total return	0.23	−0.39	−0.22	0.19	−0.15
EMBI total return	0.37	−0.33	−0.17	0.22	−0.38
(EMBI spread return)	0.56	0.42	0.07	0.29	−0.70
Average	0.40	−0.20	−0.26	0.31	−0.33

Note: Standard deviation move in the EM asset class in response to a one standard deviation move of each macro driver. US HY and UST are expressed in spread and yield terms, respectively. *Source:* Bloomberg, authors' calculations. Index data courtesy of JPMorgan Chase & Co., copyright 2020, as of 31 December 2018.

equal influence. EM rates are the exception again, where US rates are only the third most important driver, after S&P 500 (i.e. risk) and the USD.

The table also shows that the macro drivers are far from stable. When comparing the impact of a one standard deviation move in the macro assets in the 2003–2012 period to the 2013–2018 period, a few changes are important to note. First, the impact of global macro drivers on EM returns has generally weakened. In particular, the impact of the S&P, as well as the USD, has meaningfully decreased for EM assets. The impact of commodities and US HY has weakened by less. As a result, US HY has become the most important driver for EMBI total returns as well as spread returns. Changes have been even more pronounced with respect to US rates. US rates went from being not overly important for EM rates in the 2003–2012 period to being the most important driver in the 2013–2018 period. Even more striking is the impact of US rates on EMFX. Prior to the 2013 tapering, lower UST rates meant that EMFX traded poorly. Higher US rates were not harmful because they were correlated with stronger growth conditions, and these stronger growth conditions were global (otherwise, the

USD would not have been in a bear market). Post 2013, however, the correlation between US rates and EMFX flipped. Higher rates became a negative for EMFX, largely because the stronger growth was to a large extent a US phenomenon, which was also reflected in the stronger USD during that time. That 2013 would be such a major break in the global macro correlations was actually not that hard to see, and at the time there was a broad consensus that the tapering by the Fed would be EM negative. Still, the episode serves as a warning to remain open-minded about whether there is a case for a changing correlation structure in global macro land, rare as it may be.

One other way to analyse the importance of global drivers for the different EM asset classes is to investigate how much alpha could be added to trading EM if investors had an edge forecasting the relevant macro driver. We do this by running strategies where perfect foresight is assumed regarding how the relevant macro factor will behave over the next month. If it is known to move in a direction favourable for EM, the strategy goes long EM. If the macro driver is known to move in the opposite direction, the strategy goes short the relevant EM asset class for that month. The resulting information ratios are shown in Table 2.3. High information ratios suggest that the macro driver is very significant, and investors should invest some resources in forecasting that particular driver. The analysis confirms that the relevant G10 asset class is usually the most important macro driver with respect to each specific EM asset class. EUR-USD remains the most important macro driver for EMFX, SPX for EM equities, and EM high yield for EM sovereign spreads. Once more, EM rates are the exception, as US HY is a more important macro driver than UST. Furthermore, across asset classes, US HY ranks as the most important macro driver. Periods of rising US HY spreads are therefore the most important times to avoid long EM positions across asset classes.

From time to time, local factors can become dominant drivers. This happens relatively frequently on a country level, often around important political events. However, it can also happen on an asset-class level, sometimes because important local developments in a large and important emerging market can lead to contagion to the rest of the asset class. At other times, a broad EM asset class can decouple from its global driver even without the local story in one big country being the obvious culprit. To our mind, such a decoupling often creates opportunities, as EM assets eventually recouple.

TABLE 2.3 US HY is an Underrated Global Macro Driver for EM.

Factor	EMFX	GBI FX hedged	EMBI	EM equity
Commodity	1.48	0.40	0.97	1.42
EUR	2.13	0.63	0.86	1.31
US HY	1.74	1.73	2.14	2.14
UST	0.14	1.27	(0.55)	(0.02)
SPX	1.53	1.08	2.04	2.29
VIX	1.09	0.94	1.47	1.55

Note: Information ratio assuming perfect foresight for the relevant macro driver.
Source: Bloomberg, authors' calculations. Index data courtesy of JPMorgan Chase & Co., copyright 2020, as of 31 December 2018.

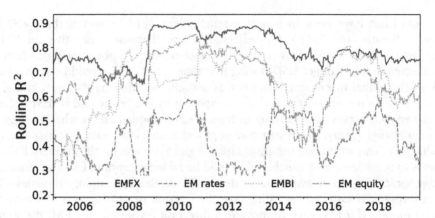

FIGURE 2.2 Idiosyncratic Factors Can Become Important for Short Periods of Time.
Note: Rolling R^2 of regression of EM returns on global macro factors.
Source: Bloomberg, authors' calculations. Index data courtesy of JPMorgan Chase & Co., copyright 2020, as of 31 December 2019.

This is illustrated in Figure 2.2, which charts how much of the returns are explained by global macro factors over time for all four asset classes. For example, between 2012 and early 2013, only 20–30% of the variation in EM rates was explained by global factors. At the time US rates had started to rise, driven by improved US activity, at a time when EM rates were still falling, largely driven by a very dovish BOJ and ECB. These low correlations turned out to be an opportunity to position for a recoupling, as EM rates then proceeded to sell off drastically when the taper tantrum started in mid-2013. Similarly, the very low correlation of EM rates to global macro factors in 2008 also turned out to be a huge opportunity. Initially, EM rates sold off hard even with rallying US rates, due to weaker EMFX. But this behaviour changed soon enough, and EM rates recoupled to DM rates in late 2008 and 2009. It is very hard for EM assets to decouple for good, which implies that observing correlation patterns can be an important tool to find profitable dislocations.

Having established the importance of global macro for EM investing, we want to investigate in more detail several key global macro events and how they impact EM. The most important events are US recessions and Fed hiking and easing cycles. We also investigate in more detail how the DXY cycle, the commodity cycle, and risk aversion impact EM assets.

2.2 WHEN THE US SNEEZES, THE WORLD (STILL) CATCHES A COLD

Among the more important global macro events that occur on a regular basis are US recessions. US recessions are more important for global macro and the EM asset class than recessions in the rest of the G3. In decades past, when trade flows were still the key driver of international finance, the US was special because it was clearly the dominant economy by size. As of the mid-1980s, for example, the US accounted for more than 30% of global GDP. The European Union did not exist as a single market, and China was still largely irrelevant for global macro. Unsurprisingly, when the US sneezed, the whole world reliably caught a cold. Today, after the advent of the EUR, and given the secular rise of China, US dominance over the global business cycle is not as uncontroversial a view as it used to be. But to us, the exceptionally important role of the US is likely to survive for longer: partly because at around 24% of global GDP, the US is still the single largest economy; partly because of the strong links between the US and China; and partly because of the importance of the USD for the global financial system and the status of the Fed as the most important central bank. US recessions will therefore likely remain central to the global business cycle. The problem (or rather, the world's good fortune) is that US recessions are quite rare. This makes a study of their impact on EM more speculative. But we are willing to live with conclusions based on very few sample points as long as they are in line with what common (economic) sense dictates.

As a first step, we are interested in the economic linkages, i.e. whether a US recession typically causes an EM recession. We analyse this question by examining which of the EM countries were going into their own recession in parallel (or slightly after) the last two US recessions of 2001 and 2007/8, which are the two recessions for which we have high(er)-quality EM data. As is shown in Table 2.4, during the relatively mild US recession starting in early 2001, every emerging market experienced negative GDP growth in year-over-year (yoy) terms. And for every country, with the exception of Hungary, the negative yoy growth lasted for at least two quarters. Furthermore, every country experienced a sharper yoy contraction in GDP than the US. Hardest hit was Asia, which is unsurprising, given that the focal point of the US recession was the deflating Nasdaq bubble. Asia in general, and Taiwan, South Korea, Hong Kong, and Singapore, in particular, were closest to that particular fire, thanks to the deep integration of emerging Asia into the US tech cycle. Technology-heavy Israel was also severely impacted. But the shock for local activity was very significant even for countries not directly linked to the bursting US technology bubble. One reason is that business cycles in EM tend to be more volatile than they are in the US, partially because the share of GDP of volatile manufacturing is higher, while the share of less volatile services is usually lower. As such, we tend to observe deeper recessions in EM, even when the recession originates in the US.

Interestingly, the first quarters of negative yoy GDP growth in many EM occurred before the US formally entered a recession in March 2001. The median emerging market already printed negative GDP growth two quarters before the US was in recession. While this may hint at causality running both ways, we think this pattern also speaks to the fact that it only takes a minor US slowdown for the rest of the world to be severely impacted, at least if the recession originates in a sector of the US economy that has strong international links. In this instance, the deceleration in US growth started after Q2 of 2000, and the impact on EM was very fast. In a few countries, such as Brazil, a local crisis was made worse by the US recession.

The 2007/2008 US recession was much more severe than the shallow US recession of the early 2000s. Once more, every country followed the US into a recession, with the worst point of the yoy GDP contraction for the median country being −4.1% rather than −2.7% in the 2001 case. The 2007/08 US recession originated with the US housing

TABLE 2.4 There is No Decoupling From US Recessions.

US recession start	First neg Q Mar-01	Worst Q (yoy)	Re-cession (y/n)	Lead (neg) Lag (pos) in Qs	First neg Q Dec-07	Worst Q (yoy)	Re-cession (y/n)	Lead (neg) Lag (pos) in Qs
Brazil	Dec-00	−2.1%	y	−1	Dec-08	−5.7%	y	4
Chile	Jun-00	−1.7%	y	−3	Jun-07	−3.4%	y	−2
Colombia	Mar-01	−1.5%	y	0	Mar-08	−4.4%	y	1
Mexico	Dec-00	−2.2%	y	−1	Sep-08	−4.7%	y	3
Peru	Jun-00	−5.5%	y	−3	Sep-08	−3.3%	y	3
Latam - median		−2.1%	100%	−1		−4.4%	100%	3
Hong Kong	Jun-00	−3.5%	y	−3	Jun-08	−4.6%	y	2
China	Sep-00	−0.8%	y	−2	Sep-07	−2.3%	y	−1
India	Mar-00	−2.6%	y	−4	Mar-08	−4.4%	y	1
Indonesia	Sep-01	−1.6%	y	2	Dec-08	−2.0%	y	4
South Korea	Mar-00	−4.0%	y	−4	Mar-08	−5.4%	y	1
Philippines	Dec-00	−1.4%	y	−1	Dec-07	−2.4%	y	0
Singapore	Dec-00	−5.5%	y	−1	Jun-08	−5.8%	y	2
Thailand	Jun-00	−3.5%	y	−3	Dec-07	−4.1%	y	0
Taiwan	Dec-00	−5.4%	y	−1	Jun-08	−6.2%	y	2
Asia - median		−3.5%	100%	−2		−4.4%	100%	1
Czech	Dec-00	−2.1%	y	−1	Sep-06	−3.7%	y	−5
Poland	Mar-00	−2.1%	y	−4	Mar-08	−2.5%	y	1
Hungary	Sep-00	−1.0%	n	−2	Sep-08	−4.6%	y	3
Russia	Mar-00	−3.2%	y	−4	Jun-08	−7.9%	y	2
South Africa	Sep-00	−0.7%	y	−2	Mar-08	−2.0%	y	1
Israel	Jun-00	−3.9%	y	−3	Dec-07	−1.9%	y	0
Turkey	Sep-00	−9.9%	y	−2	Jun-08	−7.4%	y	2
CEEMEA - median		−2.7%	86%	−2		−4.1%	100%	1

Source: Bloomberg.

bubble, which initially was a highly domestic affair. But through its impact on the US banking system, it spread widely. The small open economies of Asia were again severely impacted, but this time Latin America and Central and Eastern Europe, Middle East, and Africa (CEEMEA) had similarly deep downturns. The lags were somewhat longer, ranging from zero to four quarters, as it took some time for the shock to spread from US housing to the global financial system to the rest of the world. 2008 illustrates that even domestically focused shocks that hit the US economy impact the rest of the world, partly because the US is such a crucial nexus for the global financial system.

2.3 EM CENTRAL BANKS STIMULATE AS FAST AS MARKETS ALLOW

From a trading perspective, the main opportunities going into and during US recessions are potential receivers (i.e. positions in interest rate swaps that benefit from lower interest rates). If EM central banks are able to follow the Fed in interest rate cuts (which is not always the case), it often happens with a lag – and lags create opportunities. Long USD positions can also work, but the direction of the USD during these recessionary episodes is much less clear than the direction of US rates. After all, since 1971, the USD has appreciated four times and depreciated twice against the EUR (or its predecessor, the DEM) when the US entered a recession. We therefore study next the extent to which EM central banks are able to follow the Fed in cutting interest rates. As data availability is especially limited for EM interest rates, we again focus on data from the last two US recessions. The results are shown in Table 2.5. In 2001, central banks reacted rapidly after the Fed started to cut, largely because the fall in output in many EM followed the decline in US output very quickly. Only four countries were still raising rates once the Fed started its easing cycle.

In 2008, the lags were long. The median emerging market central bank only started to cut interest rates 15 months after the Fed. This was the case because many EM had inflation problems at the time. There also was a widespread belief that EM had decoupled from the US because the US housing crisis was seen initially as a mostly domestic US phenomenon. And the commodity spike of 2007 kept EM assets stable well after the US had already entered a recession. As a result, most EM actually continued

TABLE 2.5 Risk Aversion Be Damned: EM Central Banks Follow the Fed.

	2000 Last hike	First cut	Lag of cut	2007 Last hike	First cut	Lag of cut
US	May-00	Jan-01	NA	Jun-06	Sep-07	NA
CZK	NA	Feb-01	1	Feb-08	Aug-08	11
TWD	Jun-00	Dec-00	−1	Jun-08	Sep-08	12
KRW	Oct-00	Feb-01	1	Aug-08	Oct-08	13
CNY	Jul-93	Feb-02	13	Dec-07	Oct-08	13
INR	Jul-00	Feb-01	1	Jul-08	Oct-08	13
ILS	Nov-98	Feb-99	−23	Aug-08	Oct-08	13
MYR	NA	Sep-01	8	Apr-06	Nov-08	14
PLN	Aug-00	Mar-01	2	Jun-08	Nov-08	14
COP	NA	Mar-01	2	Jul-08	Dec-08	15
IDR	Jul-01	May-02	16	Oct-08	Dec-08	15
THB	Jun-01	Dec-01	11	Aug-08	Dec-08	15
PHP	Oct-00	Dec-00	−1	Aug-08	Dec-08	15
HUF	Aug-01	Sep-01	8	Oct-08	Nov-08	14
ZAR	Oct-00	Jun-01	5	Jun-08	Dec-08	15
MXN	NA	NA		Aug-08	Jan-09	16
CLP	Mar-00	Sep-00	−4	Sep-08	Jan-09	16
BRL	Jul-01	Feb-02	13	Sep-08	Jan-09	16
RUB	NA	Nov-00	−2	Dec-08	Apr-09	19
Median			2			15

Source: Bloomberg.

their hiking cycles even after the Fed started to cut. But those hikes turned out to be a policy mistake and were subsequently unwound. A good rule of thumb to generate alpha is to look for countries that still have an inflation problem at a time when the US stops growing. Receiver trades in such countries are often profitable because the lags versus the US are likely long and variable, which can result in attractive opportunities. We will delve more into how to identify such opportunities in Chapter 6.

2.4   WHEN BULLISH ON US RATES, EM RATES OUTPERFORM EM CREDIT

We have shown that EM economies largely follow the US script in terms of recessions and how EM central banks follow Fed actions going into recessions. But recessions are singular events, and the question is whether the Fed determines the direction for EM assets even outside of recessions. There are conceptually two ways to go about such an analysis. Either we could investigate how EM assets behave around Fed meetings, or we could investigate how US rates impact EM more broadly. The latter is preferable in our view, as there is no reason to expect Fed policy to impact EM if it does not impact US rates.

Having said that, we want to quickly discuss one important regularity with respect to the Fed cycle, before we examine the impact of US rates on EM more broadly. This regularity is that significant and volatile sell-offs in US rates occur at two distinct times in the US rates cycle: around the last Fed cut and around the first Fed hike. During other times, sell-offs at the back end of the curve are typically much more restrained.

Table 2.6 illustrates this pattern by showing all the sell-offs of the US 10-year swap of more than 80 basis points (bp) over two months that were not interrupted by a major fall in rates.[2] The analysis goes back all the way to when the Fed began explicitly setting a target rate. All of these large sell-offs happened either around the last cut or the first hike, at least for the period when the Fed was using its target rate as its primary tool. During QE days, we think we should interpret the announcement of QE2 as the last cut, because the mindset of the market at the time was that QE2 would probably put an end to the malaise of the US economy. Tapering would then be equivalent to a first hike. The table also shows that periods of large and volatile US rates sell-offs are very dangerous periods for EM assets. EM rates are hurt the most consistently, in line with the idea that contagion spreads most directly within the same broad asset class. Typically, the beta of EM rates is less than one on an index level, with tapering being a clear exception. EMFX reliably weakens during such sell-offs in US rates (a negative sign indicates a depreciation of EMFX against the USD). The biggest EMFX sell-off occurred in early 2009, followed by a quite large sell-off during tapering. EM credit (in spread terms) was impacted the least consistently. During the six large and volatile US rates sell-offs,

---

[2] The sell-off in May 2009 is not counted as a separate sell-off, given how little rates came off after the early 2009 sell-off. But for the sake of completeness, we note that this sell-off was partially driven by QE1, announced in March 2009, which generated a bullish EM environment.

TABLE 2.6 Large US Rates Sell-Offs Happen at Turning Points.

Start	End of 2m	UST in bp	EM ylds in bp	EMFX in %	EMBI sprd, bp	
5/26/03	7/21/03	0.90	−0.02	0.00	−0.08	Last Fed cut Jun 2003
3/10/04	5/5/04	0.86	0.64	−0.01	0.11	First Fed hike July 2004
1/1/09	2/26/09	0.89	0.70	−0.08	−0.08	Last Fed cut Dec 2008
10/13/10	12/8/10	0.89	0.52	−0.02	−0.12	QE2 Nov 2010 = last cut?
4/29/13	6/24/13	0.87	1.40	−0.05	0.31	Tapering Jun 2013 = first hike?
10/20/16	12/15/16	0.86	0.56	−0.04	0.00	Trump election Nov 2016 and "proper" start of hikes Dec 2016

Note: Negative EMFX moves denote EMFX depreciations.
Source: Bloomberg.

EMBI spreads widened only twice, and they narrowed three times (and were flat once). The poor performance of EM credit during tapering was in this sense more an exception than the rule, as rising US rates often lead to narrower EM credit spreads.

Once a hiking cycle is ongoing, high-volatility sell-offs, which tend to be the most destabilizing for EM, are much rarer. The 2004 tightening cycle is a good example. Back then, a long Fed tightening cycle led to very little disruption in risky asset prices, including EM, though we admit that the emergence of China also served as a stabilizing factor during that period.

Broadening the discussion from those few periods of high US rates volatility to a more comprehensive analysis mostly reinforces the message but also leads to a some-what more nuanced picture of how US rates impact EM assets. Figure 2.3 shows that EM local rates are the only EM asset for which returns have a consistently positive beta to UST returns. This means EM rates on average, and on an index level, tend to trade like a risk-free UST asset. This is in spite of the fact that for individual countries, rates frequently move higher during times of risk aversion due to a weakening EMFX. But on an index level, periods of wider EM rates, in spite of lower US rates, are much too infrequent to distract from the meaningful positive impact of lower US yields on EM duration. When bullish on US rates, investors should add duration and not worry too much about the impact of rising risk aversion on EM rates.

EM credit (in spread terms) has a consistently negative (and fairly large) beta to UST returns, largely because US yields typically rise during strong growth periods, which are usually credit positive and lead to tighter spreads. This suggests that investors should avoid EM credit (US rates hedged) when bullish on US rates but be long credit (US rates hedged) when expecting higher US rates. Thus, during US rate sell-offs, which often coincide with Fed hiking cycles, investors should be biased to external debt (hedging the US rates component) over local, and investors in local debt should reduce duration and consider FX hedges (though the hit ratio of long USD trades during periods of rising US rates is much lower than just paying rates). For unhedged EM credit positions, the calculus is not as clear, as a higher US rates component would partly offset the impact of

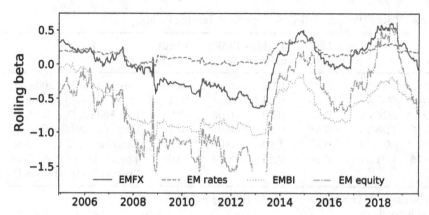

FIGURE 2.3 UST Rallies Help EM Duration But Hurt EM Credit.
Note: The beta with 3yr look back is for weekly return indexes for the various EM asset classes with respect to a UST return index.
Source: Bloomberg, authors' calculations. Index data courtesy of JPMorgan Chase & Co., copyright 2020, as of 31 December 2019.

tighter credit spreads; but, at least for high-yield issuers, credit spread tightening tends to win out.

EM RATES DIVERGENCE FROM US RATES AS AN OPPORTUNITY

As indicated, on average, the beta of EM rates to US rates is positive. It can become negative from time to time, but extremely negative betas are quite rare and can signal an opportunity. Strongly negative betas are in most instances related to broad-based risk aversion in global markets, which spills over into EM. In these instances, such negative correlations should be faded (which is, of course, easier said than done). Figure 2.4 shows the beta of EM rates to UST (calculated on daily observations for three months) versus yields of the GBI-EM. We can see that in 2008, the beta spiked to -0.4 on the back of the Lehman Brothers bankruptcy. This was the mother of all receiving opportunities across EM markets. A similar level was reached in 2018, which also turned out to be a strong receiving opportunity for EM rates. Less negative readings were less reliable, in particular in 2008. On the other side of the coin, it is not true that very high betas are a warning sign. On the contrary, positive betas are to be expected, and times of intense pressure for lower yields and resulting high betas are, if anything, a bullish sign for EM rates.

(Continued)

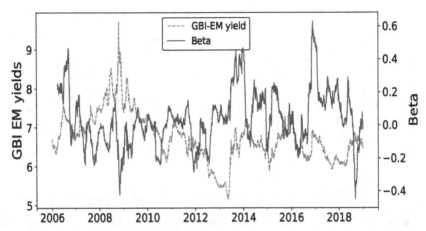

FIGURE 2.4 Highly Negative Beta of EM Rates Versus US Rates is a Sign to Receive.
Note: Beta of GBI yields to UST versus GBI yields.
Source: Bloomberg, authors' calculations. Index data courtesy of JPMorgan Chase & Co., copyright 2020, as of 31 December 2018.

For EMFX (and similarly for EM equities) the beta to US rates is not overly consistent. As has been pointed out, on average, the beta of EMFX to EM rates was negative until 2013, meaning higher rates coincided with stronger EMFX, largely because risk aversion was ebbing and growth was improving when US rates rose. But this shifted in 2013, when higher rates were associated with higher USD-EMFX in the aftermath of the Fed's tapering. We have a few more comments regarding when investors have to be especially cautious about EMFX with respect to US rates sell-offs.

First, size matters. We have already shown that large and violent sell-offs in US rates surrounding major changes in direction for the Fed have typically undermined EMFX. Figure 2.5 makes the point more broadly by charting the returns of the 7- to 10-year UST bucket over three months, and the three-month spot change in EMFX. A 5% negative return over three months in US rates usually matters and undermines EMFX. Smaller sell-offs have a less consistent impact, as for example in late 2017/early 2018, where 10-year rates sold off by 60 bp and EMFX was very strong. During those smaller sell-offs, it clearly matters whether other macro factors are supportive or not, as we will discuss below.

Our second observation is that sell-offs in real rates are more dangerous than sell-offs in nominal rates. This is largely the case because break-evens are mostly driven by oil. And, as we will see, stronger oil prices have been broadly EM positive – even for oil importers. Rising real rates in the US, on the other hand, make capital more expensive without offering the benefit derived from higher oil prices and therefore tend to be more pernicious. This stylized fact is illustrated by Figure 2.6, which shows the rolling betas for both real rates and break-evens to EMFX. While the one-year rolling

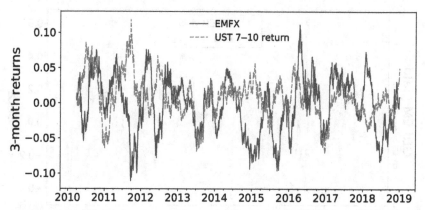

FIGURE 2.5   UST Sell-Offs by More Than 100 bp in Three Months is Reliably EMFX Negative.
Source: Bloomberg.

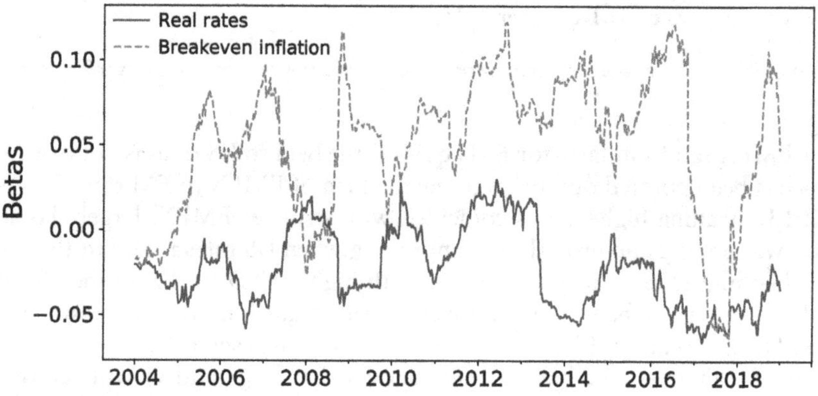

FIGURE 2.6   EMFX Gets Hurt When US Real Rates Rise.
Note: Betas of EMFX to US real and nominal rates.
Source: Bloomberg, authors' calculations.

betas are relatively volatile, it is clear that on average, higher real rates suggest weaker EMFX, while higher break-evens suggest stronger EMFX. There was a major deviation in betas during 2016, shortly after the US presidential election. But this divergence was corrected fairly quickly once fear of a border-adjustment tax began to fade.

2.5   WHEN BULLISH ON EUR, OVERWEIGHT CEEMEA OVER ASIA

The single most important factor as to whether EMFX can do well even with higher US rates is the DXY. If higher US rates lead to broad USD strength, maybe because there is healthy growth in the US, but weak growth elsewhere, EMFX trades very poorly. But if the whole world is growing, and higher US rates do not lead to a stronger USD, EMFX

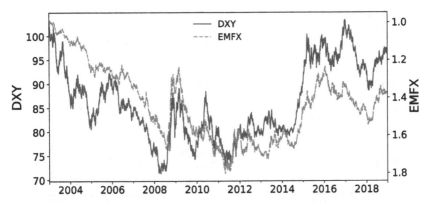

FIGURE 2.7   EMFX is All About DXY!
Source: Bloomberg.

can trade well during a move higher in US rates. Of course, even without higher US rates, a stronger USD is very negative for EMFX. To us, the DXY is actually the most important global macro driver for EMFX. Figure 2.7 shows how similarly the DXY and our EMFX index behave.

On a very basic level, this is the case because the various USD crosses are highly correlated. Some EM currencies are either traded explicitly against the EUR and have a very strong economic relationship with the Eurozone (CZK, PLN, HUF) or are explicitly or implicitly linked to a USD basket (SGD, CNY, and, to some extent, RUB). And even currencies that are not directly linked to the EUR have a very high sensitivity to the DXY.

But the other EM asset classes also tend to do better in a weak USD environment. This is highlighted by Figure 2.8, which shows the rolling betas of returns of each EM asset class to the DXY, which we proxy here with EUR. While the beta for the return of EMFX to the EUR is usually the highest and most consistent, betas of returns of EM rates and returns of EM credit to EUR tend to be positive, too. These betas only very rarely move below zero. When it happens, those events are very short lived and, at times, reverse in a very violent fashion. For example, when the correlation of EM credit to the EUR fell into negative territory in mid-2007, late 2008, mid-2015, and early 2018, it should have been a warning sign for EM credit investors. Similarly, when the correlation of EM rates with EUR fell to zero in early 2013, it should have been a warning sign for EM rates investors. Unusual correlations are important to watch – often they lead to a rapid subsequent normalization, as the underlying market structure changes only very rarely.

There are a few reasons for this strong USD impact across all EM asset classes. With respect to EM rates, the importance of FX for inflation in EM fundamentally links the behaviour of the DXY to EM rates. And for EM credit, a weaker currency increases the size of external debt as a percent of GDP, given that EM are typically net debtors and often have at least some USD-denominated debt on either the sovereign or corporate level. The DXY also matters for EM equities. After all, a weaker USD leads to capital inflows into EM. Such inflows get transmitted through the local banking systems and

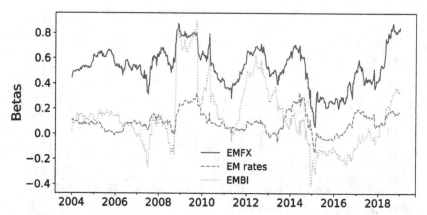

FIGURE 2.8 When Betas to EUR Fall Hard, Be Careful!
Note: Rolling betas of EM asset classes' returns to EUR.
Source: Bloomberg, authors' calculations. Index data courtesy of JPMorgan
Chase & Co., copyright 2020, as of 31 December 2018.

often turbocharge credit creation. This channel then generates higher domestic growth and pushes local equity markets stronger.

There is also a more indirect channel through which a stronger USD impacts EM. Typically, a stronger USD is associated with lower commodity prices. As the emerging market universe contains a high share of commodity producers, lower commodity prices hurt the asset class. Lower commodity prices hurt both EMFX and EM credit through deteriorating terms of trade. EM equities also can be negatively impacted through this channel, because often there is a high concentration of commodity exporters in the relevant equity indexes. We will discuss this issue in more detail in the section on commodities.

But the negative impact of a stronger DXY is most consistent for the case of EMFX, not only across time but also across regions and individual countries. As can be seen in Table 2.7, not a single EM currency has a negative beta to the EUR. The highest betas are found for ZAR, TRY, and BRL, which are the currencies most negatively impacted by EUR weakness. Interestingly, even the EUR crosses have a positive beta to EUR: i.e. if the EUR strengthens against the USD, then PLN, CZK, and HUF strengthen by even more against the USD, and vice versa. The lowest betas are to be found in Asia, even though, more recently, the beta of CNY has risen as policy makers have allowed CNY to become more flexible.

Given that the lowest betas to EUR are found in Asia, while the highest are in CEEMEA, benchmarked investors should be overweight CEEMEA FX against Asia FX whenever an outperformance of EUR is expected. Asia is preferable to Latam as a short, given that a stronger EUR is correlated with stronger commodities, which are supportive for Latam currencies. In order to illustrate the importance of the EUR, we run a thought experiment where we assume that an investor has perfect foresight regarding whether

TABLE 2.7 Not a Single EMFX Can Reliably Decouple from USD Strength.

FX	Beta to EUR	FX	Beta to EUR
ZAR	78%	INR	21%
TRY	62%	MYR	21%
BRL	52%	THB	20%
RUB	43%	IDR	18%
CLP	40%	TWD	17%
KRW	36%	EURPLN	14%
SGD	35%	PHP	14%
MXN	33%	EURCZK	10%
COP	31%	CNY	5%
EURHUF	22%		

Note: Jan 2003 to Dec 2018.
Source: Bloomberg, authors' calculations.

the EUR ends the month higher or lower. The investor then allocates 100% of her Asian FX risk to CEEMEA when she expects the EUR to go up for the month. And she allocates 100% to Asia when she sees EUR going down over the next month. We plot the resulting P&L in Figure 2.9, next to the FX component of the GBI-EM index. The simulated P&L has very few drawdowns, which illustrates that even a small edge on getting EUR right can lead to substantial outperformance in EM. Of course, forecasting the EUR is extremely challenging, and as such we doubt that this rule is overly helpful in practice. But at least it illustrates what investors are betting on when they have big allocation differences between CEEMEA and Asia.

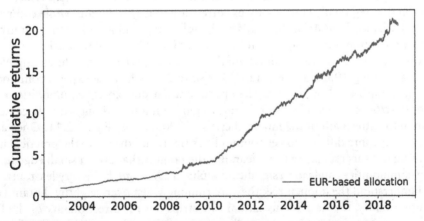

FIGURE 2.9 Go Long CEEMEA Versus Asia if EUR Strength is Expected.
Note: CEEMEA overweights against Asia based on perfect foresight on EUR.
Source: Bloomberg, authors' calculations.

2.6   WHEN BULLISH ON COMMODITIES, OVERWEIGHT LATAM OVER ASIA

Commodities are also an important global macro factor for EM. Of course, there are many different commodities, and using a commodity index risks oversimplifying the story. However, returns of different commodities are often highly correlated, and from a global macro perspective, it may therefore be sufficient, in a first cut, to focus on a commodity index. We will go into more detail with respect to individual commodities later in this chapter.

The reason for the importance of commodities for EM returns is twofold. First, and as already mentioned, many EM, especially in the EM credit indexes, are commodity exporters. This is likely the case because commodity exporting EM were more readily given access to external debt markets. After all, USD revenues from exporting commodities reduce the risk of USD-based lending. Exporters have a natural hedge in place. Second, there has also been an argument that commodity wealth can hold back overall economic development, either due to "Dutch disease," i.e. overvaluation of exchange rates due to income from natural resources, or, because fighting over how to allocate existing resources may detract from other forms of value creation (Sachs and Warner 1995). But given that commodity-rich countries like Canada, Australia, New Zealand, and Norway became very wealthy developed nations, this second argument may not be broadly applicable. Even focusing just on Asia, the main commodity consumer, and Latam, the main commodity producer, does not show a negative correlation between wealth (GDP/head) and commodity sensitivity (net exports in percent of GDP), as can be seen in Figure 2.10. We therefore believe that the large share of commodity producers in EM indexes is less because of the development argument and more because commodity producers find it easier to tap capital markets with USD debt issues.

Given that regionally commodity exporters are mostly in Latam, while commodity importers are mostly in Asia, this leads to the following trading rule: when an investor is bullish on commodities, she should be overweight FX in Latam against an underweight in Asia. Once more, we illustrate this with our perfect foresight example of an investor allocating 100% of the Latam FX risk to Asia when she expects commodities to end the month weaker. She does the opposite when she expects commodities to end the month stronger. This rule also generates significant alpha, though it only came into its own in the aftermath of the financial crisis of 2008, as per Figure 2.11. Once again, it is obviously quite difficult to get commodities right, and therefore the practical utility of pointing out this regularity is unclear. But the point is that even a small edge in forecasting commodities can lead to significant alpha in EM. And at the very least, investors should understand the implicit risk they are running when overweighting Latam versus Asia. Importantly, the Asia versus Latam rule strips out the directionality of the DXY, which is important in our view. After all, there is a debate about whether the old correlation of higher commodity prices with a weak USD is going to remain with us or not (more on that later). Therefore, it is important to express a commodity view in relative value terms – for example, across regions – rather than to go long EMFX against the USD when bullish on commodities.

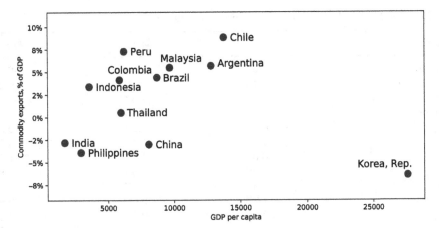

FIGURE 2.10 Latam Producing, Asia Consuming Commodities.
Source: Bloomberg, UN Comtrade.

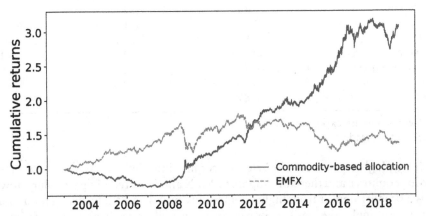

FIGURE 2.11 Go Long Latam FX Versus Asia When Commodity Strength is Expected.
Note: Latam overweights against Asia based on perfect foresight on commodities.
Source: Bloomberg, authors' calculations.

Using a commodity index is helpful, but it is advisable to dig one level deeper and focus on the relevant commodities for the various countries. Table 2.8, where we focus on the countries that are included in the most common local market indexes (which exclude the Middle East), shows which commodities matter to whom. In aggregate, and for local market purposes, the median emerging market is a large exporter of food, a small net exporter of minerals and metals, and a large net importer of energy. But the median tells only part of the story. There are important energy players (Russia, Colombia, Malaysia), meaningful exporters of minerals (copper in Chile, copper and gold in Peru, gold and platinum in South Africa, iron ore in Brazil), and foodstuffs (soy in Argentina, fish and wine in Chile, and rice in Thailand).

TABLE 2.8 The Median EM Exports Softs, Imports Energy.

Country	Softs	Metals	Energy
Argentina	5.6%	0.7%	−0.6%
Brazil	2.1%	2.5%	−0.2%
Chile	4.1%	7.6%	−2.8%
Colombia	−0.1%	0.3%	3.9%
Mexico	0.7%	−0.2%	−0.6%
Peru	1.8%	6.4%	−0.9%
China	0.0%	−1.7%	−1.3%
Korea	−1.3%	−1.3%	−3.8%
India	0.3%	−0.4%	−2.7%
Indonesia	1.9%	0.6%	0.9%
Malaysia	2.6%	−0.2%	3.1%
Philippines	−1.7%	0.2%	−2.5%
Singapore	−0.7%	0.2%	−4.4%
Thailand	4.1%	0.9%	−4.5%
Czech Republic	−0.4%	0.2%	−1.9%
Hungary	2.1%	0.1%	−3.2%
Poland	1.8%	−0.4%	−1.4%
South Africa	0.8%	2.9%	−1.0%
Russian Federation	−0.5%	0.4%	10.4%
Turkey	0.8%	−0.9%	−1.0%
Median	0.8%	0.2%	−1.2%

Note: Net commodity exports as % of GDP.
Source: UN Comtrade.

Clearly, higher prices for the relevant commodities improve external balances for exporting countries and therefore support EMFX and EM credit in particular. However, there is a broader impact from higher commodity prices on EM. Focusing for a moment on oil, interestingly, the positive impact of higher oil prices has in the past not been limited to oil exporters. Even the currencies of oil importers often have gained against the USD when oil prices rose. This can be seen in Figure 2.12, where we show the betas of FX to oil on the y-axis and net oil exports as a % of GDP on the x-axis. The betas are expressed for USD-EMFX, i.e. a negative beta means strength for the relevant currency against the USD when oil is rising. The interesting finding is that virtually all betas are negative, i.e. EMFX strengthens very broadly with higher oil for almost all countries. Obviously, importing countries' currencies have a less negative beta and therefore do not strengthen as much as the currencies of exporters with higher oil prices, but on average they strengthen rather than weaken in spite of the negative impact on their terms of trade and current accounts.[3] Directional views on oil should therefore

---

[3]Domac and Isiklar (2014) suggests that for the case of Turkey, for example, this may be because for every USD the current account in Turkey loses due to higher oil prices, Turkey's capital account improves by more than that USD of extra spending, as petrodollars start to flood in from the gulf region.

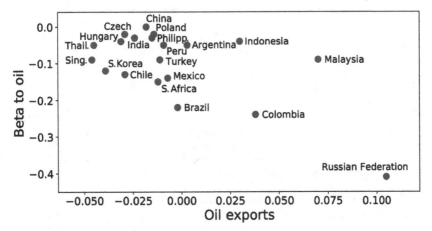

FIGURE 2.12 Even FX of Oil Importers like Higher Oil.
Note: Oil net exports as a % of GDP and USD-EMFX beta to oil.
Source: Bloomberg, UN Comtrade.

be implemented in relative value terms or with an oil exporter basket. Investors should avoid buying USD against oil importers when oil is expected to rise or selling USD versus oil importers when oil is expected to fall.

There are two factors at work explaining this observation. First, higher commodity prices often are the result of high global growth (which is particularly true for base metals), and high growth is a positive for EM broadly. This is even true for exporters of manufactured goods (at least, as long as inflationary pressures in the US are not leading to the risk of the Fed hiking rates, which undermines the positive impact of high growth). Furthermore, as mentioned earlier, it is typically true that higher commodity prices are coincident with a weaker USD. While this relationship is not as consistent as often assumed (see Figure 2.13), there are a few reasons why, on average, we should expect this correlation to persist. This topic merits a longer discussion by itself. But, in summary, there is the translation effect, because commodities are quoted in USD. Then there is the perception that the ECB, as a headline inflation targeter, is more sensitive to higher oil prices than the Fed, which has a dual mandate and targets core inflation. And finally, there is the view that oil producers in the Middle East invest their oil proceeds in non-USD assets, essentially recycling their petrodollars into EUR. Still, we do not overly stress the negative correlation between commodities and the DXY, because the correlation is unlikely to remain as stable as it was during the times of QE.[4] Furthermore, with the US having become an energy exporter, the USD is now a petro currency, also weakening that correlation. This is another reason we prefer to express views on commodities in a relative value space, rather than against the USD.

---

[4]See also Moldaschl et al. (2017).

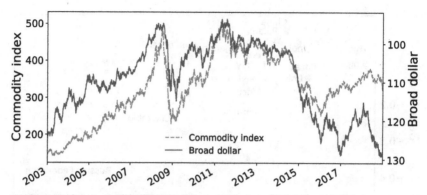

FIGURE 2.13 US Broad Dollar and Commodities are (were?) Highly Correlated.
Source: Bloomberg, authors' calculations.

2.7 RISK AVERSION BARELY HURTS EM RATES

EM are thought of as an asset class that trades poorly when it is risk off. *Risk off* is often used synonymously with lower equity markets. But there are big differences across the various EM asset classes, as well as across countries. Figure 2.14 shows how the betas of returns of the different EM asset classes to the VIX (implied volatility of the SPX, as a proxy for risk aversion) developed over time. Clearly, risk aversion impacts returns for EM credit the most significantly and returns for EM rates the least. EMFX is closer to EM credit than to EM rates but is more prone to decouple from risk aversion than EM credit. The beta of EM rates broadly fluctuates around zero, but with a slightly negative median. This is the case because EM rates have a larger UST component than EM credit does, and UST do well during times of risk aversion. However, it is interesting that typically, the beta for EM rates returns is negative, suggesting that the positive impact from the US rates channel is often not enough to create a positive performance for EM rates in this environment. The negative performance by EM credit, on the other hand, is partially driven by the performance of US credit, which trades poorly during times of a rising VIX. It is therefore no surprise that the beta for returns of EM credit to VIX is consistently negative.

The relationship between risk aversion and EMFX is more interesting than it seems. Typically, EMFX trades poorly during periods of risk aversion. Investors should avoid running EMFX risk when they expect risk aversion to rise. As illustrated in Table 2.9, not a single emerging market has a consistently appreciating currency during rising risk aversion. And this is true even for currencies of countries that sport a current account surplus or are net creditors to the world, like Singapore, South Korea, and Israel. This is remarkable because such strong fundamentals with respect to the external position could in theory lead to a JPY effect, where repatriation during times of crisis strengthens the currency. But it turns out that even SGD, KRW, and ILS tend to depreciate with rising risk aversion. USD strength during rising risk aversion is clearly too broad for EMFX

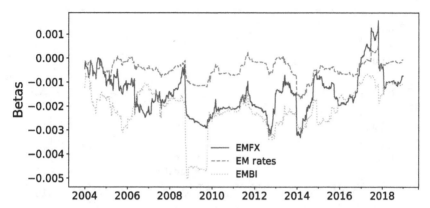

FIGURE 2.14 Risk Aversion is Negative Not Only for EMFX and EM Credit But Also (Slightly) for EM Rates.
Note: Betas of VIX to return indexes for EMFX, EM rates, and EMBI.
Source: Bloomberg, authors' calculations. Index data courtesy of JPMorgan Chase & Co., copyright 2020, as of 31 December 2018.

to decouple. Empirically, only heavily managed currencies come close to being able to decouple from VIX. Of the main currencies listed in Table 2.9, it is really only CNY that can decouple, largely because official intervention is keeping the beta low. But the beta of CNY to risk aversion will rise going forward, as Chinese authorities plan to move toward a more flexible exchange rate, one step at a time.

The reaction of EMFX to rising risk aversion also depends on whether the DXY trades well during a particular bout of risk aversion. It is well known that the DXY usually appreciates during risk aversion, which is one side of the famous USD *smile*, a

TABLE 2.9 Even Net Creditors Cannot Decouple from Risk Aversion.

Country	NIP	CAD	VIX beta	Country	NIP	CAD	VIX beta
Singapore	248%	18.8%	(37.2)	Philippines	−14%	−0.7%	(20.1)
Thailand	−7%	10.8%	(21.9)	Peru	−37%	−1.3%	(14.5)
S Korea	16%	5.1%	(46.9)	India	−16%	−1.5%	(35.1)
Malaysia	−2%	3.0%	(37.2)	Chile	−21%	−1.5%	(46.5)
Israel	41%	2.8%	(34.8)	Mexico	−48%	−1.7%	(57.7)
Hungary	−53%	2.7%	(22.5)	Indonesia	−33%	−1.7%	(20.5)
Russia	−7%	2.3%	(77.2)	South Africa	11%	−2.5%	(64.7)
China	0%	1.4%	(8.8)	Colombia	−48%	−3.4%	(59.7)
Poland	−66%	0.2%	(21.2)	Argentina	4%	−4.9%	(5.3)
Brazil	−33%	−0.5%	(74.2)	Turkey	−54%	−5.6%	(56.4)

Note: Net investment position, current account deficit, and beta to VIX.
Source: Bloomberg, IMF, authors' calculations.

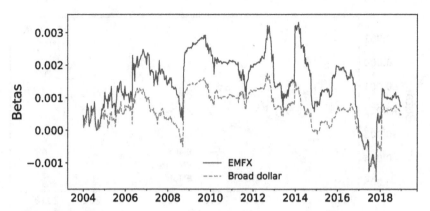

FIGURE 2.15 EMFX with Negative Beta to VIX as a Warning Sign.
Note: Rolling 1yr beta of weekly returns of DXY and USD-EMFX to VIX.
Source: Bloomberg, authors' calculations.

term originally coined by Stephen Jen. The smile means that the USD does well when the US economy does well, and it does poorly when the US economy does moderately well or moderately poorly; but then, the USD does well again when the US economy does extremely poorly, as risk aversion usually sets in under such circumstances. Still, there are episodes where DXY depreciates during an episode of risk aversion. During these periods, the beta of EMFX to risk aversion drops, though it usually stays positive, as can be observed during Q3 of 2017 in Figure 2.15. Such periods of DXY depreciation during risk aversion are rare and short-lived. Whenever the beta of DXY to VIX drops meaningfully below zero, investors have to prepare for those betas to pick up again sooner rather than later, and potentially very quickly. In the period shown in Figure 2.15, a negative beta was observed only twice: in early/mid-2008 and in late 2017. Both episodes were followed by meaningful USD strength.

EMFX has a higher beta to VIX than the broad USD. The beta of EMFX to VIX became negative only once, in late 2017. During that episode, EMFX largely ignored rising risk aversion. But this also did not last long, and 2018 saw meaningful EMFX weakness. Negative betas for DXY and/or EMFX with respect to VIX during times of rising risk aversion are a clear warning sign to, at the very least, avoid short USD positions and consider long USD trades.

While it is, of course, somewhat obvious that investors should avoid EMFX risk during rising risk aversion, it is less obvious what to do with duration risk. Given the betas discussed earlier, it is plausible that investors should not run any duration risk during periods of rising VIX. To examine the issue in more detail, we investigate a perfect-foresight rule that cuts duration to zero when VIX is moving up and goes long the same duration as the GBI-EM index in months where VIX is moving lower. The performance of this rule is strong. However, just owning the index would be even better. While the VIX-based strategy led to significant outperformance during 2008 and 2013, it underperformed considerably during the relative quiet times from 2004 to 2007, and then again from 2010 to 2013, as can be seen in Figure 2.16. The information ratio for

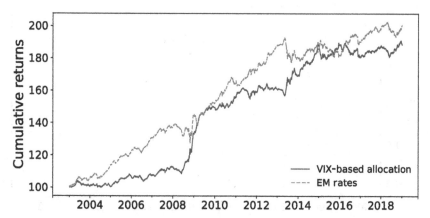

FIGURE 2.16 Avoiding EM Rates During Rising VIX Does Not Add Alpha.
Note: Duration is brought to zero during periods of rising VIX, based on perfect foresight.
Source: Bloomberg, authors' calculations.

the index is also superior at 1.6, compared to 1.4 for the VIX rule. Smaller moves higher in VIX are not overly negative. Investors should cut EM rates risk only if they fear very major shifts in risk aversion. On average, aligning EM rates trading with US rates views generates alpha, irrespective of the fact that lower US rates are at times coincident with a rising VIX. Periods of an explosive VIX, where this rule of thumb does not hold, are too infrequent (and too hard to predict) to invalidate the overall result that investors should align the EM duration view with their US rates view.

2.8 RISING US HY SPREADS WORSE THAN RISING VIX

The last remaining global macro driver we investigate is US HY. As can be seen in Figure 2.17, the betas to US HY are consistently above zero for all EM asset classes. While it is obvious from the previous discussion that higher US HY spreads will impact EM credit very directly, it is interesting to see that the beta of US HY returns to EMFX returns is very similar to that found for EM credit. Interestingly, the beta of US HY returns to returns of EM rates is also consistently positive (albeit meaningfully lower than for the other two asset classes). This low but positive beta is somewhat surprising because higher US credit spreads typically imply lower US rates, which should be beneficial for EM rates. But it turns out that a negative beta for EM rates returns with respect to US HY returns is extremely rare (and fleeting). With respect to the other side of the coin, we found two episodes where low, positive betas spiked into meaningfully higher territory: 2006 and 2014. Both were largely driven by a spike in the correlation between US HY and EMFX, which then spilled over into EM rates. The larger of the two sell-offs for EM rates was in 2014, when the oil collapse drove US HY spreads up and EMFX lower, which, in turn, caused EM rates to widen. As US HY is likely to remain much more sensitive to oil prices than in the past, in the aftermath of the US

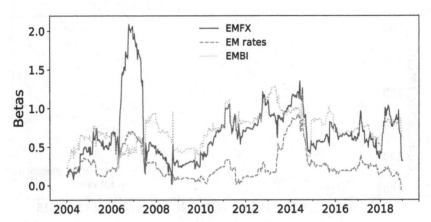

FIGURE 2.17   Rising US HY Spreads Negatively Impact all EM Asset Classes.
Note: Betas of US HY returns to EM asset returns.
Source: Bloomberg, authors' calculations. Index data courtesy of JPMorgan
Chase & Co., copyright 2020, as of 31 December 2018.

shale boom and the significant issuance by shale companies, the correlation of US HY to EM assets will likely be structurally higher going forward.

2.9   SUMMARY

Getting the global macro right is extremely important for EM trading and leads to major alpha opportunities. As a rule of thumb, around 65% of returns on an index level can be explained by global macro for EMFX, EM credit, and EM equities. Only local rates are mostly driven by local factors. There are a few simple rules that are helpful for the top-down investment process.

At times, reactions of EM assets to a changing macro environment are lagged, which can lead to opportunities in EM even after the macro environment has already changed. For example, when the Fed changes its tune and turns dovish, receiving EM rates offer better risk reward than buying UST, as it usually takes some time before EM policy makers react to a weaker global outlook. This can lead to superior entry points for EM rates. More broadly speaking, opportunities from a changing macro environment can be identified by a collapse in the typical macro correlations. Usually, the way the world works does not change, and those correlations pick up again.

Duration overweights are advisable when bullish on US rates, and vice versa. The exception is falling US rates due to rising risk aversion. However, such periods are too rare to invalidate the overall view (and too hard to forecast), even though during periods of falling rates *and* rising VIX, duration underweights are the appropriate investment stance. With respect to EMFX, higher US rates only tend to hurt during the most violent sell-offs, when the sell-off is driven by US real rates rather than nominal rates, and, especially, when the higher rates generate DXY strength.

During periods of rising risk aversion, EMFX risk should be avoided. When the USD depreciates during rising risk aversion, it usually is a warning sign of EMFX stress to come. During periods of EUR strength, CEEMEA FX overweights and Asia underweights are appropriate, and vice versa. During periods of expected commodity strength, Latam FX overweights and Asia underweights are profitable, and vice versa. But it is noteworthy that typically, all EM currencies benefit from higher commodity prices, not just commodity exporters. In terms of risk aversion, we note that rising US HY spreads tend to be more negative for EM asset returns than rising VIX or falling SPX. Rising HY spreads also impact EM rates negatively, in spite of the inherent US rates component in EM rates.

CHAPTER 3

China: The Only Emerging Market that Counts

3.1 GLOBAL BUSINESS CYCLE MADE IN CHINA

In the last chapter, we discussed how emerging markets are pushed around by global factors in general and by the Fed in particular. This characterization of EM as rudderless boats on the global macro sea is, in our view, the correct metaphor.

The feedback loop from EM to the Fed, the de facto setter of global monetary policy, is extremely weak. The most serious EM crisis over the last few decades was the Asian financial crisis in 1997. Yet that year, the Fed still hiked interest rates.[1] From Asia, the crisis spread eventually to Russia. The Fed cut interest rates the following year. But interest rates were not cut because the Fed was aiming to calm the stormy emerging market seas; they were cut because the Russian default led to serious troubles at Long-Term Capital Management, a seemingly systemically important hedge fund in the US. These troubles were serious enough to be reflected in the performance of the S&P 500. In the end, US equity weakness caused the Fed to change course more than a year after the EM crisis began. It behooves investors to remember that the Fed has a domestic mandate: it will only react to stress abroad if there is a direct spillover to the US economy. With foreign revenues of US companies having risen to about 40%, troubles in far corners of the world are transmitted to the US faster than used to be the case. However, almost none of the EM countries are sizable enough on their own to trigger a major slowdown in the US economy. This is why the Fed usually ignores EM. The *Powell Put* is a S&P put; it is not an EM put.

There is one important exception, which is somewhat recent: China. The rise of China started with its accession to the WTO in December 2001. Letting China into the WTO under quite favourable terms must count as one of the most underappreciated events in recent market and maybe world history. At the time, markets barely took any notice of this monumental event. Since then, China's GDP growth has averaged

---

[1] Apparently, a carefully crafted study by the bank's staff on the international impact of a Fed hike went straight into the filing cabinet – untouched by decision makers.

9% per year, exports in USD terms have grown by 15% per year, and the current account balance has ballooned from less than USD 20 billion per quarter to USD 420 billion at the 2007 peak. In the process, China has become the largest (in PPP terms) or second-largest (in market exchange rate terms) economy in the world. By 2030, China will likely overtake the US in terms of market exchange rates, too. It is highly integrated in the supply chains of the US business sector, as it has become the manufacturing floor for the world.

While the Trump administration is trying hard to turn back the clock, doing so will not be easy. The US effort will reduce Chinese exports to the US. But the dynamic will be counteracted by increasing exports from China to the rest of the world and by increasing exports from the rest of the world to the US, unless the economic logic of producing in China changes for everyone and not just US companies. To be fair, thanks to rising labour and other production costs, the economics of using China as a manufacturing hub had already been changing for certain manufactured goods even prior to Trump, irrespective of the latest US effort, but at this stage China is still difficult to replace.

Given the size and growth of China, it is not surprising that it has become a major driver of the global business cycle. This has caused the Fed to pay attention. While it is very hard to prove, many observers believe that there was a "Shanghai Accord" on the sidelines of the G20 meeting in February 2016, where then Fed Chair Yellen might have agreed to soften the Fed's hawkish stance in order to generate a weaker USD, which would in turn help engineer a weaker CNY on a trade-weighted basis without having to deal with the negative tremors from a sharp move higher in USD-CNY. While we cannot be sure if such an arrangement really existed, it is certainly true that Chair Yellen surprised the market on the dovish side at the March 2016 FOMC press conference and again in her speech in late March at the Economic Club of New York. China's relevance was even more visible in the Fed's reaction to the one-off devaluation of the CNY in early August 2015. The shock likely led the Fed to pause its hiking cycle at the September meeting. Given the vulnerabilities in the Chinese economic makeup it is worrisome that China is of such high importance to the global business cycle. For China, it is somewhat reassuring that its importance means global policy makers will have to react to its woes, which is not the case for virtually any other emerging market country.

If China is important for the US business cycle, it is even more important for other EM. Table 3.1 shows Chinese imports as a percentage of the GDP of the export country. In theory, we should adjust for supply chain effects, but we think even the un-adjusted numbers are good enough as a first approximation.[2] Vietnam, Malaysia, Korea, and Singapore stand out. The importance of China is first and foremost felt in its Asian neighbourhood. This is a typical phenomenon – a large fraction of a country's trade volume tends to be local. Note that many commodity exporters also appear high on the list.

[2]For a more detailed analysis, see Chua and Kim (2019).

TABLE 3.1 China: The Importer of Choice.

Country	Exports to China % of GDP	Country	Exports to China % of GDP
Vietnam	22.9%	Brazil	2.9%
Malaysia	17.4%	Indonesia	2.8%
Rep. of Korea	11.5%	Russian Federation	2.6%
Singapore	10.6%	Germany	2.6%
Thailand	9.1%	EU	2.1%
Chile	7.6%	Czech Republic	1.7%
South Africa	7.0%	Colombia	1.2%
Peru	6.2%	Mexico	1.0%
Philippines	6.1%	USA	0.8%
Uruguay	4.5%	Argentina	0.7%
Japan	3.4%	Poland	0.6%
Hungary	2.9%	India	0.6%

Source: UN Comtrade.

3.2 THE COMMODITY LINK

The impact of China on commodities deserves special attention. China is important for commodity exporters because its growth has been highly commodity intensive. Infrastructure build-out and other fixed asset investments have been a big part of that growth. Table 3.2 illustrates this along two dimensions. First, it shows how important China is in terms of global demand for key commodities. Even more importantly, the table shows how significant China has been for the demand growth in those commodities, which is much more relevant for commodity prices. Between 2006 and 2016, China was responsible for 97% of the incremental demand for copper and more than 60% for iron ore. Even for oil, which is less directly linked to infrastructure investments, China has been responsible for almost 40% of the demand growth over those 10 years. We have discussed how important commodity exports are for EM. It is therefore no surprise just

TABLE 3.2 China Dominates Demand for Many Commodities.

	2006 global demand	China demand	2016 global demand	China demand	China net imports	% of global demand	% of 16/06 demand growth
Iron ore	1,031	601	1,606	1,161	1,025	72%	97%
Copper	10,950	3,571	22,414	10,610	9,502	47%	61%
Soybeans	1,546	549	3,370	1,022	882	30%	26%
Sugar	143,039	11,500	173,573	17,500	6,000	10%	20%
Crude	85,728	6,479	99,310	11,662	7,593	12%	38%
LNG	153,400	–	267,700	24,300	26,000	9%	21%

Source: Liao et al. (2019)

how important China has become for emerging market growth. While there is a lively debate about the extent to which the future growth of China will be less raw material intensive, we think such a structural change will be slow. Economies do not change their structure overnight. While consumer goods require less raw materials than infrastructure projects, the resource requirements of an increasing housing stock, increased car penetration, a build-out of the electricity grid, etc., should not be underestimated. And even with lower growth rates in commodity demand, we're talking about a much larger base. It is therefore not surprising to us that the beta of copper to the China Purchasing Manager Index (PMI) has, if anything, increased in the last five years, even though the variability of the PMI has come down. We firmly believe that China will remain the key driver for commodity demand globally, even if (possibly) to a slightly lower extent than in the past.[3]

The commodity angle leads to a second measure of dependence on China. Figure 3.1 shows China-sensitive commodity exports as a percentage of GDP for each commodity-exporting country. The maximum of this number and the percentage of exports to China gives us a good proxy of the impact of China on a given country. It does not matter if iron ore is exported to China or somewhere else; any iron ore exporter would be impacted by weaker Chinese demand, which drags prices lower. The results of this approach are depicted in Figure 3.1. Malaysia, Korea, Singapore, and Thailand stand out for direct exports, but Russia, Chile, and Peru are similarly sensitive through the commodities channel. Central and Eastern Europe, India, Mexico, and Turkey are the least sensitive to China from an export perspective.

One way to illustrate the importance of China for commodity-linked EM assets is to analyse two leading indicators for Chinese growth: the monetary conditions

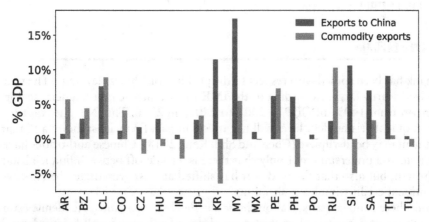

FIGURE 3.1 Dependence on China Comes From Either Direct Exports or Commodity Exports.
Source: Bloomberg.

---

[3] For a more sceptical view on what China can deliver for EM going forward, see Lubin et al. (2019).

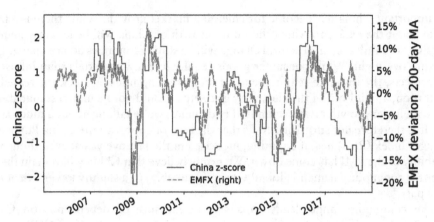

FIGURE 3.2   China Stimulus is Instrumental for Commodity-Sensitive EMFX.
Note: Z-score of China monetary conditions and credit impulse versus
commodity EMFX index, deviation from the 200-day moving average.
Source: Bloomberg, authors' calculations.

index and the credit impulse index. Figure 3.2 plots the sum of the rolling z-scores of those two indexes next to a de-trended version of a basket of commodity EMFX. The ebbs and flows of China's economic stimulus clearly are reflected in the performance of commodity currencies. Sometimes the two charts are coincident, and sometimes FX leads. But there were times, such as the fading of the stimulus impact in 2017, when the FX market reacted slowly to a delta in Chinese stimulus, offering important trading opportunities.

3.3   ON LEVERAGE

Much ink has been spilled with respect to the problem of Chinese leverage. The numbers are indeed scarily large. According to the IMF, total domestic non-financial sector debt has grown from 140% of GDP in 2007 to 240% in 2016. The IMF goes on to worry that this quickly rising debt level will negatively impact financial stability and that any adjustment may be disruptive (Chen and Shik Kang 2018). Chinese authorities have also taken note and understand not only that there is a trade-off between financial stability and growth, but also that the trade-off has shifted against growth, as the effectiveness of additional credit stimulus is shrinking.

Still, there is no consensus about how much debt is too much. Academic estimates are going up over time, and at this stage plenty of otherwise-well-behaved countries are significantly above levels that would have been deemed dangerously overleveraged as recently as 10 years ago, with few ill effects in evidence. We remember distinctly the first "China is bust" scare of our careers, in 2004! Fifteen years later, the numbers have become scarier, but the story remains the same. Furthermore, one mitigating factor is that the whole country is mostly one balance sheet, allowing regulators to shift resources around as needed. So yes, Chinese policy makers do have more tools than their counterparts in other countries. And Chinese regulators have taken notice of risks emanating from sky-high leverage and are trying to reduce vulnerabilities.

So where do we come out on the China bust question? Clearly, very high leverage at time of falling nominal GDP growth will create stress. Furthermore, increased reliance on foreign capital will make managing that stress much more difficult for the authorities than in the past (more on that shortly). Whenever the bust happens, it will be a major negative event for EMFX and EM credit, and the impact will be large enough to also impact EM rates negatively in some countries. But the timing will be very difficult to get right. Our best guess is that a meaningful quantity of Chinese assets will have to be foreign-owned before authorities will find it impossible to control a potential credit bust. But the increase in foreign ownership is still in early innings. As such, we keep a very open mind with respect to Chinese hard-landing scenarios, but we will not trade under the assumption that the long-awaited Chinese bust is around the corner.

3.4 CURRENT ACCOUNT SURPLUSES NO MORE

There is one more issue to discuss on the trade side. As of the end of 2019, it appears likely that the days of current account surpluses for China are numbered. For 2018, the Chinese current account came in at +0.4% of GDP, down from a peak of +10% in 2007. While 2019 saw a slight improvement, partly on lower oil prices, China is likely to move to a current account deficit by 2022. This is in a sense not a surprising development, as the growth in China's middle class is leading to increased imports of consumer goods. And such increased import demand is happening at a time when China's market share gains in the global manufacturing value chain have likely topped out and are probably reversing, due to increasing real wage pressures in China, trade restrictions from the West, and increased competition from other EM. Furthermore, tourism has become a major negative contributor to the Chinese current account, and this factor is also likely to grow with increasing purchasing power for the Chinese middle class. But even though the move into a negative current account is likely an inevitable consequence of the increasing wealth of China, it is nevertheless a major challenge from the point of view of Chinese policy makers. A current account surplus offers a country a margin of protection during downturns, as such a country does not have to rely on foreign savings in general and foreign portfolio investment flows in particular. This reduces the country's vulnerability to sudden stops of capital flows during downturns (Lubin et al. 2019). In the Chinese context, it is unlikely that China could have accumulated the current stock of debt over GDP without a crisis, if it had had to rely on foreign savings in a meaningful way. The implication of this assessment is that the Chinese authorities are likely to aim to at least slow the deterioration of the current account balance, partially by trying to keep the currency sufficiently cheap. But any policy response will probably only slow the inevitable, especially because currency valuation is not the main determinant of current account balances. With current account deficits on the horizon, we now shift to a discussion of the Chinese capital account.

3.5 ENTER THE CAPITAL ACCOUNT

For most EM countries, capital account links are a much more important transmission mechanism than trade flows. This is not yet the case in China. As of 2019, the financial and capital account linkage between China and the rest of the world is still much more limited than for the average emerging market country. China's capital account was mostly closed and is only slowly being opened. The gradual opening of the capital account is a smart policy, since many an emerging market crisis has had its root cause in unfettered inflows of foreign capital that the local banking systems were ill equipped to channel toward profitable and credit-worthy ventures. A major reason for the slow pace in opening the capital account is the fact that China can rely on Hong Kong as a controlled conduit for foreign financing, which makes it less urgent to open the onshore financial system.

Be that as it may, at the end of 2018, foreign ownership of domestic A shares sat at only 3.2%. Foreign ownership of local bonds stood at 2.8%, though the China Government Bond (CGB) market has a larger foreign ownership share, at around 7.9%. As a result, the correlation of A shares to the S&P 500 is among the least consistent ones across the various emerging equity markets, fluctuating widely between -0.4 to close to 1. The correlation appears to be slowly rising over time, though, as can be seen in Figure 3.3. Having said all that, we need to point out that even with fairly limited portfolio investments into China, there has been a significant rise in external debt issuance by Chinese corporates. This means that China is already hemmed in with respect to its economic policies to some extent, at least with respect to FX markets. Still, so far, the relative closedness of the Chinese capital account is a source of strength when it comes to managing the Chinese economy.

Going forward, the capital account will become more important. Chinese policy makers face challanges on two fronts. First, large inflows of foreign exchange from the current account surplus are a thing of the past and cannot be relied upon to finance capital outflows. Second, there is continued demand for geographic diversification by

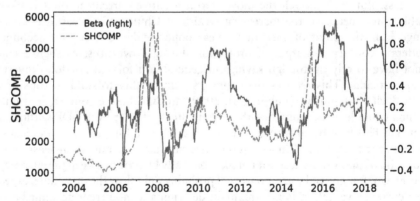

FIGURE 3.3 Beta of Chinese Equities to the SPX is Highly Unstable But Rising. *Source:* Bloomberg, authors' calculations.

Chinese investors. As a result, outflows of domestic capital are likely to continue for the foreseeable future. Demand for asset diversification is understandably high in a country that has generated considerable – but also unevenly distributed – wealth, and where the protection of individual property rights is not as strongly anchored as in most Western countries. The Chinese authorities see foreign capital inflow as a solution to outflow pressures, rather than overly relying on the sale of accumulated FX reserves.

The steps toward capital account liberalization started out modestly but have recently gained steam. On the equity side, initially, foreign investors were mostly limited to the H-shares market, which consists of Chinese equities listed in Hong Kong. In 2014, HK Connect was launched, widening the scope of foreign participation in the USD 8 trillion onshore A-share markets (Shanghai and Shenzhen) compared to earlier schemes, such as the Qualified Foreign Institutional Investor (QFII) and a related scheme for offshore renminbi (RQFII). HK Connect is a collaboration between the Hong Kong, Shanghai, and Shenzhen Stock Exchanges and allows international and mainland Chinese investors to trade securities in each others' markets through the trading and clearing facilities of their home exchange. HK Connect is still subject to quotas, though. In May 2018, 234 China A shares were added to the MSCI indexes with a 5% inclusion factor. This resulted in Chinese A shares accounting for 0.7% of the MSCI EM Index. During 2019, MSCI increased China further to 3.4% of the MSCI EM Index. The FTSE Russell index is adding China during 2019 and 2020 with a 25% inclusion factor. The importance of China in international benchmarks will only continue to increase. After all, if Chinese equities were to be added in line with global market capitalization, they would amount to around 20% of the MSCI EM Index. Jerry Peng expects foreign ownership of Chinese A shares to rise from a low 3.2% to around 8% in his base case (Sun et al. 2019, p. 3–8). From an index-provider point of view, it is clear that the preferred strategy is for China to enter the various indexes gradually, since otherwise China would swamp the indexes and drown out some of the smaller EM countries.

On the fixed-income side, the bulk of the trading initially took place offshore as well, in the form of "dim sum bonds" that did not require approval from the People's Bank of China (PBOC). In 2013, the PBOC opened access to the USD 9 trillion local bond market to institutions approved under the QFII or RQFII scheme. In 2016, the China Interbank Bond Market Direct (CIBM Direct) access was launched. This was followed by a Bond Connect scheme in 2017. After many years of lobbying by the Chinese government, in March 2018, Bloomberg agreed to add China to its flagship global aggregate index starting in April 2019. Because of the huge size of the Chinese bond market, the inclusion is being phased in over 20 months. This index inclusion could bring around USD 150 billion of foreign inflows into the bond market. China has also entered the JPMorgan GBI-EM. While this index is followed by much less assets under management (AUM), it adds to the inflow of foreign capital into China. The FTSE Russell World Government Bond Index (WGBI) is another index that eventually is likely to start to include China. Flows from those three index inclusions are expected to take foreign ownership of CGBs to around 14%. (Sun et al. 2017, p. 3–8).

In the past, index inclusion of other EM countries led to inflow well in excess of the estimates based strictly on fund assets managed against the relevant indexes. This is because countries often have to implement meaningful reforms to the micro-structure of their bond markets as a condition for entry. Such reforms attract other investors who are not indexed, indexed, who buy the bonds due to the improved liquidity as a result of index inclusion. If this behaviour holds for China, foreign ownership could rise to 20% by 2023.

While the idea of using foreign inflows to counteract asset diversification by domestic investors is appealing at first glance, the price to pay is deeper integration with world markets, which can transmit shocks between China and the rest of the world more easily (in both directions). Although indexed money is typically sticky, the non-indexed money following on the heels of the indexed money is usually much less so. There is no free lunch. China will be more vulnerable to global shocks going forward. This development should be watched carefully by investors (and policy makers). Given the amount of leverage in the Chinese economy, greater susceptibility to external shocks will make the global economy more precarious.

3.6 READING THE CNY TEA LEAVES

One financial asset price already matters intensely to global markets: the CNY. Currency trading also started out with an offshore version (CNH), but foreign investors now also actively trade the CNY, and they do so to a much greater extent than Chinese bonds or equities. That the CNY matters to global markets is a relatively recent development, too. For the longest time, the CNY was pegged, and trading it was therefore a sleepy affair. China was, as a matter of fact, almost the only significant emerging market that did not de-peg during the Asian financial crisis in the late 1990s. The global economy still owes China a thank-you note for managing through the pressures of that crisis without resorting to a devaluation. A Chinese de-peg would no doubt have made the Asian crisis much worse.

But starting in 2005, China made the CNY more flexible. Perhaps the authorities realized that a pegged exchange rate was not the optimal FX regime for an economy with a large export sector. The authorities were also aiming for the renminbi to match China's newfound status as the second-largest (and soon the largest) economy in the world. To become a plausible competitor to the USD as both a transaction vehicle and a savings vehicle, the CNY will eventually have to be a floating currency. This objective has recently increased in importance, given that the US is arguably abusing the central role of the USD by cutting individuals or companies off the USD-based financial system to increase the effectiveness of economic sanctions.[4]

Moving from a pegged FX regime to a floating one is difficult. The longer a peg lasts, the more USD liabilities accumulate, only some of which are out in the open, and many of which are sitting in unexpected spots. These USD liabilities accumulate

---

[4]We note, though, that the view that Chinese policy makers aim to move to a flexible CNY is not necessarily consensus. David Lubin, in his excellent book *Dance of the Trillions*, argues that China feels uncomfortable with market exchange rates and may therefore stick with a system of managed convertibility for a long time to come (Lubin 2018).

because interest rates are usually lower in USD than in the domestic currency, creating an arbitrage as long as the peg is expected to last. It follows that a transition to a more volatile exchange rate regime will inflict losses on some domestic agents with material FX mismatches. Such a transition therefore has to be very carefully orchestrated. In the past, many EM countries were forced to float by unruly markets, where the float was happening in days rather than years, creating major economic dislocations along the way. China is in a much better spot, as it is to some extent in charge of its own destiny. Its large war chest of FX reserves and general control over economic agents onshore affords it a slow, managed move toward a floating exchange rate. However, even with an uncharacteristically high level of control by the standards of a market economy, the process could be accident-prone.

THE 1.9% THAT SHOOK THE WORLD

On 11 August 2015, the PBOC allowed the CNY to move by 1.9% in a single day. This was unprecedented and the single largest move of the CNY in more than a decade. The policy action was explained to the market as being in line with a commitment to move to a more flexible exchange rate, and something that would be positive for financial stability (and would be required for the CNY to be included in the IMF's SDR basket). But the market was unprepared, partially because the trading range for the previous five months had been very tight, with CNY hugging the 6.20 level. Markets reacted fiercely, especially when the CNY move weaker continued the next day.

The S&P 500, after initially weakening only slightly, fell by more than 10% in just four days – according to some measures, the largest sell-off since the Great Recession – as illustrated in Figure 3.4. Two-year US rates fell from 0.97%

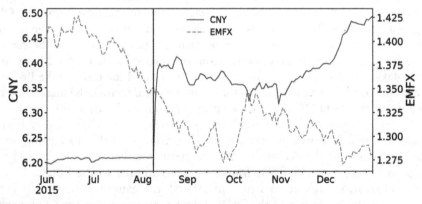

FIGURE 3.4 EMFX Suffering from an Indigestion Made in China.
Note: USDCNY on left axis, Lower EMFX means depreciation. Vertical line marks day of Chinese devaluation.
Source: Bloomberg.

(*Continued*)

to 0.78% in the following days. That was a large move, given the prevailing yield level, and it was driven by the market perception that the Fed might not go ahead with the planned rate hike at its 17 September FOMC. And indeed, the FOMC blinked and did not hike. The FOMC statement suggested that conditions for a rate hike were now not only the classic two (labour markets and inflation), but also international (read Chinese) conditions. US two-year rates kept falling, bottoming out at around 0.66% in mid-October. China had just changed the path of US monetary policy.

Interestingly, the positive impact on EMFX from the Fed blinking was not tradable. After a brief rally, EMFX continued to sell off and only troughed out in early 2016, when USD-CNY peaked out. This trading behaviour demonstrated in very stark terms that a shaky China is so negative for EM that even the Fed becoming meaningfully more dovish is not necessarily enough to offset such an important negative. And for USD-CNY to peak took a massive intervention by China, where FX reserves fell from close to USD 3.6 trillion in July 2015 to around USD 3.2 trillion by the end of February 2016, eventually troughing out at USD 3 trillion in early 2017. And it is debatable if even this aggressive selling of FX reserves would have been able to stabilize USD-CNY by itself. After all, the stabilization of CNY also coincided with the bottom in EUR-USD. This means that to this day, it is not fully clear whether China was able to stem the tide due to intervention and increasing capital controls, or whether China just got lucky as the DXY turned, changing expectations for the CNY. Given this uncertainty, it is unlikely that Chinese authorities will move with undue haste again in the future.

At this stage, China is managing the CNY against a basket. The basket weights are known and are loosely linked to the trade weights. But in practical terms, the CNY is trading to a basket of USD and EUR. Each day, the market is observing the fix for the CNY to see whether it is stronger or weaker than the market moves of the currencies in the basket imply. If the fixings deviate from the theoretical fixing by a large margin for a few days (usually against the most recent direction of the USD, as the PBOC may then have enhanced the employment of the *countercyclical* factor), the market interprets this as a signal by the PBOC that a correction in the direction (or at the very least, the pace) of CNY moves is desired. Typically, market participants oblige. This is illustrated by Figure 3.5, which shows the five-day moving average of the forecasting error by financial firms next to the actual fix. A 10 bp error in either direction often leads to a change in direction of the CNY. Markets listen carefully to the PBOC. In a calm environment (which is the normal state of affairs), the game for the market is much more to anticipate the desires of the PBOC rather than to take on the Chinese central bank. But there are, of course, exceptions to this rule. The 2015 episode was one where the market was not easily guided and where the PBOC had to spend USD 1 trillion of FX reserves to calm the market. But the shock has to be large for something like this to occur. The reason is a combination of large FX reserves, the possibility of offering

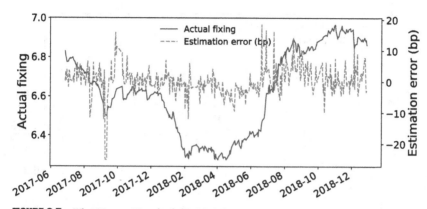

FIGURE 3.5 The Heavy Hand of the PBOC.
Note: Five-day MA of fixing error and actual fixing.
Source: Bloomberg, authors' calculations.

strong guidance to the state-owned and private sector banks about how to behave in the market, and the fact that the capital account is still heavily controlled.

Going forward, the volatility of USD-CNY is likely to increase, as the capital account will become more open. Furthermore, there is also a question about whether the PBOC can really fully control capital outflows in a strong USD environment. After all, and as discussed in the box, it is plausible that capital outflows only stopped because the DXY turned in early 2017. And the history of capital controls does suggest that if an expected depreciation of a currency becomes too large, local citizens find ways to circumvent even strict capital controls.

It should also be noted that even though CNY trading is very active among foreign investors, CNH is often still the preferred vehicle for offshore investors. The reason is that given still relatively tight controls on the CNY fix by the PBOC, the CNH is more volatile. Especially on the bearish side, long USD-CNH trades typically outperform, as the CNH can significantly weaken relative to the CNY. This is why the ratio of CNH to CNY is a good indicator to judge how mature a given sell-off of CNY is at any given time. Even better is to use the 12-month CNH forward, as it is often the main vehicle to express negative China bets. As per Figure 3.6, the 12-month CNH being more than 5% weaker than the CNY spot has been a good indicator in the past to call for an end to an upmove in the CNY, though to analyse longer time frames, this chart needs to be adjusted for rates differentials between the US and China. Once a CNY move has become extreme on the weak side, a CNY bullish positioning should best be expressed in CNH rather than in CNY as well.

The importance of the CNY for the EM overall comes from the fact that in many ways, the CNY works like an accelerator for USD strength against EMFX. If the EUR weakens against the USD, USD-CNY tends to move up, which in turn often leads to weaker EMFX. The fundamental justification is that a higher USD-CNY reduces demand for commodities. Furthermore, a weaker CNY requires weaker currencies for the countries competing with China for exports into Europe and the US. Between commodity exporters and countries that compete with China in manufacturing, a large

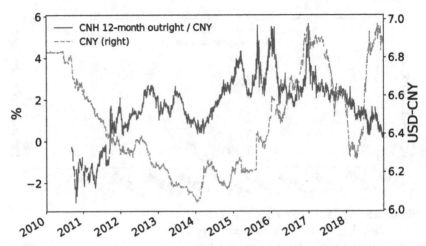

FIGURE 3.6 Twelve-Month CNH: A Warning Signal for Extended Positioning.
Source: Bloomberg, authors' calculations.

part of the EM universe is impacted by a higher USD-CNY. In practice, though, the link between CNY and EMFX is not just about fundamentals; to a large extent, it is also about market psychology.

On a country level, the currencies most impacted by CNH can be seen in Figure 3.7. In this chart, we calculate betas to 12-month CNH for the principal EMFX and G10 currencies. We first control for EUR-USD moves, though. Controlling for EUR is important, as otherwise betas are overstated due to the fact that the EUR is a key driver for all EMFX, including CNY, given that CNY is managed against a EUR-heavy basket. As one would expect, the main China impact is on commodity currencies (ZAR, CLP, AUD, COP, NZD) and Asian currencies (AUD, NZD, KRW), where betas range from around

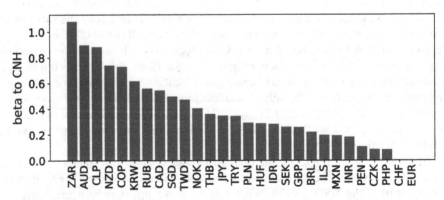

FIGURE 3.7 EM Asia and Commodity FX in China's Cross Hairs, With the MXN as the Safe Haven.
Note: Twelve-month beta to CNH, controlled for EUR.
Source: Bloomberg, authors' calculations.

0.5 to just above 0.9. Next in line, at just below 0.5, is a second set of commodity and/or Asian currencies (JPY, CAD, RUB, TWD, SGD, and NOK). On the other side of the spectrum are some currencies with limited China risk, which are not part of the Chinese supply chain. Among EMFX, MXN sticks out on this front and is, according to our numbers, almost as safe as the Swiss Franc when it comes to China fears! This is interesting, as Mexico is a competitor with China in the all-important US end market. But more recently, MXN is also seen as benefiting from the China-US trade war, as some of the Chinese supply chain will be re-shored not to the US, but to Mexico. As such, we would expect MXN to outperform, in a negative overall environment for EMFX during periods of escalation in the China-US trade conflict.[5]

Going forward, the CNY has a plausible chance to become a dominant global currency. But the internationalization of the CNY is still moving fairly slowly. As of early 2019, the CNY's share of international payments was sitting at just below 1.9%. As per Swift, it is growing quickly in importance, though, helped by the 2016 inclusion into the IMF's SDR basket. Furthermore, usage of CNY for cross-border payments is gaining share fast for countries that are part of the Chinese Belt and Road Initiative (Swift 2019). And from a trading perspective, as of late 2018, the CNY was already the third-most-traded FX after the EUR and JPY. Furthermore, the CNH already anchors most of Asia FX – at at this stage, much more so than the JPY. As can be seen in Figure 3.8, the correlation of USD-CNH to USD-Asia is both higher and more stable than the correlation of USD-Asia to the JPY. While this is partially due to the higher correlation of the CNH with the EUR, it is very likely that the CNH will be the dominant currency in the Asia time zone in the not-too-distant future.

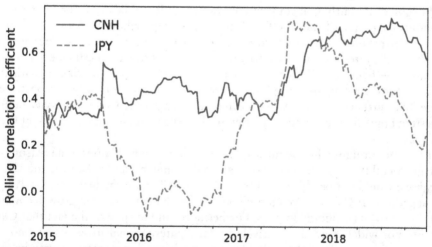

FIGURE 3.8 The Sun has Set for the JPY.
Note: Rolling correlations of USD-Asia to the JPY and CNH.
Source: Bloomberg, authors' calculations.

---

[5] See also Revilla et al. (2019).

3.7   CGBS: THE JGBS FOR MILLENNIALS

Interest rates in China are also less transparent than in most other EM; but again they are extremely important to watch, given the importance of China for EM and global macro. The PBOC has neither a classical inflation target nor a clear way of setting interest rates to achieve any specified economic goals. While the PBOC sets a benchmark lending rate, recently the central bank has preferred other measures to impact monetary conditions. The most high-profile measures have been changes in the required reserve ratios (RRR), which leads to an immediate liquidity injection for the banks. Sometimes, such RRR cuts can be targeted to particular banks or industries. Other measures have been the adjustments to the MLF (medium lending facility: 3 months to 1 year), SLF (standing lending facility: short-term liquidity provision to banks), and reverse repo rates. Alternatively, the liquidity provision volumes for MLF or reverse repo can be adjusted. Having said that, it is a goal of the Chinese regulators to move away from quantitative tools and toward a clear price-based framework, as per the 13th 5-year plan (2016–2020). But for now, the market focus is firmly on the seven-day repo rate. After all, the PBOC is mainly using seven-day reverse repos for its daily open market operations. The seven-day repo rate is also the floating rate for the large and relatively liquid Non-deliverable interest rate swap (ND-IRS) market. This repo rate includes transactions by banks and non-banks: therefore, not only is it determined by conditions in the money market on any given day, but it also may at times include a credit component. As a result, the depository institutions' seven-day repo rate is gaining in importance as a potential future target policy rate, especially since it has been mentioned in the PBOC's monetary policy report.[6]

In spite of its fairly non-transparent way of setting policies, in the bigger picture, the monetary policy of the PBOC has been relatively orthodox. Around six months after a deceleration in activity has started, monetary easing commences. Therefore, even though interest rates are not necessarily the most potent tool to ease financial conditions in China, the five-year ND-IRS swap has a relatively strong correlation with the Li Keqiang index, one key measure for activity in China. This is clearly demonstrated by Figure 3.9. Furthermore, bond yields often have lagged the Chinese activity numbers, suggesting opportunities to add alpha by trading the Chinese business cycle in Chinese fixed income.

Also interestingly, Chinese rates are more volatile than US rates. One reason is that the true volatility in Chinese growth may well be much higher than for the US, even though we would not be able to tell from the officially published Chinese GDP figures. This suggests that China is even more relevant for changes to global growth conditions than the size of its economy implies. Furthermore, and in spite of the fact that Chinese rates are not widely traded as actively by large international investors, we note that there is information about the global business cycle in Chinese rates. As can be seen in Figure 3.10, US rates and Chinese rates clearly have a common driver. Plus, Chinese rates often lead US rates, especially at troughs. For example, in 2009 rates stopped

---

[6]For a more detailed description, see Sun and Mathur (2016).

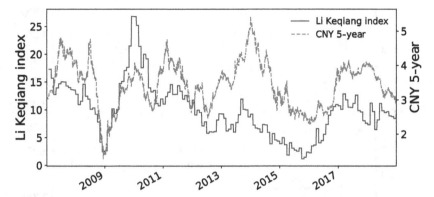

FIGURE 3.9 Chinese Yields Lagging the Chinese Business Cycle.
Source: Bloomberg.

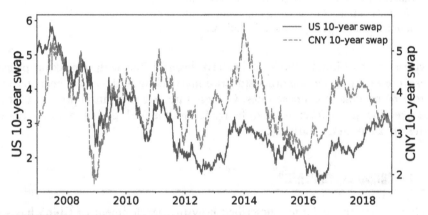

FIGURE 3.10 But Chinese Yields Often Lead US Rates.
Source: Bloomberg.

falling in China before they had clearly bottomed in the US. Chinese rates also led US rates ahead of the taper tantrum (albeit, impractically, by almost a year) and again in 2016 (by six months). In terms of peaks in yields, US rates appear to be more often leading. But Chinese rates often peak in a more volatile fashion, making peaks for US rates easier to identify. And the big rally in Chinese rates starting in March 2018 was a signal that the US rates sell-off in early 2018 was extremely mature. Finally, a bottom in Chinese rates is also often a bullish event for Chinese equities. In the old days, global macro investors spent a significant amount of time on JGBs, given their importance for the global business cycle. CGBs are the JGBs for the new millennium, and it pays to watch the signals of Chinese rates to get the global macro cycle right.

To make this strong correlation between Chinese and US rates tradable, we regress Chinese rates on US rates and plot the residuals of a 52-week rolling regression next to Chinese yields in Figure 3.11. While this is a very simplistic model, it is nevertheless

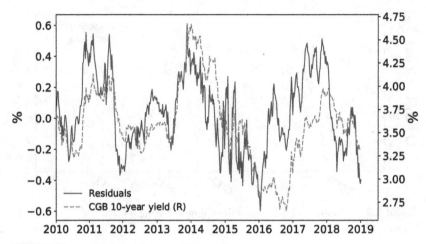

FIGURE 3.11 Calling for Turns in Chinese Rates.
Note: Residuals of a 52-week regression of China on US rates.
Source: Bloomberg, authors' calculations.

noteworthy that residuals above 50 bp have been in line with a peaking process of Chinese interest rates. On the other side, residuals below −50 bp have been in line with a bottoming process in Chinese rates. Chinese rates are now an important part of the global fixed-income market and can be traded in line with global factors – for which US rates are a summary statistics.

3.8 THE GRAND DECOUPLING?

This chapter has so far largely described how the development of China has shaped EM ever since it joined the WTO in 2002. But there is, of course, a question of whether the next decade could be qualitatively different. From the point of view of Chinese policy makers, there is no reason to change a fantastically successful playbook. However, the perception of China by the US government and, to a lesser extent, by the rest of the world has clearly changed for the worse, and there is a heightened desire across the political divide in the US to change the rules of the game in favour of the US. Given rising tensions, a new Cold War, where the world is split into US and Chinese spheres of influence, becomes an increasingly plausible base case. However, we doubt that even in such a scenario the impact of China on EM will be much diminished. After all, the linkages we have described are economic, not political. The importance of China is mostly the result of the size of its economy and its fast growth, and the relative size of China will only increase. The comparison to the Cold War with the Soviet Union is not overly apt, largely because the Soviet Union cut most economic linkages to the West. In the 1980s, exports and imports each were only around 4% of Soviet GDP. Total trade with the US amounted to around USD 2 billion per year in the late 1980s. Of course, if China were to cut itself off from the global economy, the Soviet analogue would become much more relevant. But this would be a very extreme measure that we consider unlikely even in a Cold War scenario.

3.9 SUMMARY

China is already a key driver for the global business cycle, which implies that the Fed cannot ignore China when setting monetary policy. This is a positive for China, as it is the only emerging market that can expect a helping hand from the Fed in times of trouble. The importance of China will only grow going forward, both because its relative size will continue to increase and because its financial markets will become more tightly integrated into global financial markets. This integration, especially when combined with the disappearing act of the current account surplus, increases the risks, and the world will have to get used to managing global shocks emanating from China. The commodity link makes EM especially vulnerable to these shocks. EM Asia will also be at the receiving end of future shocks from China. Mexico is one of the few beneficiaries from a US trade war with China.

But even before Chinese financial integration advances much further, investors should be intensely focused on both CNH and Chinese interest rates. With respect to the former, it typically pays off to position in line with the policy signals sent by the authorities through the fixing mechanism. With respect to Chinese interest rates, they are eminently tradable in line with the Chinese business cycle. Furthermore, the Chinese bond market has at times been a great leading indicator for US rates and should be part of the dashboard of any global macro and EM investor.

CHAPTER 4

How to Trade EMFX

EMFX trading has gained market share from G10 FX trading over the last decade, as briefly discussed in Chapter 1. And it is plausible that EMFX is even more important for alpha generation than its rising market share suggests. This is likely the case because one of the more popular strategies to extract alpha in FX is the carry strategy. With carry in G10 having collapsed in the aftermath of the financial crisis, EMFX has become more important for carry-hungry currency investors, even though carry in EM has admittedly also fallen for some time now. While to our mind, EMFX is a very macro asset class, there are also micro features that can be exploited to generate alpha. This chapter outlines how we propose to go about doing that.[1]

4.1 ONLY THE JPY IS SPECIAL

We start off with a quick discussion of how to define what an emerging market is for the sake of FX trading.[2] It turns out that it is actually very hard to find a dividing line that neatly separates EMFX from G10 FX. In Chapter 2, we found that EMFX is driven to a large degree by global macro factors, and in particular by equities/risk aversion, US credit, commodities, and, in some periods, US rates. When analysing the correlation patterns of both G10 FX (where we ignore CHF, as it is mostly driven by EUR) and EMFX with these major macro drivers in more detail, as we do in Table 4.1, it turns out that the only currency that is "special" is the Japanese Yen, because it appreciates relatively reliably with rising risk aversion and to some extent, for the same reason, rallies when US rates are falling. No other currency (again excluding CHF) has a consistently strongly positive correlation with risk aversion, be it a G10 or an EM currency. The EUR comes relatively close, though. It also has a positive beta to the US HY index, a slight negative beta to VIX, and a positive beta to the SPX. But the betas are much smaller than for the JPY, and the relationship is less consistent. But for

---

[1] We would also point the reader to Donnelly (2019) for a very worthwhile discussion of FX trading. Donnelly is more focused on technicals than we are but also lays out the fundamental principles of FX trading extremely well.
[2] As we are interested in the trading behaviour of the various assets, rather than in a unified theory of what constitutes an emerging market, we think that the definition should be asset-class-specific.

TABLE 4.1   It is Hard to Distinguish Between EMFX and G10 FX.

	UST 10yr	SPX	US HY	VIX	BBG commodity
USD-BRL	4%	−28%	−82%	2%	−39%
USD-MXN	8%	−25%	−79%	2%	−26%
USD-CLP	3%	−21%	−58%	2%	−28%
USD-COP	0%	−44%	−125%	3%	−48%
USD-KRW	3%	−19%	−58%	2%	−22%
USD-TWD	1%	−8%	−25%	1%	−10%
USD-INR	3%	−10%	−31%	1%	−9%
USD-CNY	1%	−1%	−5%	0%	−6%
USD-MYR	3%	−16%	−67%	1%	−19%
USD-IDR	1%	−17%	−53%	1%	−14%
USD-SGD	5%	−6%	−25%	0%	−15%
USD-PHP	2%	−4%	−24%	1%	−5%
USD-THB	4%	−8%	−29%	1%	−14%
EUR-PLN	2%	−12%	−31%	1%	−7%
EUR-CZK	0%	0%	−2%	0%	−1%
EUR-HUF	2%	−9%	−16%	1%	−5%
USD-RUB	−7%	−48%	−135%	5%	−62%
USD-TRY	5%	−20%	−36%	2%	−17%
USD-ZAR	9%	−36%	−84%	3%	−38%
Median EM	3%	−16%	−36%	1%	−15%
USD-JPY	16%	26%	27%	−3%	−4%
USD-EUR	6%	5%	2%	−1%	−19%
EUR-NOK	1%	−21%	−66%	2%	−18%
EUR-SEK	−1%	−10%	−26%	1%	−4%
USD-CAD	1%	−17%	−51%	1%	−35%
USD-AUD	4%	−25%	−64%	2%	−32%
USD-NZD	8%	−12%	−42%	0%	−23%
Median G10	4%	−12%	−42%	1%	−19%

Note: Betas of FX to US rates, SPX, US HY, BBG commodities, and VIX.
Source: Bloomberg, authors' calculations.

any G10 currency other than the JPY and maybe the EUR, the betas are very similar to the betas of their EM peers. On the EM side, the one currency that comes closest to behaving like a risk-free currency is EUR-CZK, followed by CNY (given that it is highly managed). And if we create a basket of the G10 commodity currencies (NOK, AUD, NZD, and CAD) and compare its correlation structure to an EM commodity basket (RUB, ZAR, CLP, COP, BRL, PEN, IDR, and MYR), the betas to those global macro market drivers are very similar and at times even lower for the EM commodity basket than for the G10 commodity basket. We conclude that when it comes to their trading behaviour with respect to global macro, G10 and EM commodity currencies are more similar than different in most respects. Therefore, it is more helpful to distinguish between commodity producers and commodity consumers rather than between G10 and EM currencies.

But when abstracting from global macro correlations, we do find important differences between G10 and EM currencies that become obvious on closer inspection. One distinction is that the institutional framework is often weaker in poorer countries than in richer countries (and the classical delineating feature between EM versus G10 is, of course, GDP per head). While on most trading days this difference is irrelevant, it becomes episodically very important, especially during election time. A lot more damage can be caused if a market-unfriendly candidate wins in the average emerging market than when this happens in the average G10 country, presumably because personalities often are able to dominate institutions in EM more easily than they can in DM, where checks and balances are more pronounced. EM currencies take such risks into account to a larger extent than G10 currencies do – but only when elections are close. Weaker institutions also make policies like capital controls more likely. Later in this book, we are going to illustrate how these events can be traded in EMFX.

4.2   NO HELPING HAND FROM EM RATES

Another key difference between EMFX and G10 FX is that interest rate spreads explain an important part of the trading behaviour of G10 FX, but such spreads explain very little for EMFX. In particular, for G10, more hawkish central banks typically lead to widening spreads of interest rates versus the US, which then results in a stronger currency. This is not true for EMFX, where local rates often move higher with weaker FX. We illustrate this pattern in Figure 4.1. The chart shows a simulated P&L for a strategy that assumes perfect foresight on two-year interest rates. When spreads of

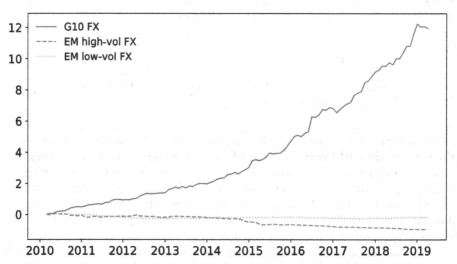

FIGURE 4.1   And This is What Makes EMFX Different from G10 FX.
Note: P&L of a perfect-foresight strategy for EM and G10 FX using two-year swap rates.
Source: Bloomberg, authors' calculations.

domestic interest rates against US rates rise, the strategy goes long the currency in question against the USD. The opposite trade is put on when the interest rates fall versus US rates. We apply this strategy to G10 FX and to EMFX, where we distinguish between low-volatility and high-volatility EMFX. The argument for making this distinction is that low-volatility EMFX is unlikely to sell off by enough to generate inflation fears and rate hike expectations, cutting off one of the possible channels that tie higher rates to weaker FX. As can be seen, the results vary drastically for the three classes of currencies. For G10 currencies, the simulated P&L moves higher, almost in a straight line and without major pullbacks. In EMFX, however, the P&L is heading slowly but consistently lower, also with little reprieve. The downward slope is more pronounced for the high-volatility EMFX, but even low-volatility EMFX loses money when traded in line with interest rate differentials. As it turns out, even for low-volatility EMFX, rising risk aversion can lead to a strengthening USD, which then also pushes up EM rates, mostly in a coincident fashion.

And even controlling for risk aversion and USD directionality more directly, G10 FX and EMFX behave differently when it comes to interest rates. This becomes clear when we implement the same strategy once more, but this time apply our trading rule separately to EMFX and to G10 relative value crosses. In this exercise, we make sure that both currencies for a given cross are similarly volatile. This approach largely strips out the impact from rising risk aversion given that it removes any USD directionality. With this exercise, we obtain results for G10 FX that are very similar to before. If we had perfect foresight on rate differentials in G10 space, the P&L when going long the currency where rate spreads are rising, and vice versa, is consistently positive. The pattern for EMFX is different, though. Instead of pointing straight down, the P&L chart goes mostly sideways, neither making nor losing much money. This is an important finding. It suggests that even once we have controlled for episodes of rising risk aversion, it is still the case that more hawkish central banks are not necessarily bullish for EM currencies. One reason is that many EMs are attracting large capital inflows when local bonds are in a bull market, which is often the case when central banks are cutting rates. Such bond inflows can lead to currency strength in spite of lower rate differentials.

The correlation of FX with their domestic interest rate is for us the key distinction between EMFX and G10 FX. Either rates differentials are important to trade FX, in which case the currency quacks like a G10 FX, or they are not, in which case we should treat that currency like an EM currency, even if the country is not categorized that way by more traditional definitions.

Using this approach, we can identify the "true" EM currencies, at least from a currency trading perspective. Table 4.2 shows the mean returns, volatilities, and information ratios (IRs) by currency resulting from the perfect-foresight strategy of the USD crosses. The true EM currencies are the ones that have negative IRs. The results are mostly as one would intuitively have expected. In Latam, the BRL, MXN, COP, and PEN all behave like true EM currencies, while the CLP does not. In CEEMEA, the TRY, RUB, ZAR, and HUF behave like EM currencies, while the PLN, CZK, and ILS do not. In Asia, most currencies behave like G10 currencies. Here the results are less intuitive, as the currencies that trade like EM currencies are the TWD and, to a lesser extent, the SGD, which are not the typical high yielders that appear in Latam and CEEMEA.

TABLE 4.2   Some EM Currencies Behave like G10, Mostly in Asia.

FX	Mean	Volatility	IR
AUD	18.1%	12.9%	1.41
CAD	11.9%	9.4%	1.26
CHF	13.7%	11.6%	1.18
EUR	11.5%	9.5%	1.21
JPY	10.1%	9.9%	1.01
NOK	15.7%	12.2%	1.29
SEK	15.9%	12.0%	1.33
CNY	2.5%	3.0%	0.83
INR	0.7%	8.0%	0.09
KRW	3.6%	12.0%	0.30
MYR	3.9%	7.2%	0.54
SGD	−0.4%	5.4%	(0.08)
THB	1.6%	6.8%	0.23
TWD	−7.2%	4.9%	(1.48)
CZK	10.3%	12.0%	0.86
HUF	−13.3%	14.4%	(0.93)
ILS	0.4%	7.9%	0.05
PLN	4.4%	13.7%	0.32
RUB	−12.4%	15.0%	(0.83)
TRY	−20.7%	14.5%	(1.43)
ZAR	−20.5%	16.9%	(1.21)
BRL	−10.6%	16.0%	(0.67)
CLP	5.2%	10.3%	0.51
COP	−6.6%	11.8%	(0.56)
MXN	−7.9%	11.3%	(0.70)
PEN	−4.8%	5.9%	(0.81)

Note: Mean returns, volatility, and IRs for a perfect-foresight strategy for two-year swaps.
Source: Bloomberg, authors' calculations.

4.3   CARRY WORKS – IF YOU ARE JAPANESE

For now, we have only established that rising or falling interest rates, i.e. interest rate changes, do not act as a systematic driver for EMFX. But maybe the level of rates does work: after all, buying a basket of high-yielding currencies is the classic carry trade that often attracts investors to EM in the first place.[3] From a practitioner's point of view, there are a few ways to investigate this question. First, investors could try (and have tried) to buy the top yielders outright, often against the USD, but also against the EUR or JPY, depending on the relevant home currency. These strategies have done well in the heydays of EM currencies, but their performance has been mostly uninspiring

---

[3]For some academic studies, see also Brunnermeier et al. (2008), Gilmore and Hayashi (2011), Burnside et al. (2007), McCauley and Scatigna (2011), and Heath et al. (2007).

FIGURE 4.2   Carry Returns Funded in JPY Outperform Over the Cycle.
Note: Carry returns of the top four highest ranked carry currencies in
USD, EUR, and JPY terms.
Source: Bloomberg, authors' calculations.

since 2012. Against the USD, peak performance was reached in 2011. This is not
surprising, as 2011 marked the beginning of the broad USD bull market. While the
carry trade funded in USD returned to its peak performance levels in late 2017, it faded
again in 2018. The EM carry trade has left USD-based investors without any profits
since 2011, as can be seen in Figure 4.2. Investors funding EMFX in EUR or JPY are
obviously performing much better in the recent USD bull market. When considering
performance during the earlier USD bear market, the advantage of EUR or JPY funding
is no longer clear. Still, while the cumulative returns for USD- and EUR-funded carry
trades are almost identical between 2003 to 2018, the EUR-funded trade has a much
higher Sharpe ratio. And the JPY-funded cumulative returns are significantly higher
than EMFX returns funded in either USD or EUR. The popularity of the carry trade
in Japan is therefore not overly surprising. Still, with USD-funded EMFX trades being
prevalent in markets, we conclude that the carry trade in its simplest form has been
eaten up by the USD bull market. We encourage even investors not based in the
Eurozone or Japan to consider diversifying the funding for EM carry plays.

One (slight) improvement can be implemented by taking volatility into account.[4]
If we rank currencies by carry over realized volatility and then go long the top four
versus the bottom four in a volatility-adjusted way (where the weight of each currency in the basket depends on how volatile it has been over the previous year), the
P&L improves (slightly), as demonstrated in Figure 4.3. Trading EMFX pairs on a
volatility-adjusted basis is actually something that we find improves alpha opportunities more broadly, also in a single currency pair setting, as has been demonstrated by
Willer and Dabholkar (2019a).

One obvious culprit for the degradation of the simplest carry strategy could be that
the level of carry has fallen, also in risk-adjusted terms. This would be in line with

---

[4]See also Moreira and Muir (2017) and Menkhoff et al. (2012) for a more academic treatment.

FIGURE 4.3 Taking Volatility into Account Helps.
Note: Rank of carry adjusted by volatility, and positions weighted by volatility.
Source: Bloomberg, authors' calculations.

the outperformance of the JPY-funded strategy, given that carry over the period under study was highest when funded in JPY. However, Figure 4.4 suggests that this is not the full story. True, carry was meaningfully higher in the early 2000s, when the carry strategy was doing well. It was again meaningfully higher than it has been more recently following the 2008–2009 crisis, when the carry strategy also did well. But since the carry strategy largely stopped working in 2011, carry has been at times meaningfully higher than it was during the good old days of either 2007 or 2010. As such, lower carry offers only a partial explanation for the degradation of the performance of the carry strategy. Adjusting carry for (realized) volatility is not suggestive of carry being

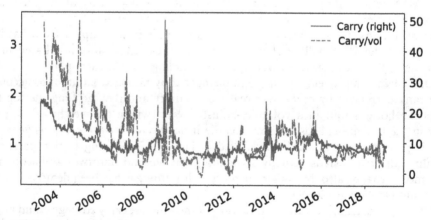

FIGURE 4.4 Lower Rates Alone are Not To Blame.
Note: Average carry of the carry strategy outright and adjusted by realized volatility.
Source: Bloomberg, authors' calculations.

extremely low, either. It is plausible that we need yields for EM currencies to rise quite substantially, maybe to the levels of the glory days of 2004, for the carry strategy to come back into favour. But this is unlikely in a global low interest rate environment. We therefore conclude that the carry strategy in its simplest form no longer provides sufficiently attractive returns, at least unless the DXY turns.

Investors have been trying several approaches to improve on the simple carry strategy. One early attempt was to strip out the USD directionality by converting it into a long-short strategy, where investors short the lowest-yielding EM currencies against the highest yielders. Picking the four top ranked against the four bottom ranked currencies survived the 2008 risk-aversion spike relatively well (performance not shown in a chart). However, the overall performance is directionally very similar to the long-only carry strategy, and the high watermark of 2011 had not been reached again by the end of 2018. And cumulative performance is considerably worse than it is without the short leg of the basket. But just as with the long-only version, volatility adjustments improve performance. Figure 4.5 illustrates the P&L when longs and shorts are picked from a ranking of volatility-adjusted carry. The sizes of the positions are then normalized by volatility as well. This strategy makes new highs after 2011 and, for now, peaks out in 2016. It performs better than the long-only strategy that picks only the top four currencies with the highest volatility-adjusted carry.

In the end, all of these strategies need to be judged by focusing on the IRs. We summarize these ratios for the various USD-funded carry strategies in Table 4.3. While the long-short setup lowers the volatility of the strategy, this comes at the price of lowering returns, too. In terms of IRs, a long-short carry strategy beats the EMFX index but does slightly worse than the long-only carry strategy. Volatility-adjusting the long-short carry strategy again leads to improvements. But, once more, the IR is actually lower than it is for the volatility-adjusted long-only strategy, as returns fall by more than volatility. With the volatility-adjusted long-short strategy making new highs in P&L terms in 2016, it is premature to claim that carry is dead. But at the very least, returns have clearly deteriorated during recent years.

FIGURE 4.5 Long-Short is Expensive, But Volatility-Adjusted is Less So.
Source: Bloomberg, authors' calculations.

TABLE 4.3　Volatility Adjustments Are a Good Idea!.

Strategy	Mean	Vol	IR
Long carry	8.7%	10.6%	0.83
Vol-adjusted long carry	8.6%	7.4%	1.16
long-short carry	6.9%	8.8%	0.78
Vol-adjusted long-short carry	7.2%	6.8%	1.05
EMFX benchmark	4.8%	6.2%	0.79

Note: Mean, Vol, and IR calculated from 2003 to 2018.
Source: Bloomberg, authors' calculations.

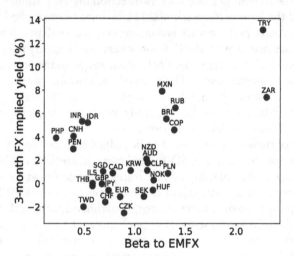

FIGURE 4.6　Finding the Best Hedges.
Note: As of December 2018.
Source: Bloomberg, authors' calculations.

In spite of having demonstrated the high costs of hedging/running a long-short strategy, it is an important concept that there are currencies that are volatile, have a strong correlation with global risk, and are low positive or at times even negative carry. Such currencies offer the best hedging opportunities. As an illustration, Figure 4.6 shows the state of affairs as of the end of December 2018. The three most interesting currencies, with a beta greater than one and negative carry, were the HUF and SEK. To be less dependent on idiosyncratic country developments, the EUR and CZK may also be added to such a hedge basket.

The subsequent average spot performance of those four currencies in 2019 was −3.4%. The volatility-adjusted spot performance of our EMFX index over the same time was −0.4%. 2019 was therefore a banner year for such hedges, given that the spot performance does not even account for the positive carry of the basket.

The strategy to use the cheapest hedge actually works relatively well when applied systematically. We illustrate this point by always finding the cheapest hedge for our

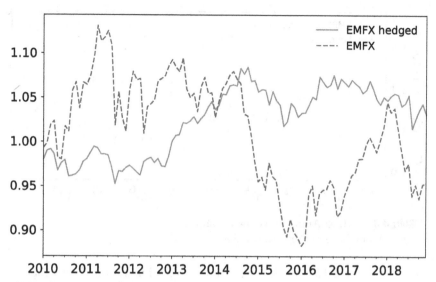

FIGURE 4.7 Low-Cost Hedges At Work.
Source: Bloomberg, authors' calculations.

EMFX index by comparing the carry of each potential hedge after adjusting for the beta to the EMFX index. We then pick a basket of the three cheapest hedges to reduce the impact of idiosyncratic shocks. We go long our EMFX index and hedge with this hedging basket. Figure 4.7 illustrates the resulting P&L. The hedged EMFX index either goes sideways (2010 to 2013, and then again 2015 to 2018) or makes money (2013 to 2015). While being long a hedged version of the EMFX index clearly is not making anyone rich, the hedge works relatively well.

Other refinements of the carry strategy are to time the onset of risk aversion, which is usually carry negative, and to reduce carry strategies at those times.[5] Rising risk aversion is typically identified by rising implied volatilities. But which risk the market cares about can be different in every cycle. It can be equity risk, as in 2001–2002; it can be US rates risk, as in 2013; or it can be risk from oil, as in 2015. FX volatility, for both G10 and EMFX, can also be a useful warning indicator. Even though the volatilities for different asset classes are often highly correlated, we believe it is most relevant to focus on the maximum of such volatilities, rather than on the median or average. This is the case because EMFX reacts poorly even if only one important global macro driver starts to deteriorate. To be precise, we define our risk index as the maximum z-score (with a two-year lookback), of the implied volatilities for EMFX, G10 FX, US rates, the S&P 500, and oil. The risk index cuts out the long EMFX exposure whenever the index moves above two standard deviations, and re-enters the long EMFX index when it falls back below two. The analysis only starts in 2010 because the implied volatility index for oil begins in April 2009, and we found that implied volatilities are clearly

---

[5]For an academic treatment, see also Menkhoff et al. (2012), Egbers and Swinkels (2015), and Mulder and Tims (2018).

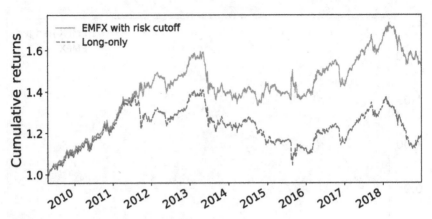

FIGURE 4.8   EMFX: Afraid of its Own Shadow.
Source: Bloomberg, authors' calculations.

superior to realized volatilities for signalling danger. Figure 4.8 shows that this risk overlay significantly improves the return even when compared to our volatility-ranked and volatility-adjusted EMFX long-only carry index.[6]

4.4   CURRENT ACCOUNTS: MEASURING RISK THE OLD-FASHIONED WAY

Given that the carry strategy has recently been, at best, a qualified success, we now investigate the second most important fundamental factor (after interest rates) for a country when it comes to FX: the current account. Large current account deficits are negative for currencies during episodes of rising risk aversion, as such deficits have to be financed, which is increasingly difficult when investors start to flee for the safety of their home markets. On the other hand, countries with a current account surplus benefit during crisis times as capital outflows stop (or even reverse), leading to appreciation pressures thanks to a strong current account. Therefore, a positive current account makes a country safer at times of rising risk aversion. The problem is that the performance of the current account factor, here expressed as top four versus bottom four currencies, ranked by current account balances, is overall money losing. As illustrated by Figure 4.9, the main episodes of outperformance were the 2008 crisis, the 2013 tapering episode, and, to a lesser extent, the collapse in crude oil in 2014–2015. In 2018, the strategy also performed well, largely due to idiosyncratic country issues that came to the fore in both Argentina and Turkey. But those episodes of stress have not been enough to make the current account factor a profitable strategy unless it is coupled with a strong view on when risk aversion is going to rise.

---

[6]See also Gill (2018). Gill proposes to be long EM only when an EM risk index containing global economic surprises and data momentum, an EM sovereign bond index, implied volatility of EMFX options, change in assets in EM ETFs, and EM high beta to low beta correlations is in its lower 50 percentile.

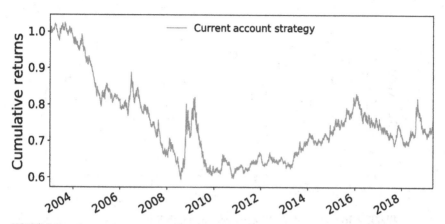

FIGURE 4.9 Playing It Safe Does Not Pay.
Note: P&L of a strategy that is long four best current account balances versus short the four worst. We assume zero slippage and transaction costs.
Source: Bloomberg, authors' calculations.

The problem with the current account factor is that countries with a current account surplus often have low (real) rates. This is the case because such countries do not need high rates to compensate investors for the additional risk inherent in a weak external balance. Therefore, the current account strategy is often exactly the opposite of the carry strategy. This is why the current account strategy does not perform well during good times, when money is flooding into higher interest rate countries.[7] Figure 4.10 loosely illustrates this relationship for the end of 2018, where real rates are calculated as (nominal) FX implied interest rates minus current CPI. Countries with a current account deficit of more than 3% of GDP all offer high real rates. The current account surplus crowd can get away with much less. Exceptions are few, even though a country like Russia, for example, chooses to have high real interest rates in spite of the fact that the market would likely give the central bank room to adjust rates lower without undermining its currency.

The case of Russia raises the somewhat obvious question of whether those two factors can be combined into a strategy where high carry *plus* a decent balance of payments would make up the longs, while countries with low carry with a poor balance of payments would constitute the shorts. Of course, to get large carry with a strong balance of payments position is very rare – and at times can signal other issues (elections, fiscal, etc). But to illustrate the concept, we test a strategy where we rank countries by current account balances as well as by carry and then add those two ranks. We then go long the top four versus the bottom four. However, the results are not overly encouraging (no chart shown). One issue is that the current account numbers move very slowly, and as such, the rankings are very sticky and do not react much to either improvement

---

[7] We note that some of the academic literature also focuses on factors other than current accounts, such as low FDI, credit buildup, low reserves, and currency overvaluation, that are associated with large currency crashes (Frankel and Rose 1996). But the basic idea that such risk factors are usually more than compensated for by carry still often holds.

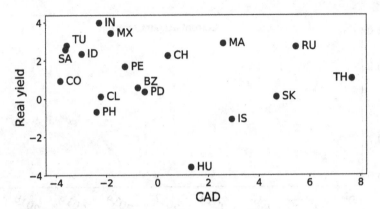

FIGURE 4.10   Only Risky Borrowers Pay High Rates.
Note: Real rates calculated as three-month FX implieds minus current CPIs, Dec 2018.
Source: Bloomberg, authors' calculations.

or deterioration on a timely basis. We therefore also investigate whether an improving current account is helpful, as long as carry is sufficiently high. For improvements, we analyse changes in the trade balance. While the trade balance is a much narrower concept than the current account, the majority of the variation in the current account usually comes from the trade balance. Furthermore, publication lags are much shorter for most countries. We define an improvement or deterioration as a six-month change in the trade balance as percent of GDP. We rank currencies by both this trade improvement and carry, add those two ranks, and then construct a basket that is long the top four currencies against the bottom four. Figure 4.11 shows the P&L, which is much better than the one with a static current account focus. Our conclusion is that the best

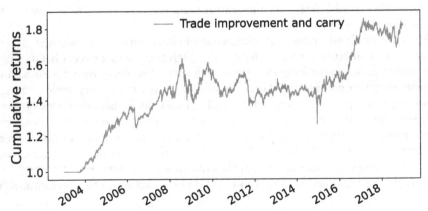

FIGURE 4.11   Carry Combined with Trade Improvement Works Better.
Note: top 4 against bottom 4 currencies when adding ranks for carry and 6 m change in trade balance.
Source: Bloomberg, authors' calculations.

way to use current accounts is to look for improvements, rather than for levels, and that carry needs to be taken into account together with any current account model to generate alpha.

INDIA ESCAPES THE CLUB OF THE FRAGILE FIVE

2013 was the year of tapering by the Fed. As usual, the onset of tightening by the Fed had significant negative spillover effects on EM. Morgan Stanley is credited with coining the term *Fragile Five* for the group of countries that were going to feel the impact of the liquidity withdrawal in the most acute fashion. Those five fragile countries were Indonesia, South Africa, Brazil, Turkey, and India. As is typical when worrying about quickly disappearing liquidity, those countries were largely chosen based on the size of their current account deficits. The five countries sported current account deficits ranging from -3.2% in Indonesia to -6.7% in Turkey. India certainly fit well into the group, with a current account deficit of around 5% of GDP (and a consolidated fiscal deficit of around 7% of GDP). The currencies of the Fragile Five were the worst performers in spot terms in 2013, and again, India fit in well, with the INR weakening by almost 12% that year.

But then external balances started to improve in India. The 12-month rolling trade balance bottomed out in June 2013, an event that became obvious by September 2013. The improvement was initially driven by general government belt-tightening measures and by lower gold imports (due to the government imposing a 10% import tariff on gold, which is important in India: it accounted for around 25% of India's trade deficit at the time). In July 2013, the INR started to meaningfully outperform IDR (which we use as a funding currency to remove the overall directionality of USD-Asia). As can be seen in Figure 4.12, the

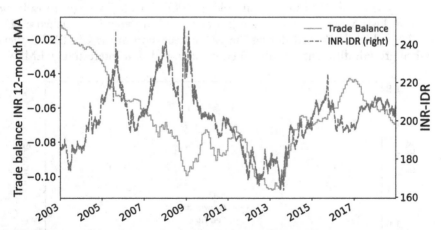

FIGURE 4.12 INR Changes Trend with Improving Trade Balances.
Note: Twelve-month MA of Indian trade balance versus INR-IDR.
Source: Bloomberg.

(*Continued*)

INR outperformance started at a time when the current account deficit was still reasonably large. But the change in trend, combined with continued intervention by the RBI, was enough to convince the market that India was on its way to becoming less fragile. In a second leg, falling oil imports also contributed to the current account adjustment as oil prices started their large sell-off in the second half of 2014 – a lucky occurrence that the Indian government used to lower subsidies for fuel prices, cutting oil demand on a more permanent basis. By 2015, the current account deficit stood at -1.3%: fragile no more.

4.5   GOING FOR GROWTH

Other than carry and external position, the other major attraction of EM has been that growth tends to be higher than in DM, as EM are catching up with the living standards and know-how of developed countries (although we note that recently, not much catch-up has been in evidence). Historically, periods of strong EM growth have on average been good for the performance of EMFX. But the correlation is not as strong as a naive discussion would suggest. The reason is that at times of high global growth, the Fed typically hikes rates. Such rate hikes often undermine the positive impact of strong EM growth. The most beneficial part of the growth cycle is early on, when growth differentials start to improve in favour of EM but the Fed is still in the initial phase of its hiking cycle where monetary policy is still relatively easy. This interplay between growth differentials and the Federal Reserve is illustrated in Figure 4.13. The 2004 to 2006 Fed tightening cycle is a case in point. Initially, EMFX performed well as growth differentials between EM and G3 started to increase, even though the Fed also started its tightening process. But then, from 2005 onward, EMFX started to go sideways in spite of a continued rise in growth differentials. The Fed hikes had started to bite. Only when the Fed moved on hold in 2006 did EMFX begin to rally again. The peak in EMFX performance came just as growth differentials reached a peak of around 7%, which happened during the Great Recession in the US. EMFX then fell hard when growth differentials subsequently narrowed. But interestingly, EMFX then

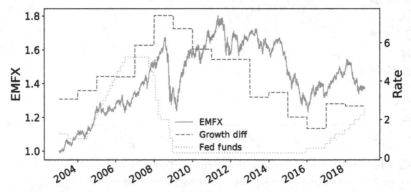

FIGURE 4.13   High EM Growth Differentials and Easy Money are Bullish for EMFX.
Source: Bloomberg.

recovered and largely range traded even as growth differentials moved lower. Only when growth differentials entered a new range of around 1.5 to 3%, did EMFX start to sell off more significantly. The story was the same during the Fed hiking cycle that started in December 2015. The early part of the Fed hiking cycle was tolerable for EMFX, as growth differentials started to improve again. It was the latter part of the Fed hikes that began to undermine EMFX at a time when growth differentials stopped rising.

A more precise and higher-frequency approach to analyse the importance of the growth factor is to focus on the economic indexes: for example, those produced by Citi's excellent quant FX group. Those indexes are constructed as a MA of the economic growth surprises vis-a-vis Bloomberg expectations, with a weighting that is in line with the importance of the indicator for the FX markets. While we found that bottoming economic surprise indexes for EM are not overly supportive for EMFX, we note that whenever the EM economic surprise index starts to move more strongly into positive territory, the likelihood for EMFX to put in a short-term bottom, followed by a significant EMFX rally, rises significantly. This finding makes intuitive sense to us because those surprise indexes are by construction moving to zero over time, even if nothing really changes, just as previous negative (or positive) surprises drop out. And moving to zero does not appear to move the needle for EMFX. It takes actual positive growth surprises to get the index into positive territory, and that does move the needle for EMFX.[8] Noual has demonstrated the utility of the surprise indexes for G10 FX trading more broadly (Noual 2015).

Figure 4.14 illustrates the performance of a strategy that goes long EMFX when Citi's EM economic surprises cross the zero line from below and short EMFX when surprises cross back below zero. The P&L is meaningfully positive and relatively

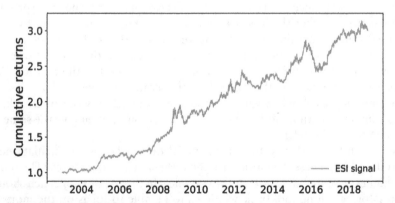

FIGURE 4.14 EMFX Likes Growth.
Note: P&L of a strategy that uses crossovers over the zero line of the Citi EM economic surprise index. We assume zero slippage and transaction costs.
Source: Citi, Bloomberg, authors' calculations.

---

[8]This has also been demonstrated for the EMFX asset class by Willer, Costa, and Garg (Willer et al. 2019). Kasikov has demonstrated that the strategy also works in a cross-sectional context where the currencies with the volatility-adjusted highest surprise indexes outperform (Kasikov 2018).

consistent. Interestingly, the strategy performs less well when the spread against the US economic surprise index is used. At the end of 2018, the growth factor was the most consistently profitable factor for EMFX trading. We conclude that growth does play an important role for trading EMFX, even as the focus on surprises suggests a more subtle relationship than the classical focus on growth differentials.

4.6 MODEST VALUE IN VALUATION

For most asset classes, valuation is an important aspect of trading, as it often can serve as an anchor for how far asset prices can move. The bad news in the case of FX is that valuation means very little. While there are a few classical concepts for how to value FX, they are, in our view, not overly compelling. Maybe this is why chartists are especially prevalent in the FX business. Without a valuation anchor, a focus on charts and technical analysis can become irresistible. In spite of the difficulties in applying valuation concepts to FX, extreme readings should be taken into consideration in the investment process, and we therefore go through some simple concepts of valuation for FX.

The most straightforward way to think about valuation is to generate a long history of real effective exchange rates (REERs) and analyse how cheap a currency is compared to its past. Here, the "real" aspect of the REER concept corrects exchange rates for inflation differentials, which can be done using PPIs, CPIs, or unit labour costs (Harberger 2004). The "effective" aspect takes the composition of the export and import destinations into account. But all other fundamentals are assumed to stay constant, which clearly is an oversimplification that is rarely reflective of reality. The other problem with the REER concept is that the indexes were at some stage arbitrarily set to a predetermined initial value before they started to move in line with spot FX moves and inflation. But as the initial starting point was not necessarily set to a time period when the currency was fairly valued, it is very hard to interpret the level of the REER index. Still, investors use deviations from the REERs, partly because the view is that the concept of valuation can only work when valuations are very significantly out of whack. At such extremes, simple valuation models, like REER-based ones, often give the same answers as more complicated models.

One straightforward way to implement REER models is to calculate deviations from a rolling MA. These deviations are then translated into z-scores. The model goes long the highest z-scores and short the lowest ones. In theory, this approach should work principally for very long lookback windows to be able to focus on the more extreme readings. In Figure 4.15, we use a lookback window for the z-scores of 10 years and, as usual, choose the top four z-scores against the bottom four on a volatility-adjusted basis. However, as can be clearly seen, the results are far from impressive.[9]

---

[9]In the academic literature, it is also demonstrated that for G10 FX, simple valuation measures like REER and HP-filtered REER do not generate alpha, though filtering currencies included in a carry strategy for extreme over- or under-valuations has proved to be more useful (Nozaki 2010).

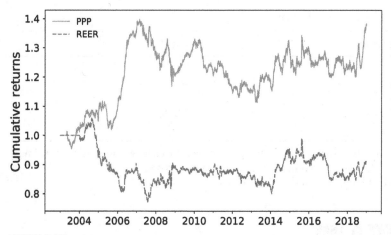

FIGURE 4.15 Valuation: Focus on PPP.
Source: Bloomberg, IMF, authors' calculations.

The second strategy plotted in Figure 4.15 uses the same ranking approach, but for purchasing power parity (PPP) rather than REER. The PPP approach was popularized to get around the fact that REER depends on arbitrary initial conditions. The PPP valuation measure suggests that similar goods should cost similar amounts of money across countries. If they do not, free trade should go into overdrive, quickly correcting such arbitrage opportunities. Of course, for many goods, transaction costs can be substantial. Still, given that in the last 20 years, the US outsourced the bulk of its manufacturing capacity to China, it does not seem to be the case that transaction costs are large enough for the PPP concept to break down. There is a question of which basket of goods to apply the PPP concept to. The *Economist* magazine popularized one version of the PPP: the Big Mac index. This is almost certainly too narrow a measure. We use PPP indicators from the IMF, which are much broader, though we imagine that in the age of big data and web scraping, much more reliable PPP measures can be constructed going forward. But given that we mostly care about big picture, glaring misvaluations, the marginal effort to improve FX trading should be exerted elsewhere. Interestingly, the P&L of the PPP strategy is overall much stronger than that of the REER-based strategy. While the two P&Ls behave similarly during most periods, PPP outperformed significantly in both 2005–2006 and then again in 2018. We have the sense that currently, REER has more mind share with investors than PPP does, maybe because it is updated more frequently. This is a mistake, and we urge investors to focus more on PPP than on REER.

We don't think that our finding of better returns from PPP is very model-specific. Table 4.4 shows the IRs for both strategies in relation to the lookback window for determining the z-score. PPP is superior across all look-back windows. Another interesting finding is that for both strategies, there is a relatively consistent improvement, the longer the lookback period. In both cases, the 10-year window offers the best IR (data availability prevents us from testing even longer time horizons). To the extent that valuation adds any alpha, it does more so for investors who have a very long-term perspective on valuation.

TABLE 4.4   The Longer, The Better.

Lookback (years)	IR – REER	IR – PPP
1	−0.41	0.0
3	−0.24	−0.01
5	−0.26	0.19
7	−0.18	0.29
10	−0.06	0.35

Note: IRs for valuation strategies going long the four cheapest against the four most expensive currencies. We assume zero slippage and transaction costs.
Source: IMF, Bloomberg, authors' calculations.

4.7   TERMS OF TRADE

A slightly more sophisticated version of a valuation strategy aims to take account of the fact that a country's competitive position does not remain constant over time. In particular, REERs should get more expensive if the productivity growth of the country in question outpaces the rest of the world, or if the terms of trade (ToT: Export prices divided by import prices) of the relevant country improve significantly.[10] With productivity being relatively stable over short horizons (and also being notoriously hard to measure), changes in ToT are more relevant for short-term trading horizons. Significant changes of the ToT over a short period of time are typically due to changes in the prices of commodities that a country imports or exports, largely because commodity prices are much more volatile than prices of manufactured goods or services. For that reason, our focus is on commodity ToT, which assumes implicitly that the prices of non-commodity imports and exports remains constant in relation to each other. In this discussion, we use Citi's commodity terms of trade (CTOT), also produced by the Citi FX quants, to adjust our simple REER framework.[11] In particular, we run a five-year rolling regression of the log of the REER of the relevant currency on its CTOT. We then calculate z-scores of the residuals with a two-year lookback window. While a longer lookback window would likely be preferable, given Table 4.4, the more limited history of the CTOT indicator forces us to shorten the window. Two years is a good trade-off between data availability and model fit. As the next step, we volatility-adjust the currencies and create a top four against bottom four basket according to the z-scores. The result is shown in Figure 4.16 for the period from 2008 to 2018. The strategy has an IR of 0.4, a significant improvement over the (full sample) period IRs for the simple REER strategy, as well as for the IR of the simple REER strategy for

---

[10]See also Coudert et al. (2008) and Cashin et al. (2004).
[11]Stephens demonstrates that momentum in the CTOT indicator results in profitable trading strategies, but only for commodity currencies in Latam and CEEMEA. Those results were better than using momentum in the currencies. The strategy worked particularly well during time of high commodity volatility (Stephens 2010).

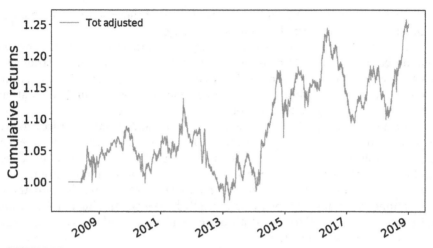

FIGURE 4.16   ToT are Helpful for FX Valuation.
Note: P&L of a strategy that adjusts REER by CTOT. We assume zero slippage and transaction costs.
Source: Citi, Bloomberg, authors' calculations.

the period from 2008 to 2018. Our conclusion is that adjusting valuation for changes in the CTOT is helpful. Even so, an IR of 0.4 likely means that valuation is not tradable as a standalone strategy.

4.8   TECHNICALS TO THE RESCUE

Given that the IRs of some of the classic fundamental rules for FX trading are at times quite low, considerable effort has been placed on technicals. The absence of a strong valuation anchor has made technicals even more relevant for FX than for other asset classes. This book will not go through all the various technicals that have been proposed over the decades. Our view is generally that we need a precise trading rule for how to use a specific technical. Many technicals are not precisely defined, especially with respect to exit conditions, but are used by practitioners as an art form rather than a science. This reminds us of astrology before astronomy came along! Today, astronomy – in the form of increased computing power – arrived for FX, and we can backtest proposed technicals more carefully. Doing this leads both to discarding many popular technicals and to false discoveries of new technicals due to overfitting. While this research is evolving, we think there are three very basic concepts on which most technicals rely in one way or another: momentum, mean reversion, and breadth. Obviously, the first two concepts are the opposite of each other; but they can both be helpful, largely because they can work on different time horizons. Here, we discuss one basic technique that is helpful in generating alpha for each category of technicals. While there are more refined techniques that can work better, we illustrate the basic concepts and capture the main sources of alpha that can be generated by purely technical rules. If those simple rules completely break down, more sophisticated ones may also struggle.

We start with momentum. There are many different ways to implement momentum-based trading rules. In its simplest form, a momentum strategy suggests that investors buy the currencies that went up the most over a certain period and sell the ones that fell the most over the same time. The behavioural foundation for momentum is that investors tend to follow herding behaviour. And there is nothing better than quickly rising prices to create greed (or quickly falling prices to trigger fear) and to lead investors to buy (or sell). There are absolute and relative momentum strategies. Absolute momentum invests in assets that go up more than a certain threshold, while relative momentum ranks all FX pairs based on momentum and then goes long the top momentum pairs against the lowest-ranked momentum pairs. Most CTAs (commodity trading advisors, who typically have a fast trading mindset) combine several strategies across relative and absolute momentum with varying performance windows that measure momentum.

Table 4.5 shows the IRs for the various relative momentum strategies in EMFX. We show results for long-only momentum (top four currencies) and for long-short momentum (top four versus bottom four). We also show the volatility-adjusted version for both strategies. Volatility adjustment is done in two respects. First, the actual momentum is volatility-adjusted; and second, the weight of the currencies in the basket is adjusted for volatility. We also add a (volatility-adjusted) absolute momentum strategy. The absolute momentum strategy could be long four currencies, short four currencies, or long two and short two, for example, depending on how many longs or shorts appear in the top four currencies ranked by absolute momentum. We have a few observations. First, for all specifications, using short-term momentum works best. For four out of the five strategies, one-month momentum displays the strongest returns, while for one strategy, three-month momentum is slightly better than one month. Second, volatility-adjusted momentum is superior for all strategies and time horizons. This is similar to the improvements we found when using volatility adjustments for the carry strategies. And finally, the long-only momentum strategy creates higher IRs than the long-short version, both outright and volatility-adjusted.

Figure 4.17 shows the one-month, volatility-adjusted P&L for the long-only and long-short momentum strategies over time. While an IR of 0.86 should be tradable,

TABLE 4.5   Momo Works, in the Short Term.

	Long-only momentum	Vol-adj. mom.	Long-short momentum	Vol-adj. mom.	Absolute momentum
1M	0.64	0.86	0.38	0.62	0.75
3M	0.37	0.56	0.07	0.27	0.79
6M	0.35	0.60	0.20	0.36	0.55
12M	0.20	0.42	0.06	0.33	0.30

Note: IRs, assuming zero slippage and transaction costs.
Source: Bloomberg, authors' calculations.

FIGURE 4.17 Momentum: Not Bad, But Not the Good Old Days, Either.
Note: One-month momentum, volatility-adjusted. We assume zero
slippage and transaction costs.
Source: Bloomberg, authors' calculations.

we point out that there are meaningful drawdowns. Furthermore, it does appear that
the heydays of the strategy were prior to the Great Recession of 2008, rather than
during the last 10 years. More encouragingly, the long-only and long-short momentum
strategies display negative correlation, especially during drawdowns of the long-only
strategy in 2008 and 2014. Combining both strategies should therefore improve results.

For mean reversion, the basic idea is that assets can go in one direction for only
so long. At some stage, no potential sellers (or buyers) are left, causing the asset to
reverse from such oversold conditions. For mean reversion, we tend to focus on longer
time horizons: not so much because there cannot be mean reversion on shorter horizons
(there likely is), but because we are not overly interested in daily returns and therefore
prefer to focus on overbought or oversold conditions in the bigger picture. The simplest
way to analyse mean reversion is to just extend our momentum study further out in
time. Figure 4.18 shows the case of a momentum strategy for three-year momentum.
The long-only strategy becomes reliably negative, suggesting mean reversion setting in
on a three-year horizon. But this variety of mean reversion clearly is not tradable on a
standalone basis, as the P&L indicates. And the long-short version of the strategy still
ekes out positive returns for momentum. In practice, long-term mean reversion needs
to be combined with short-term momentum to improve results.[12]

Breadth is the third important technical concept that we need to discuss, as we found
it useful for EMFX trading purposes. The idea of breadth is that a healthy market is
characterized by most assets with similar characteristics going up together. If gains for
an asset class are driven by only a few exceptional assets, the rally is at risk of coming
to an end. This could happen as soon as those few leading assets are hit by a negative

---

[12]This has been studied by various authors, including Serban (2018). See also Gill and Dingman
(2019). The authors have some success in finding mean reversion on shorter horizons and are
able to improve on returns by focusing on currency pairs that have similar drivers.

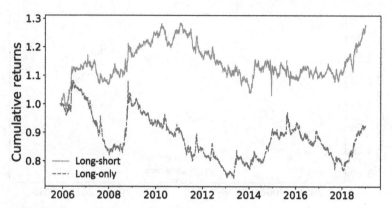

FIGURE 4.18   In the Long Run, Momentum is Dead.
Note: Three-year momentum with zero slippage and transaction costs.
Source: Bloomberg, authors' calculations.

shock, or when the gains of the leading assets come to an end as valuation differences conpared to the laggards become too extreme.

We focus on an expression of breadth in EMFX where we count the number of up days over different time periods for all the EMFX currencies under consideration. It turns out that when breadth is improving, it pays to be on the long side of EMFX. The opposite is true when the indicator deteriorates. We show the P&L of a simple version of this rule in Figure 4.19. The breadth rule is not very early or helpful in calling turns for the EMFX market. But it does keep investors on the right side of the market, even though the 2010 to 2016 performance was only sideways.

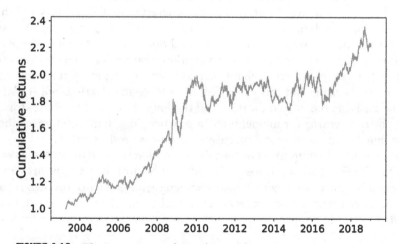

FIGURE 4.19   The Importance of Good Breadth.
Note: P&L of the MA of up minus down days. We assume zero slippage and transaction costs.
Source: Bloomberg, authors' calculations.

4.9   FLOWS FOLLOW; DON'T FOLLOW THE FLOWS

The other tool market participants focus on to a larger extent in FX than in other asset classes is flows. Again, this is because fundamentals in general and valuation in particular are much less clearly defined than in some other asset classes. There is also some fundamental justification for this sharp focus on flows, because in FX markets many players transact for reasons that are not, strictly speaking, profit maximizing. Important examples are governments intervening for financial stability reasons or to fight inflation. Furthermore, corporate hedging behaviour can lead to FX flows even when those corporates don't necessarily expect the outcome they hedge against to materialize as a base case. As a result, research on flow has become a cottage industry in the FX world. A lot of this flow research just takes publicly disseminated flow data – for example, from an equity exchange – and aggregates the flows, sometimes with a bit of data-mining on top, to determine which flows are more relevant in terms of setting prices. For longer-term flows, such an aggregation also uses balance of payments data disseminated by international or national statistics agencies. Many banks essentially engage in the same exercise, and a few are able to add their own proprietary FX flows. Recently, more and more flow data has become available, as web scraping of investor filings leads to more data along those lines.

We are broadly sceptical that flows are very useful for forward-looking analysis. To our mind, flows largely follow, or are at best coincident with, price action, rather than leading prices. We illustrate this point first with equity flows and then with FX flows. Focusing on equity flows has the advantage that the data are timely and of relatively high frequency, given that equities are mostly exchange traded. For fixed income, we don't usually have similarly rich data sets. Equity investors also typically do not FX hedge their shares, or at best do so partially; while in fixed income, the inflows from crossover investors are often FX hedged. Given that Asia is characterized by significant equity flows, while Latam and CEEMEA are more driven by significant fixed-income flows, we focus here on Asia FX and how it relates to equity inflows into Asia. We use deviations from the 200-day MA for both flows and FX to de-trend the series. As can be seen in Figure 4.20, at almost all the bottoms and tops, Asia FX is leading or is, at best, co-incident with the flows into Asian equity markets. Such flows are therefore not very useful to trade Asia FX. Having said that, there is one interesting observation to be made in Figure 4.20: the strong performance in Asia FX in 2017 was never corroborated by strong inflows into the Asian equity markets. In the end, equity flows were correct. Growth in Asia never recovered sufficiently to be supportive for Asia FX, and 2018 turned out to be a very poor year for Asia FX in particular but also EMFX more broadly.

On the FX flow side, we show the z-score of Citi's FX flows into and out of EMFX by leveraged accounts, next to the z-score of the EMFX index. We concentrate here on flows from leveraged investors, given that correlation with price action is higher for such flows, and given the perception that leveraged investors move faster than real money investors. As such, if flows were leading, we would expect this to manifest itself mostly on the leveraged investor side. But once again, as can be seen in Figure 4.21, at most times flows are coincident or lagging at both peaks or bottoms. What does happen from time to time, though, is that leveraged flows accelerate post turning points, and

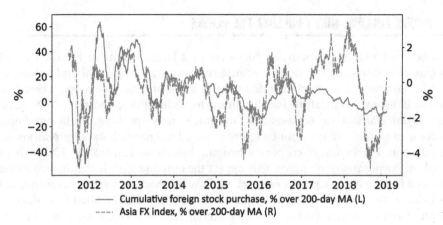

FIGURE 4.20 Asia FX Leads Equity Flows.
Source: Bloomberg, authors' calculations.

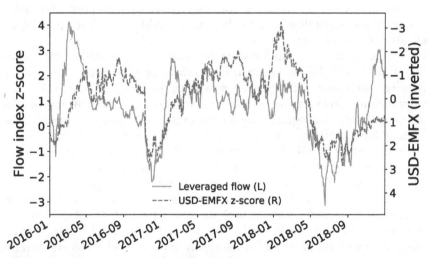

FIGURE 4.21 FX Flows are a Lagging Indicator.
Source: Citi, Bloomberg, authors' calculations.

those accelerations can be leading price action. This happened in early 2016 and then again in late 2018. As such, while we don't focus too much on flows, we do keep an eye open for surges in leveraged inflows that are not immediately coincident with too much EMFX strength (i.e. the z-score of flows moving above one, while the z-score for EMFX stays below one).

While the idea that large inflows from hedge funds are indicative of positive forward returns is not overly intuitive, especially if there is no instant gratification for such funds, the CitiFX quants have also had some success generating alpha using flows from leveraged accounts. They have found that momentum in leveraged flows on a three- to four-week basis tends to be a positive signal for the relevant currency. Flow momentum is most likely correlated with the price momentum strategy, given that flows for leveraged money are highly correlated with price action. But the CitiFX quants were able to refine the strategy by also integrating flows from real money investors. Real money investor flows are also positively correlated with price action, but to a lesser extent than flows from leveraged accounts (while flows from banks and corporate flows have no significant positive correlations with price action). CitiFX quants focus on events where momentum in flows from leveraged accounts is going in the opposite direction as the momentum of flows from real money accounts. The idea is that leveraged accounts are often moving first, and, in the end, real money will more often than not follow, creating some persistence to the overall flows. CitiFX Quants have had some success with such a trading strategy (Dingman and Gill 2018).

The other way to use FX flows is to think of them as a proxy for positioning, especially for currencies where no reliable positioning data exists. We mostly consult FX flow data for this purpose when we observe news that seems to change the prevailing consensus narrative for that particular currency. Extreme positioning, as proxied by flows, is relevant in determining whether investors should take the other side of consensus on the first sign that the consensus story may be changing. Using flows this way does not lend itself to any easy back-testing. We therefore remain careful when it comes to using flows in this manner and see it mostly as one additional reason to engage in a certain trade, but rarely a particularly important one. The following box illustrates a use case of flows for MXN.

WHICH PRESIDENT IS THE BIGGER MXN FOE: TRUMP OR AMLO?

The Mexican peso, one of the most liquid emerging market currencies, had a rough few years. First it became the most popular way to position for a Trumpian trade war, which initially was directed against the NAFTA treaty rather than against China. Therefore, the election of President Trump in November 2016 was a major hit for the MXN. Mexico stood out in the NAFTA context because investors were initially less concerned with Canada due to the more balanced trade flows between Canada and the US. The other pivotal event for the MXN in recent years was the election of President Andrés Manuel López Obrador (AMLO) in Mexico in July 2018. Prior to the election, AMLO had been perceived as a leftist politician who would likely be quite market unfriendly and, in particular, would aim to reverse the all important energy reform of the previous market-friendly administration. From a fundamental point of view, it would not have been obvious which of the two new presidents, Trump or AMLO, would undermine Mexican fundamentals more. If President Trump had pulled the US out of NAFTA without a quick replacement agreement, the damage to Mexican exports would have been substantial, given that the US administration would likely have levied major tariffs on Mexican goods in that case. But AMLO reversing the energy reform would have meant that Pemex's oil output would likely continue on a

(Continued)

one-way street lower, substantially undermining the external and fiscal position of Mexico. Ex ante, these fears would have suggested to investors that they keep buying USD-MXN after both the Trump election as well as after the AMLO election. In the event, the day after the AMLO election, the MXN swung widely but ended the day only slightly weaker. The next day, USD-MXN started to move lower aggressively, though, and the MXN kept rallying for a month. After the Trump election, on the other hand, USD-MXN exploded higher and then kept going for two more days, only peaking out two months later. The right answer, therefore, would have been to buy USD-MXN after the Trump election but to sell USD-MXN after the AMLO election, even though both elections were arguably a negative shock for Mexican fundamentals. Clearly, expectations matter, and AMLO was largely expected to win while Trump was not. But this is not the full explanation for the differing market reaction. After all, there was still a question mark regarding whether investors were really positioned for an AMLO victory, given that USD-MXN had moved lower into the election, suggesting that some investors had at the very least taken off their bearish positions. In this situation, analysing the flows would have helped. Figure 4.22 shows that leveraged money went very long MXN into the US election, with the z-score of cumulative positioning close to three. Real money investors also went long into the US election, but inflows into the MXN from real money had been on a smaller scale. With everyone long, no wonder the MXN sold off very viciously on the Trump election, and entering USD longs even after the event would have been profitable. On the other hand, going into the AMLO election leveraged money was also long MXN, but to a much lesser extent, having reduced long positions

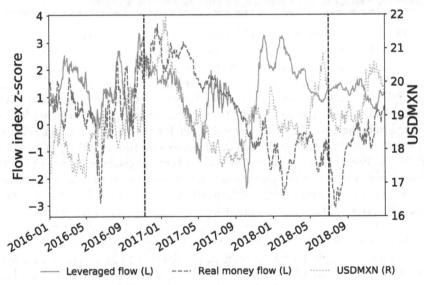

—— Leveraged flow (L)   ---- Real money flow (L)   ······ USDMXN (R)

FIGURE 4.22   Is Trump Really Worse for Mexico than AMLO?
Source: Citi and Bloomberg.

(*Continued*)

into the event. And real money had been short MXN. These flows into the event explain why the up move in USD-MXN on the day after the election was small, and why the USD turned lower very fast. It is also noteworthy that leveraged money reduced MXN longs after the Trump election but added to MXN longs after the AMLO election. Real money investors, on the other hand, added to MXN longs after the Trump election, but kept selling the MXN after the AMLO election, again highlighting the earlier point that leveraged money flows are more highly correlated with price action (though they may be following price action more than creating the price action).

4.10 POSITIONING WITH POSITIONS

Flows lead to positions, but depending on the choice of starting point, positioning can be very different from flows. Furthermore, when focusing on flows from real money investors, it is unknown whether flows result from inflows into the fund, and therefore do not lead to an off benchmark position, or whether flows are due to the fund manager implementing a new position against their benchmark based on a country call, for example. Therefore, we examine positioning separately from flows. The most widely available positioning data are the CFTC data, which the CFTC publishes for its traded future products. Sadly, for EM, only the MXN is traded in that fashion with any liquidity, though other currencies are starting to become more liquid in futures space. While there are a multitude of other positioning data around, often survey-based, we will use the MXN CFTC position as an illustrative example of how to think about positioning.

Table 4.6 buckets positioning of investors in USD-MXN into percentiles. The 90th percentile is very long MXN, while the 10th percentile is very long USD. For this

TABLE 4.6 Consensus is Good For You!

Positioning percentile	USD-MXN 3m forward	Excess returns
[0.0, 0.1]	2.4	1.0
(0.1, 0.2]	2.7	1.3
(0.2, 0.3]	1.1	−0.3
(0.3, 0.4]	0.1	−1.2
(0.4, 0.5]	4.1	2.8
(0.5, 0.6]	−1.3	2.7
(0.6, 0.7]	3.2	−1.9
(0.7, 0.8]	−1.8	3.2
(0.8, 0.9]	0.4	1.0
(0.9, 1.0]	1.2	0.2

Note: USD-MXN three-month forward returns and excess returns by percentile of speculative CFTC positioning.
Source: Bloomberg, authors' calculations.

exercise, we first translate CFTC contract data into USD numbers. After all, presumably most of the trading on the exchange is done by offshore investors, who mostly think about the risk they are taking in USD terms, rather than in MXN terms. When choosing the lookback windows to calculate the percentiles, the main consideration should be what type of moves in USD-MXN we are trying to capture. If we choose a long look-back window that includes the Great Recession, extreme readings will be very hard to come by. But too short a window creates the perception of extreme positioning much too early. We chose a lookback window of three years for this exercise, which appears to be a good compromise. We then show three-months forward returns of USD-MXN given that for our purposes, three months is a realistic time horizon to judge whether a trade "worked" or not. We also calculate excess returns, which are the return for the given percentile minus the average return over the period under study, adjusted for whether investors are long or short. From 0.0 to 0.5, a larger move up in USD-MXN than average is a positive excess return. From 0.5 to 1.0, a larger move up in USD-MXN than average is a negative excess return.

To us, the most interesting finding is that consensus usually works. For 7 of the 10 percentiles, excess returns are positive; and the average excess return is positive and relatively large at 0.9%. Furthermore, it is not obvious that more extended positioning leads to worse returns. While the 0.0 to 0.1 percentile does not generate the very best excess returns for being long USD, it does generate excess returns that are positive and considerably higher than returns for some of the lower brackets. The same is true, to a lesser extent, on the other end of the distribution. The 0.9 to 1.0 percentile also generates positive excess returns, as do several other brackets where investors are short USD, even though in absolute terms those trades are money losing, given that the period under study (post crisis: 2010 to 2018) was more often than not a USD bull market. There is no indication in the data that positioning works as a counter-indicator. If anything, going with consensus tends to make it more likely for a trade to work. We therefore would use positioning more as a momentum indicator than a contrarian indicator.

One other interesting study focuses on the EM bond index overall. In Willer and Dabholkar (2019a), it is shown that when most real money EM funds outperform in a bull market, it is typically *not* a counter-trend signal. Forward returns remain positive on a three-months basis. However, when most real money EM funds underperform in a bear market, there is usually follow-through in terms of additional negative performance. Three-months forward returns are reliably negative in that case. The reason is that real money funds are forced by price action to exit large money-losing long positions, prolonging the downmove. But they are not selling long positions when they are outperforming the index. This is in line with the famous finding by Kahnemann that a loss of one USD hurts twice as much as the pleasure gained by a gain of one USD (Kahnemann 2011). As a result, losses beget losses, and shorting EMFX in periods when the EM fund industry broadly loses money being overweight is a money-making strategy.

4.11 GOING WITH THE SEASONS

Seasonals are also given relatively high importance in FX trading. In particular, the subset of FX flows that are not driven by purely economic reasons may be partially calendar dependent. Examples are dividend payments by important corporates, year-end liquidity requirements by corporates and banks (partly for accounting

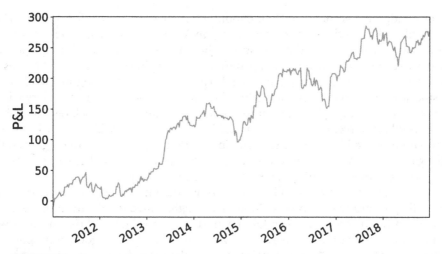

FIGURE 4.23   Respect the Seasons.
Note: P&L of positioning for weekly seasonals with excess returns of more than 1%, volatility-adjusted (rolling 1yr). We assume zero slippage and transaction costs.
Source: Bloomberg, authors' calculations.

purposes), and others. Famously, remittance flows into Mexico surge in May for Mother's Day – though this is a case where flows are too small and too well understood to impact price action much. Still, when having a choice of positioning in line with seasonal patterns that come with a fundamental explanation versus patterns that do not have an underlying logic we can fathom, we prefer to position for and with flows that we fundamentally understand. We find that such flows are often not fully arbitraged. But we have an open mind for trading seasonals even where we do not fully understand the underlying reason for the seasonal behaviour.

To study seasonals in a more methodical fashion, we use a 10-year lookback window to estimate weekly seasonals (rather than the more typical monthly seasonals). We define a week as any five weekdays, irrespective of the starting day of the week. This controls for the fact that just numbering the weeks in the year would lead to significant shifts over the years that make comparisons with respect to the same calendar days more difficult. Seasonals are defined as the median return for any given week minus the average of all weekly medians. We run this study for all of the liquid EMFX. A long-short position for our strategy is triggered when the seasonals are more than 1% higher/lower than the median. We then volatility-adjust the P&L streams for all the currencies and add them up. The results of our study are illustrated in Figure 4.23. Clearly, in aggregate, seasonals add alpha with an IR of 1.0. For individual currencies, the strategies are not quite as good; but 15 out of 21 currencies tested have a positive IR, with the highest IR achieved by the ZAR at 0.95 and the lowest by TRY at -0.4. Outside of the ZAR, other tradable seasonal strategies are found for the ILS, CLP, SGD, KRW, and THB, in that order.

4.12   VOLATILITY: FOE, NOT FRIEND

While volatility has, over the last decade, become its own asset class, in this chapter we are more interested in considering how to use volatility for directional FX trading.

To our mind, there is some confusion about what volatility means for trading. This is illustrated by the fact that banks often blame weak trading results on a lack of volatility, only to blame losses at other times on specific high-volatility events. Volatility appears to be a positive, but only when you happen to be on the right side of it. For EM investors, low volatility is seen as a major positive because, usually, investing in EMFX means investors are long carry. If volatility is low, investors are able to accrue the carry without heightened risk of capital losses. Furthermore, when investors conclude that they are in a low-volatility regime, they tend to add to carry trades, which often leads to an appreciation of the high-carry currencies in question – generating capital gains on top of the gains from carry. Often, investors rank the attractiveness of currencies by carry over volatility, where volatility can be either realized or implied.

However, it also is well established that rising volatility is a negative for carry trades, while falling volatility is a positive. Volatility is highly directional. Given that volatility is broadly mean reverting and can fall the most when it is high and rise the most when it is low, one could argue that periods of very high volatility are good entry points for carry trades, while periods of low volatility are inherently dangerous.

To analyse whether investors should be more bullish when volatility is (very) high or (very) low, we analyse the following trading rule. We go long EMFX whenever the implied volatility enters into the top fifth percentile over the last two years. We keep the holding period a relatively short six weeks, to not be at the mercy of the general bull or bear market in EMFX. We also show the P&L of the opposite strategy: going long EMFX for two weeks whenever implied volatility drops into the bottom five percentile. As is demonstrated in Figure 4.24, going long EMFX, even at volatility levels that are already very high, is still a money loser. On the other hand, buying EMFX, even at volatility levels that are already extremely low, not only makes money, but does slightly better than the index. Low volatility can stay low for a very long time and therefore is not a compelling signal of danger. The few instances where low volatility leads to compelling short opportunities are just occurring too rarely. Still, we feel that if low volatility is the main rationale to buy EMFX, it is important to make use of this low volatility by using options to express an EMFX bullish view. This also means that when ranking EMFX, using implied volatility is superior to using realized volatility.

On the other end of the spectrum, fading unusually high volatility appears to be more art than science. True, predicting volatility one month forward is slightly easier at high volatility levels, as volatility is typically not able to sustain high levels for very long. Fall it will. But as we demonstrated, simple rules to understand when to start fading the rise in volatility are difficult to come by. Furthermore, in high-volatility regimes, every minute counts. Being just one day early to fade the volatility spike (or, at times, just one minute early) can incur major losses. This means position size needs to be adjusted under the assumption that high volatility lasts longer. It is therefore difficult to catch the good entry points offered by volatility spikes in any size, as risk management dictates small sizing.

4.13   SUMMARY

This chapter demonstrates that EMFX generally behaves very similarly to G10 FX (excluding the JPY, the CHF, and, to a lesser extent, EUR, which are truly different).

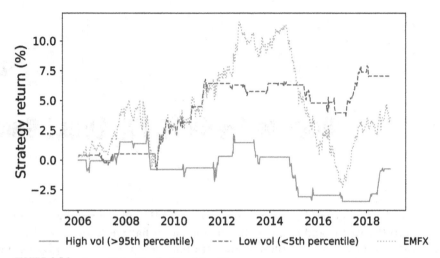

FIGURE 4.24 Low Volatility is Good for You.
Note: Strategy returns with entry upon entering the top and bottom fifth percentile of implied volatility calculated over the last two years, respectively, with a six-week holding period. We assume zero slippage and transaction costs.
Source: Bloomberg, authors' calculations.

Having said that, EMFX tends to be much less responsive to interest rate differentials than their G10 counterparts, which is important to keep in mind when trading EMFX. Sadly for FX traders, the carry strategy, which has been the go-to strategy for EM investors for many years, has deteriorated over the last decade. But the chapter demonstrates that carry still works reasonably well when expressed against the JPY and/or when implemented with volatility adjustments. Another way to improve carry strategies in EMFX is to cut positions when implied volatilities for global macro asset classes are moving higher.

Rules based on strong current accounts are overall money losing, even though improvement in trade balances can complement a pure carry strategy nicely. Valuation also is not generating easily tradable strategies, though we note that PPP clearly outperform REER-based strategies. REER strategies improve, though, once REER is adjusted for ToT shocks. But by far the best performing strategy is based on EM growth surprises rather than on valuation, external accounts, or carry.

Technicals are very important, too, and we warn against trading FX with too fundamental a view. Short-term momentum works well, especially when volatility-adjusted, while mean reversion takes over on a longer horizon. Breadth is also generating profitable signals. Furthermore, seasonals continue to generate alpha. The use of both positioning and flows, on the other hand, is much more an art than a science. On balance, we think positioning should be used as a trend indicator rather than as a contrarian indicator. But large long positions in a falling market lead to selling pressure that is tradable. Similarly, the true power of flows comes to the fore when they are used as a tool in combination with positive or negative shocks that upend consensus.

CHAPTER 5

How to Trade EMFX: Event Guide

Having laid out the general principles for trading EMFX in the previous chapter, we now go into the weeds and explore the trading rules that we found useful for more idiosyncratic events. Many of these events are relatively rare for any given country, but, given the number of countries we deal with, they are relatively common across the asset class. Most of the events we study are caused by policies that are implemented by authorities during crises (or, much more rarely, when times are "too good").

5.1 CHAINING THE FX VIGILANTES

In EM, the sensitivity of policy makers to FX moves is often very high. The reason is twofold. First, there is an economic rationale. FX is more important for inflation in EM than in DM. And there is much more USD-denominated debt outstanding than in DM, and therefore episodes of fast and outsized FX depreciation can be destabilizing by threatening a wave of defaults. But second, there is also a political rationale. Political stability in EM is typically much lower than in DM. Therefore, locals either already save in USD or can be expected to start buying USD at the first sign of economic trouble. This makes the FX rate the most visible indicator of whether the government is doing a solid job in terms of its economic management. The role being played (or maybe the role that used to be played) by the bond vigilantes in DM is played by the FX vigilantes in EM. Furthermore, from a political perspective, it is also true that governments very rarely survive a crisis where the FX moves are large enough to trigger a wave of defaults. The clean-up job in the aftermath of such a FX crisis very frequently falls into the lap of a new government.

Given this outsized role that FX plays for EM policy makers, it is not surprising that governments try to avoid large waves of depreciation. But it is very rare that the first reaction to a fast-depreciating FX is to correct the underlying economic policies, which typically would require slowing down the economy severely in order to adjust external imbalances and/or cutting government spending to adjust fiscal imbalances. In our experience, there is a clear pattern of how EM react to severe FX weakness. The first line of defense is FX intervention, at least if the country accumulated sufficient FX reserves during the bull days. If FX continues to deteriorate in spite of intervention, the next step often involves emergency interest rate hikes. If those also do not manage to stabilize the currency, the next step is either the introduction of severe capital controls or, finally, a major correction of the underlying economic policies, often with support from the IMF. Each of these steps along the way can last a considerable time. This is the case because the severe political cost paid by governments for outsized FX depreciation means that economic policy makers, just like generals, fight the FX wars to the bitter end. For example, authorities usually continue to spend FX reserves even after it has become clear to most observers that the country will shortly run out of reserves and that an outsized FX depreciation can no longer be avoided. Below we study the effectiveness of the various measures used in the typical FX war.

5.2   INTERVENTION AT WORK

FX intervention is the first line of defense because costs to policy makers are quite low. After all, carrying reserves is fiscally costly, as local rates are usually higher than USD rates. The direct costs of using FX reserves are therefore zero or even negative. FX reserves are also seen as insurance to be used in crisis situations. As such, the hurdle to use them is not very high in times of crisis, at least if the stock of FX reserves is relatively high. Having said that, the benefits are also relatively small, with the impact of an FX intervention often fleeting.[1]

FX intervention comes in various forms. In DM, the main distinction is between bilateral and multilateral intervention, with the presumption being that the likelihood of success is much higher for the multilateral kind. In EM, though, intervention is almost always bilateral, as the US Treasury does not get involved (other than granting a swap line through the Fed to increase the firepower of countries with low international reserves). The more relevant distinction in EM is whether the intervention is sterilized or not, and whether the intervention is done in spot or using derivatives. Regarding the former, economic theory suggests that sterilized intervention is extremely unlikely to succeed, given that the quantity of (unwanted) local currency in circulation does not fall. Non-sterilized intervention, on the other hand, has a higher likelihood of having a significant and longer-lasting impact. With respect to derivatives, the debate is more interesting. If FX reserves are low, countries often use derivatives for intervention. Those derivatives are usually settled in the home currency and, as such, do not deplete the stock of international reserves. Of course, upon settlement, investors would either roll the derivative forward or buy USD in the spot market, which in turn can impact reserves. Thus the use of derivatives does not offer a silver bullet for countries with low FX reserves, even though the market has a relatively high tolerance for authorities engaging in such derivative transactions.

To investigate whether FX intervention "works," the first question is what constitutes success. We have a different perspective on this issue than policy makers and most of the academic studies on this topic. We care much less about whether the intervention is supportive of the needed economic adjustment. We are also not

---

[1] See Mohanty (2013) for some reasons the effectiveness may be limited.

that interested in the long-term impact of the intervention on the adjustment of the economy under question. Instead, we mostly care whether there are profitable trading opportunities upon the announcement of the intervention. In addition, we have a relatively short horizon for this investigation. Even opportunities for trades as short as two or three weeks are very relevant to us. There have been many academic studies of the topic, typically with a fairly limited dataset that often relies on the experience of a single country. One of the papers using a more extensive dataset is Fratzscher et al. (2017), which investigates 16 years of intervention data for 33 countries, focusing on episodes of sterilized intervention. But even this investigation is not overly useful for our purposes, as for floating exchange rates the most relevant criterion for success in this study is for the currency to move in the direction of the intervention on the day of the intervention (the "event" criterion). While this may be interesting to policy makers, in a trading context, only day traders care, while traders with a slightly longer holding period are unable to benefit from this "successful" intervention.

Nevertheless, there are a few interesting lessons from this paper. First, only 61% of interventions are able to push the currency in the direction of the intervention on event day. However, for 88% of events, the slope of the FX moves five days after the intervention is lower than the slope for the five days into the event day (the "smoothing criterion"). This implies that selling volatility on event days could be profitable, though this is something we have not systematically investigated yet. Furthermore, large interventions (as percent of GDP), intervention toward fundamentals (proxied by three-year moving averages or PPP), and backing up the physical intervention with oral intervention improve the likelihood of success on event day but do not help with the smoothing criterion. The smoothing is more successful if volatility is high going into the event. With these preliminary findings out of the way, we shift our focus to the question of whether intervention can lead to somewhat longer-lasting trade ideas.

Sadly, it turns out that there are no obvious rules that fit every situation equally well. We therefore illustrate a few country-specific lessons in Latam. Brazil and Colombia intervene relatively frequently on both sides of the spectrum, and Mexico intervenes relatively frequently on the selling USD side. For those cases, we distinguish between large and/or surprising interventions on the one hand, and small and/or follow up interventions on the other. We also include USD purchasing interventions by Mexico and interventions on both sides for Chile. Those interventions happen more rarely, and we therefore do not have enough data to distinguish between different types. Presumably, all those interventions are surprising due to their rarity. Interventions in both Peru and Argentina are too frequent to consider in the context of a study of flexible exchange rate regimes; we therefore exclude those two countries. Figure 5.1 shows the cases for the countries under consideration. The charts illustrate the behaviour of the relevant currency against our EMFX index, adjusted for volatility. The line moving up means that the FX of the relevant country outperforms, and vice versa. We first focus on the case of interventions where authorities lean against weakening exchange rates.

In Brazil, large interventions (above USD 2.5 billion/day) work. When done for the first time (or when firepower is meaningfully increased within an existing programme), the BRL outperforms the EMFX index, volatility adjusted, for around 10 days by 2.5%. Small first-time interventions or programme extensions have no significant impact. This is in line with the findings from Fratzscher et al. (2017) that size matters. Interestingly, firepower reductions also do not have a significant impact, probably because authorities only dare to reduce firepower when the world is a happy place and Brazil is in a good spot, seeing plentiful capital inflows. In Mexico, the first intervention also typically works, also for around 10 trading days, and generating on average 1.5% outperformance. Subsequent interventions have a lower impact. In Chile, intervention tends to work for around 10 trading days. For Colombia, we do not find a strong pattern, though. This could be the case because Colombia uses a structure in which it sells USD options to provide or acquire USD, which are executed only if the exchange rate is lower than the average of the last 20 days. While likely helpful in dampening volatility, it is not clear that such a structure impacts the direction of spot significantly.

Figure 5.1 also gives a clue of what triggers the precise onset of the intervention. While interventionist pressures have often brewed a long time before triggering a decision by policy makers, the chart for Brazil suggests that it takes a 1.5% underperformance over five days, obviously from an already very weak position, for the central bank to intervene. In Mexico, it takes an underperformance of only 1% over more than 15 days to trigger a reaction in the right setup. In Chile, there is extreme short-term weakness that could be a trigger; but over the 20 days going into an intervention, the CLP is not particularly weak, at least against the EMFX basket. The rare interventions in Chile are likely driven by bigger-picture weakness.

We also note that at times, emerging market policy makers intervene when their currency is strengthening too much. Here, the motivation is much less political (in that a stronger currency is seen as a sign of good economic housekeeping) and is mostly driven by the harm done by the appreciating currency to the exporting sector. This case is quite different from the case of shoring up a quickly depreciating FX. First, it is usually not quite as urgent. And secondly, theoretically, it would be expected to be more successful, given that there is no hard limit to how much FX reserves a country can accumulate, while there is at least a soft limit to how much FX reserves can be sold by any country. In practice, though, there is a limit to the amount of intervention on the strong side, too. Often, the inflows that drive the appreciation lead to a local boom, especially if there is intervention to keep the currency weaker than it arguably should be. Such inflows can then create inflation pressures – and a stronger FX is often an easy way to fight such pressures. Such constraints imply that even on the appreciation side, FX intervention is not always as successful as could be imagined.

In the case of our three countries under study, the conclusions are again country-specific. Brazil is once more a case where size matters. Interventions of more than USD 2 billion tend to "work" and weaken the currency, relative to EMFX, for 20 days by almost 3%. Smaller interventions at least stabilize the upward pressure on the BRL. On the long USD side Colombia also "works," at least in the case of the first interventions, which weaken the FX in relative terms by around 1% over a bit more than 20 days. For Mexico and Chile, the interventions are also successful. In most cases, USD purchases engineer a stronger and longer-lasting impact on the local currency than USD sales. It is easier to buy USD than sell (scarce) USD.

The lesson for investors is that they should study previous interventions on a country-specific basis. For countries that intervene frequently, large interventions are

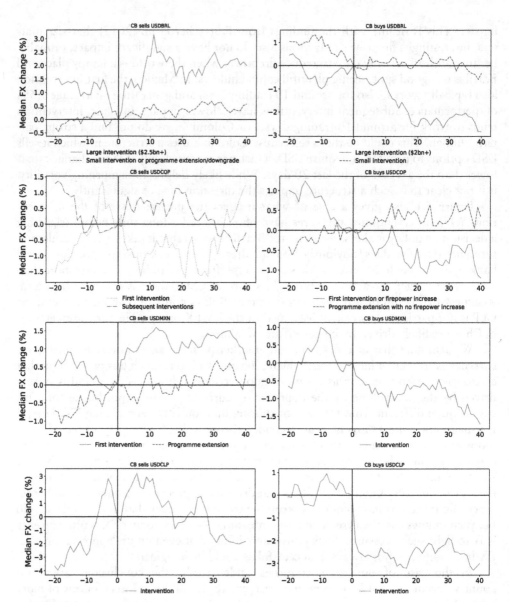

FIGURE 5.1 Intervention: Do It Rarely, or Do It Big.
Source: Bloomberg, authors' calculations.

necessary to have a market impact. In the case of Brazil, investors should go with the intervention if it is sufficiently large and they expect the central bank to follow through and engage in more USD sales if tested by the market. For countries that intervene more rarely, there is no need to distinguish between large and small, and investors should generally go with the intervention relative to the EMFX index. If the intervention takes place in a large country that has set the (negative) tone for EMFX more broadly, it is plausible that the intervention in that currency can stabilize the overall asset class. Then the trade should be attempted against the USD rather than against an EMFX index. It is actually uncanny how often FX intervention in large basket cases can turn around EMFX more broadly. For example, the intervention in USD-CLP in late 2019 was the peak for USD-EM for several weeks.

5.3   EMERGENCY RATE HIKES – ONLY FOR EMERGENCIES

Emergency rate hikes come only after FX intervention has not been able to stabilize FX markets. Costs are seen as higher by policy makers, given that emergency rate hikes slow down growth and can contribute to recessions. This is why such rate hikes often come later than the market is asking for. And the rule of thumb is that the later they come, the larger they need to be to restore confidence. When they do come, they are usually justified by saying that the FX turmoil is undermining growth even more than a higher rate would. Whether this is correct or not is almost impossible to assess. But it is a convenient argument for the monetary authorities to make to get politicians to approve emergency rate hikes (even formally independent central banks cannot easily implement emergency rate hikes without some political cover). The second argument justifying emergency rate hikes *vis-à-vis* often-unwilling governments is that they are supposed to last a relatively short time. The idea is that the hike will restore confidence, and, once that has been achieved, rates will quickly return to earlier levels.

Table 5.1 shows our sample of emergency hikes, where an emergency hike is defined as one that is either much larger than "normal" or implemented during an unscheduled meeting. As can be seen, such events are quite rare. We found 20 examples in the last 21 years, in 8 countries, i.e. 1 every 8 years per country. And this statistic does not include the numerous countries that have not implemented any emergency hikes over the last two decades. Emergency hikes are rare indeed. They also appear to be clustered across both countries and time periods. Turkey is a frequent emergency hiker, resorting to that policy every three years or so, while such hikes are very rare in Mexico. Whenever an emergency rate hike happens, the likelihood of another one occurring in short order is much higher than usual – the policy is often to hike until it "works" and the currency stabilizes. The second hike is usually significantly larger than the first one. But even in those clusters, the likelihood that a second hike is necessary is only around 25%. Third hikes are very rare.

So how likely are emergency rate hikes to "work"? We again apply the same criteria for success as with FX interventions. We are interested in whether there are useful trading rules for EMFX in the aftermath of an emergency rate hike. Figure 5.2 shows the average FX performance around day zero, the day of the emergency hike. Here we only use hikes that qualify as independent episodes: i.e. we omit second and third hikes that happen within a few days or weeks. For the three cases where there is more than one hike in a short period of time, we show the performance after the first hike and after the second hike separately.

TABLE 5.1   Emergency, Emergency!

Country	Date	Hike (bp)	Comment
Success			
TRY	25-Jun-06	225	2nd hike in 18 days, at emergency meeting
TRY	20-Oct-11	350	TRY basket used to neutralize EUR impact during crisis
TRY	28-Jan-14	425	
EURHUF	19-Jun-03	200	Hiked at emergency meeting
EURHUF	28-Nov-03	300	2nd hike in 8 days
EURHUF	22-Oct-08	300	
CZK	27-May-97	250	
ZAR	29-Jan-14	50	Surprise hike
RUB	16-Dec-14	650	
BRL	04-Mar-99	600	Fraga as new BCB president also helped
BRL	14-Oct-02	300	
MXN	17-Feb-16	50	Also announced discretionary FX intervention
ARS	01-Mar-16	585	Hiked 100 bp 1 week later, but first big hike worked
Failure			
TRY	07-Jun-06	175	1st of 2 hikes in 18 days; TRY down 8% until 2nd hike
EURHUF	11-Jun-03	100	1st of 2 hikes in 8 days; EURHUF up 3% until 2nd hike
RUB	12-Nov-08	200	Widened FX band, and S&P continued to fall
INR	15-Jul-13	300	Sold off another 13% after rate hike
ARS	27-Apr-18	300	1st of 3 emergency hikes in 7 days
ARS	03-May-18	300	2nd of 3 emergency hikes in 7 days
ARS	04-May-18	675	3rd of 3 emergency hikes in 7 days

Source: Bloomberg, authors' calculations.

Our take-away from the chart is that emergency rate hikes work. For the majority of cases, where only one emergency rate hike is implemented, the positive response to the emergency rate hike is quite pronounced but only lasts around 10 days. Subsequently, this performance is given up again; but the currency remains very stable around the point just prior to the emergency rate hike. Investors can at least earn the (high) carry, and policy makers will be happy with the result. Cases where a second hike is necessary are also interesting. For these much rarer events, the positive response to the initial emergency rate hike is very small, and the rally does not last more than a day. The second hike also does not quite "work," but the currency subsequently stabilizes nonetheless. As discussed, such events are rare, but losses for short USD trades post-hike, when the initial hike fails, are very significant. It is therefore crucial to figure out which hikes are sufficient to stabilize the FX and which ones are not.

Figure 5.2 gives a clue: The sell off into the emergency rate hike is very large. For all the cases with only one hike, it is more than 30 daily standard deviation moves over

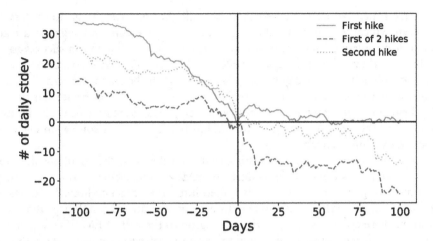

FIGURE 5.2 Emergency Hikes Often Work.
Note: FX performance around day zero, the day of the emergency hike.
Source: Bloomberg, authors' calculations.

100 days. But for the first hikes when a second hike is necessary, the sell-off into the emergency rate hike is much smaller. It is therefore likely that for events where a second hike is necessary, the currency in question did not sufficiently cheapen into the first hike. We are going to investigate this hypothesis in the next section.

To do this, we break out performance separately for cheap and expensive currencies (as defined by the deviation from an eight-year moving average REER being above or below zero). There are six cheap and eight expensive currencies in the sample. Figure 5.3 shows that for cheap currencies, there is an initial positive follow-through post emergency rate hike, and even in the bigger picture, the USD peak is in: the levels of the EM

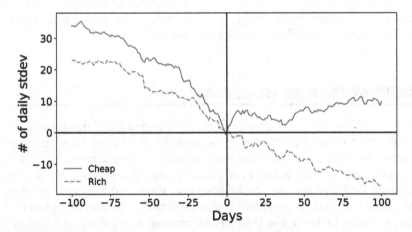

FIGURE 5.3 Don't Make That Emergency Call Too Early!
Note: FX performance around day zero, the day of the emergency hike.
Source: Bloomberg, authors' calculations.

currency from just before the emergency rate hike are not seen again for a very long time. Given typically high carry, this is a success for investors and suggests a trading rule to go long cheap currencies post emergency rate hikes. It also is a success for policy makers, as they achieve the goal of FX stabilization. For expensive currencies, the downtrend only stalls for a day before continuing with the same strength. The lesson for investors is to fade rallies induced by emergency hikes if the currency has not sufficiently cheapened into the hike. For policy makers, it suggests patience. The hikes will not work until the currency has sold off and has become at least somewhat cheap – or, even better, extremely cheap.

On another note, it is also interesting that the rule works better in absolute terms (against the USD), as opposed to against our EMFX index. One reason could be that by the time a large emerging market is forced into an emergency hike, there has been contagion to other EMFX. Then, when an emergency rate hike stabilizes the country in question, there could also be positive contagion to the rest of EM. If emergency rate hikes happen in large countries, we would therefore prefer to go short USD, rather than to go long the currency in question against the EMFX index.

To understand better what is going on, we focus on investigating why emergency hikes do not work for expensive currencies. To do this, we analyse the worst outcome for USD bearish trades post an emergency rate hike, which was the case in Argentina in 2018 (in Figure 5.3, included in the expensive basket). What was going on? As per Table 5.1, Argentina in April and May 2018 implemented three emergency rate hikes in seven days. This was in reaction to a depreciation of the ARS in the two months leading up to the devaluation of only 2% – a minuscule move for an EM currency in a two-month period. The emergency hike did not work. *Ex post*, this was not overly surprising. After all, it was not an emergency. Whenever emergency rate hikes are implemented before the FX has sufficiently cheapened, they cannot work their magic. Clearly, a 2% sell-off did not result in a sufficiently cheap Argentine Peso. Time is needed to allow the investors who are long the currency to cut their positions and for new short positions to be established. Only once that has happened can emergency rate hikes stabilize the currency, partly by increasing the costs for the shorts to remain short. In the context of emergency rate hikes, valuation is relevant.

5.4 CAPITAL CONTROLS, IMF, OR ... CHINA

In theory, a combination of a large depreciation combined with large interest rate hikes can be sufficient to start a correction of the underlying fundamentals. In practice, the depreciation and emergency rate hikes sometimes are not large enough. If FX and several rate moves do not fully stabilize the situation, the next step is either severe capital controls or an IMF package. For the longest time, those two endgames were mutually exclusive, as IMF orthodoxy prevented capital controls from being part of an IMF package. More recently, however, the IMF has warmed up to measures controlling capital flows, which opens up the possibility of a combined end game of capital controls as part of an IMF package. But for our purposes, we still treat those outcomes as largely distinct, as the capital controls in an IMF programme are typically less harsh and more limited in terms of duration.

Which of those two paths a country chooses in a crisis is often driven by politics. If an IMF package can be obtained at a reasonable cost, it is clearly desirable, as the IMF funds can spread the required adjustment out over time, which makes it more bearable. But how do we define "reasonable cost"? Costs are reasonably low if a country has goodwill with the IMF and the US administration. While the IMF and the US administration are obviously separate actors, in practice, IMF programmes are very difficult to get done if the US is opposed. If a country is part of the Western club or has strategic value to the US, the cost of a package is often relatively low. On the other hand, if a country has been on a collision course with Washington institutions and/or the US, the costs to obtain an IMF programme are very high. In the latter case, severe capital controls can be the only politically feasible option. Of course, it is also true that severe capital controls can be so painful in terms of lost output that eventually they lead to political changes and a belated IMF package. But severe capital controls can last a long time, and if a government survives the initial reaction to such controls, market mechanisms that would push the country into the arms of the IMF are significantly weakened.

In the future, a third option will become more and more prevalent: relying on the generosity (or rather, political calculus) of China. Clearly, countries not following the prescriptions of Washington and/or not on the good side of the US administration will increasingly utilize Chinese funds. In this sense, China is replacing the Soviet Union of the 1970s and 1980s as a funding vehicle for an alternate development path. And we are already seeing China growing into this role. At this stage, it is largely limited either to countries in Asia, which China sees as its natural sphere of influence, or to countries that are of strategic importance due to their commodity resources, which China has come to rely on. The most prominent emerging market where Chinese money contributed to allowing the country to avoid an IMF programme (but not capital controls) is Venezuela. But the very substantial Chinese funds for Venezuela have not been able to stabilize the economic situation. The endgame in Venezuela is likely to still involve the IMF.

For us, the key question is what traders should do when a country announces capital controls. The question is complicated to answer, largely because capital controls come in a multitude of forms, which makes them hard to study. Even very open EM (and DM) often restrict some forms of capital flows. And most countries have rules for their banking system when it comes to FX transactions, which can be seen as a form of capital control. But soft capital controls do not change currency behaviour for very long. One good example is the IOF tax in Brazil, which is a financial transaction tax the authorities used mostly to reduce inflows. These inflows had pushed the BRL into overvaluation territory, at least in the eyes of the authorities. Several hikes of the IOF tax between 2008 and 2010 had only a very limited impact in weakening the BRL. While measures to weaken the BRL continued, it took a turn in the DXY to lead to a change in the trend of USD-BRL. Soft capital controls do not appear to work very well.

Severe capital controls, on the other hand, can be real game changers, as they amount to taking a country off the grid. Such controls have been quite rare over the last decade, as the costs are very high, especially if a country runs a current account deficit and is a net debtor to the world. Severe capital controls force the current account deficits to adjust to zero overnight, which can only be achieved with a severe recession. An IMF package is therefore preferable to most countries. Still, at times, political reasons prevail over economic logic. See the following box for the case of Argentina.

To us, severe capital controls are very hard to trade. Both shorts and longs can lose money, as the fixing of the FX is set arbitrarily. For deliverable currencies, investors who are short USD and long the local currency may not be able to transfer local currency holdings out of the country. And USD longs may only be able to buy back the local currency, which they borrowed in order to short it – at an artificially strong rate. While a black market typically springs up, it is usually impossible for foreign investors to access that black market to buy all the USD needed. For non-deliverable currencies, the fixings are set by the legal documents governing the NDFs and whoever those documents determine to be the calculation agent. Calculation agents may pick an artificially strong onshore FX rate as a fixing to collapse the NDFs if there are no other obvious candidates available.

A sample of recent relatively severe capital controls also suggests that the market reaction is not as uniformly negative as one would believe, as can be seen in Table 5.2.

The only advice when capital controls are expected is to stop trading the relevant asset. However, investors can benefit from fears of coming capital controls by trading onshore-offshore spreads. Capital controls make USD trapped onshore less valuable than USD held offshore.

TABLE 5.2   Even Severe Capital Controls Come in Many Shapes.

Country	Date	Capital control	USDXXX	
			in 1 m	in 6 m
Egypt	Feb 11 to Nov 17	Indiv. with one-time 100k USD limit. Relaxed in 2014 to 100k p.a.; foreign companies needed approvals for >100k.	1%	1%
Argentina	Oct 11 to Dec 15	Restrictions on international payments in USD. Restrictions to repatriate earnings and dividends and use of credit cards abroad.	−6% (blue FX)	24% (blue FX)
Ukraine	Feb 14 to Jun 16	Cap on FX purchases by individuals ban on buying FX to invest or repay debt. Law for banks to sell 75% of FX within 90 days.	4%	40%
Nigeria	Jun 15	Importers without FX access for 40 products. ATM cards and credit cards limited to 50k p.a. Daily cash withdrawal limits of USD 300. Enforcement was phased in gradually.	8% (parallel)	18% (parallel)

Source: Costa and Vicol (2018).

AN ARGENTINE TRAP

In late 2011, the Argentine authorities fought back against rampant capital flight by implementing the *el cepo*, or "the trap," which was designed to keep wealth inside the country. The campaign began on 31 October 2011 when the government started to require exchange houses and banks, which could previously conduct individual transactions with little oversight, to submit their clients' tax identification numbers online to the federal tax agency for approval. Requests to purchase USD were often denied without a clear legal basis. The government deployed more than 4000 inspectors to oversee money changers across the country to enforce this rule. In a second step, the government also started to impose a 15% tax on credit card usage abroad, closing a loophole that had been used extensively to get around the earlier restrictions and further limiting access to USD. Unsurprisingly a black market for USD sprang up onshore, where the USD was trading almost 20% stronger than the official rate. The shortage of USD also caused a sharp drop of USD deposits in the Argentine banking system, and those dollars were used for foreign currency transactions or to gain from black market opportunities. In spite of these severe capital controls, international reserves of the central bank dropped from USD 47 billion at the time of the introduction of *el cepo* to USD 30 billion by December 2013. The loss forced authorities to speed up currency depreciation in December 2013. In spite of the shortage of USD, the trade balance deteriorated, partly due to the overvalued exchange rate and partly because imports did not weaken as much as expected. While imports pulled back right after the introduction of *el cepo*, they stayed strong throughout 2013, partially driven by over-invoicing by importers to access dollars. As such, it is very unclear what the Argentine government gained, if anything, from *el cepo*. But it took a new government under President Macri to dismantle *el cepo* in December 2015. It is generally hard for sitting governments to reverse policies, even the most costly ones.

For investors, the period of *el cepo* also proved to be interesting. Somewhat curiously, the authorities never closed one loophole that existed for investors to get USD out of the country. This loophole consisted of allowing swapping equities or bonds traded onshore (priced in ARS) for their offshore equivalents (priced in USD). For the case of equities, this mechanism used American Depository Receipts (ADRs). This swap was perfectly legal, though it did not necessarily work well for large quantities, at least without severely impacting the price (the *blue chip swap rate*). This rate was very volatile and at times reached levels 80% weaker than the official exchange rate, making it very cheap to get USD into the country and very expensive to get USD out. Not surprisingly, local bonds, evaluated at the blue exchange rate, collapsed in late 2011 and only bottomed out in late 2013 when the market slowly began to position for the possible end of the Kirchner administration, which came about according to plan in late 2015. NDFs for ARS

(Continued)

kept trading throughout this period of capital controls. This is different from some other examples of severe capital controls, where banks lost access to local currency and therefore abandoned the NDF market. Still, liquidity in Argentine NDFs was very low. NDF yields spiked with the blue swap exchange rate and peaked at 65% in late 2013. Implied yields then started to fall. The important point for investors is that the total returns of the ARS during that period was actually very strong. Figure 5.4 shows the blue FX rates next to the total return index for the ARS, based on rolling a one-month NDF. While there were many extremely severe drawdowns, overall the period of *el cepo* was a profitable one for NDF investors, highlighting that there can be compelling long opportunities even in the presence of severe capital controls.

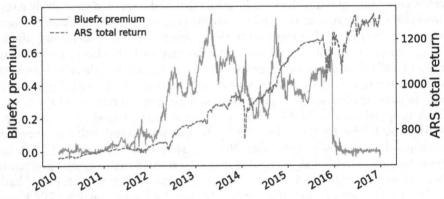

FIGURE 5.4   A Profitable *el cepo*.
Source: Bloomberg, authors' calculations.

Another example of how the capital controls in Argentina led to interesting trading opportunities was the ARS depreciation in late 2015 going into the presidential election (first round 25 October and second round 22 November 2015). The market expected a large FX depreciation following the presidential election, and as a result, the one-month NDF moved substantially higher once the election entered the one-month window of the contract. However, the incumbent administration did not allow the onshore forward market to reflect such weakness, largely to send a signal of strength into the election. Due to heavy official intervention in the onshore futures market, ROFEX, the one-month forward barely moved. Figure 5.5 shows how big a gap opened up between the onshore and offshore outright one-month ARS. This misguided policy offered a tremendous arbitrage opportunity for onshore investors, who bought USD onshore and sold USD offshore. This was a nice subsidy from Argentine policy makers to the trading class.

(Continued)

Offshore investors were also able to participate in the fun. While investors try to avoid sending money into jurisdictions subject to dicey political situations, for offshore in dicey political situations, for ROFEX, only the margins needed to be sent to Argentina.

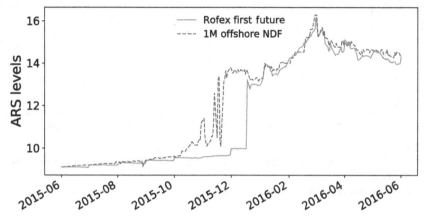

FIGURE 5.5 Fun with the Onshore Offshore Spread.
Source: Bloomberg, authors' calculations.

5.5   IMF PACKAGES STABILIZE FX – EVENTUALLY

In the more frequent case of a country running into the arms of the IMF, how does FX behave? We analysed all IMF packages since 2001 and investigated whether the announcement of an IMF programme managed to stabilize the FX. As can be seen in Figure 5.6, the relevant EMFX on average sells off quite sharply against the USD going into the announcement of the IMF package. The median performance is similar but less extreme. Interestingly, at first, the announcement does not stabilize the average (or median) FX rate. Only in the top 10 percentile of programmes does the FX change direction with the IMF package and immediately stabilizes. But around 25 trading days later, the median performance also starts to turn around, and the relevant FX starts to strengthen. At that time, a few outliers are still displaying EMFX weakness, though, such that the average performance continues to deteriorate. It takes around three months post the IMF announcement for the average trend to change. Our takeaway is that in the bigger picture, the IMF programmes are stabilizing the currencies, just not necessarily on day one. One reason for this slow turnaround could be that some IMF programmes actually require a weaker FX. In Chapter 9, we get a very similar result for EM credit and IMF packages. Investors need to be somewhat patient when positioning for successful IMF packages.

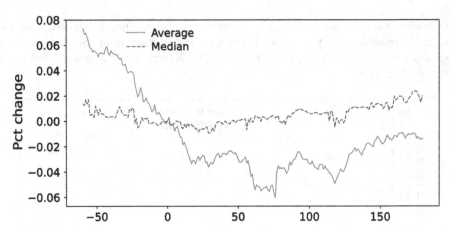

FIGURE 5.6   IMF Packages Stabilize FX in the Big Picture.
Note: FX performance around day zero, the day of the IMF package announcement.
Lower is weaker EMFX.
Source: Bloomberg, authors' calculations.

5.6   EM ELECTIONS: OF MARKET FOES AND WHITE KNIGHTS

Political risk is typically higher in EM than in DM, largely because institutions are less firmly anchored and have less credibility than their DM peers. But the market is not usually trading this feature of EM, as it is a constant risk and not susceptible to much day-to-day variation. This changes when elections approach. Elections in EM often offer candidates with starkly differing economic philosophies, which would result in starkly differing economic outcomes. In particular, many EM elections pitch one candidate who is a proponent of economic orthodoxy against another candidate who is more populist and often espouses market-unfriendly policies. Even in cases where the underlying proposed policies are not that different, the media (and maybe also the market) often display a tendency to paint one candidate as a white knight and to caricature the other candidate as a severe market foe. The market finds it difficult to look through such election risks, especially if polls are close enough to make either outcome plausible. And with the quality of polls often being quite low, many outcomes can appear plausible.

In our study, we look at 23 presidential elections in Latin American countries. We focus on Latam largely because politics is calmer in many other regions (with some notable exceptions). Latam is famous for its swings to populism and back. We include in our sample only elections that were justifiably market moving due to investor fear of a leftist candidate. Whether those fears were justifiable is proxied by the *ex post* election outcome. To be included in our sample, a market-unfriendly candidate has to garner at least 25% of the popular vote. This way, we exclude elections where all plausible candidates offered similar market-friendly or neutral policy prescriptions, or

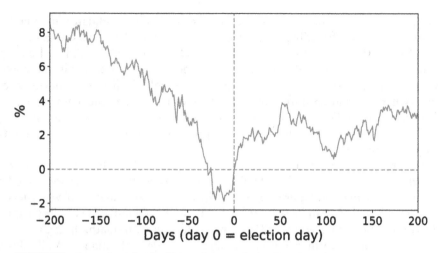

FIGURE 5.7 Don't Be Afraid of Your Average Left-Wing Populist.
Note: FX performance around day zero, the day of the election. Lower is weaker EMFX.
Source: Bloomberg, authors' calculations.

where it was obvious from the beginning who would win.[2] Using these commonsense rules narrows our sample to nine elections since 1999. If there were two rounds, we select the one where the "leftist fear" was settled through either a victory or elimination of the market-unfriendly candidate.

Figure 5.7 shows the average path of the currency (against the USD) in the run-up to and aftermath of a contentious election. We find that election uncertainty, in the form of rising volatility and a weaker currency, generally begins six months prior to the event and accelerates at about the three-month mark. But just a month before the election, the trend stalls out, and the currency turns around with two weeks to go. It often goes on to rally meaningfully after the election. This is a highly consistent pattern. Within our sample, all the elections resulted in a depreciation between three months and two weeks before the event. On the flip side, the currency strength from two weeks before an election to three months after showed up in all but one episode.

Given the relatively small sample, we need a plausible underlying theory for why this pattern should persist, in order to have sufficient confidence to actually trade it. Otherwise, the risk of overfitting the data is too high. Without a plausible theory, it is possible that investors just got lucky with respect to the market rallies post elections. After all, ever since the 1990s, elections in EM have usually resulted in market-friendly

---

[2]One notable exclusion was the 2010 presidential election in Brazil. Dilma Rousseff, riding on Lula's coattails, was generally perceived by the market as a market-neutral candidate, despite hailing from the Workers' Party.

outcomes. And even if they did not, the market-unfriendly candidates often ended up implementing market-friendly policies regardless, like President Lula did in Brazil after his election in 2002 and Andrés Manuel López Obrador (AMLO) did, at least on the fiscal front, in Mexico in 2018. As the saying goes, "Political power is like playing a violin. You grab it with the left, but play it with the right." There were of course a few elections where the market-unfriendly candidate won, who then ended up implementing market-unfriendly policies. But even in these cases, it was quite rare for a policy maker to implement such negative policies on day one on a sufficient scale to undershoot fairly negative expectations.

Investors often forget that even late Venezuelan President Hugo Chavez, who may have been the most market-unfriendly EM leader in recent history, was not immediately a negative for the market. Figure 5.8 shows the relative performance of Venezuela USD bonds versus Brazil. As can be seen, most of the politically induced volatility happened prior to the election of 6 December 1998. In the election's aftermath, the big moves were for Venezuelan *out*performance versus Brazil, not *under*performance. While this was, no doubt, helped by the strong oil rally at the time, it was also generated, somewhat ironically, by market fears about Lula going into the 2002 Brazil election. Of course, Lula turned out to be one of the more market-friendly (or maybe just lucky) presidents on record. With respect to Venezuela, it took several years before the market recognized the Chavez regime for what it was. After being elected to his third term in December 2006, Chavez pronounced his "21st century socialism," nationalizing key industries, and, in 2007, expropriated Exxon's oil fields. Only then did Venezuelan USD bonds start to underperform Brazil. So much for the long-term forecasting accuracy of markets!

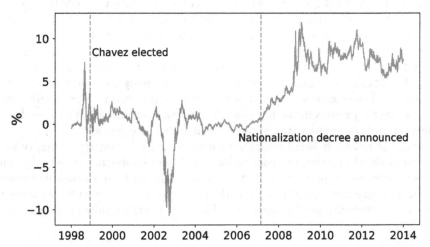

FIGURE 5.8 Wait, When Did Chavez Come to Power Again?
Note: Spread difference Venezuela over Brazil.
Source: Bloomberg.

The underlying reason for this pattern is that the incentives for an incoming president, who is seen sceptically by markets, to sound market friendly are very high. After all, the main alternative is to have to deal with an immediate collapse of FX markets, which will generate inflation and a negative growth impact. Most market-unfriendly administrations therefore decide that it is better to boil the frog slowly, rather than to pour boiling water on the market. Therefore, we strongly believe that the typical relief rally post-election has not been just a case of luck, but a strong underlying psychological pattern that shapes how asset markets behave around elections. Thank God for the FX vigilantes! We also note that most recently, the pattern has continued. For example, the election of AMLO in Mexico in July 2018 resulted in a relief rally post-election even though he was clearly a market-unfriendly candidate, who did not have much interest in placating markets. In spite of that, the usual rally happened (see the following box).

MEXICO TURNS POPULIST

On 1 July 2018, the Mexican people elected AMLO to be the new president of Mexico. This was the populist's third attempt to reach the presidency, and his prior attempts had been, at times narrowly, thwarted by the Mexican establishment in the form of the PRI or PAN. AMLO had campaigned on a populist/nationalist agenda. Promises made during the campaign included self-sufficiency in energy space (by building refineries) and rolling back the energy reform of his predecessor, additional aid for the poor, as well as fighting corruption. At the same time, AMLO also favoured a responsible budget and an independent central bank, though local observers were highly sceptical of how a responsible budget would be possible in light of expensive fiscal promises. AMLO's victory had actually been foretold by the polls for some time. But the surprise on election night was that his party, Morena, was much more successful in the coincident parliamentary elections than had been envisioned. This was an important development because one important safety valve from the market's point of view had been the expectation that the general economic structure in Mexico (including the energy sector) was mostly safe from tampering by AMLO. His party was not expected to control Congress, much less secure a supermajority to be able to change the constitution, which was necessary to fully reverse the energy reform. Those views turned out to be wrong, as Morena put in such a good showing that a constitutional amendment would be feasible with a minimal coalition-building effort. No more safety valves. It is therefore very interesting to see that the Mexican peso rallied, regardless, in the aftermath of the election – just as it did in the previous two cases when AMLO lost. This trading pattern of USD-MXN is illustrated for the last three elections in Figure 5.9.

(Continued)

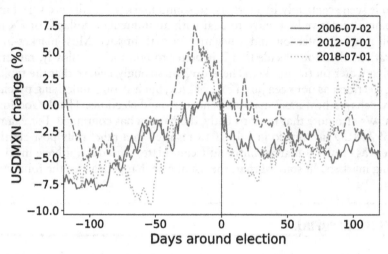

FIGURE 5.9   Nothing Ever Changes South of the Rio Grande.
Source: Bloomberg, authors' calculations.

While the rally was partially driven by a market-friendly acceptance speech, there were no clear-cut reassurances to the market by the new administration. And a second speech, geared toward the local population, was much less reassuring. The large move lower in USD-MXN after the election owed less to actions by AMLO and more to the fact that local investors had become extremely bearish and built large long USD positions. Those positions were partially stopped out post-election. The meaningfully negative carry from holding long USD-MXN positions reduced staying power. In an ironic twist, which is actually typical for market behaviour, it was only after most USD longs had been stopped out that the AMLO administration carried out its first market-unfriendly act: the cancellation of the new Mexico City airport. In this way, AMLO did eventually undermined the peso, if only for a short period.

5.7   TRADING DATA

As we highlighted in the Chapter 2, EMFX is an asset class that is mostly driven by global factors. Therefore, global data are most important for most currencies, and certainly for the EMFX index. And the most important global data releases are, or rather used to be, the nonfarm payroll release (NFP) from the US. For the longest time, it was possible to position for follow through of the daily momentum observed on NFP days. As of late 2018, this is unfortunately no longer the case, as reversals of the price action, often as soon as the day after the NFP print, have become much more frequent than prices showing quick follow-through. In another development, Chinese data have become of global importance. Adding Chinese data to our study of how to trade economic data is therefore crucial. In Figure 5.10, we more systematically investigate the question of which global data releases still have good follow through (in terms of price action) for both US and Chinese data. In addition to NFP, we pick the US manufacturing ISM, the US CPI, and the FOMC meetings as events to study. On the Chinese side, we choose both the manufacturing PMI and total social financing (TSF) as the indicators with the highest market impact. But how do we know whether a release surprised the market or not? While Bloomberg estimates are available for all the indicators under study, we feel that the "true" market consensus is often different from the published Bloomberg consensus. This can be the case because some contributors to the survey do not update their submissions on a daily basis, which leads to stale estimates. Or it can be because economists, who mostly produce those estimates, generally hold on to their views well after turning points, given that it can be reputationally costly to change views too frequently. This also may bias official estimates toward the status quo, especially during uncertain times. We therefore prefer to rely on the price action on the day of the release as an indicator of whether the release was a surprise for the market. For the US data, we use moves in two-year US swaps to define a surprise, given how sensitive Fed expectations are to the data releases under consideration. For Chinese data, we use moves in the AUD to define a surprise, given how closely the Australian economy is linked to the fortunes of the Chinese business cycle (and given that Chinese rates do not have a sufficiently long trading history for our exercise). Our basic view is that if asset prices of either US rates or the AUD do not move by more than one standard deviation on the day of the release, the data cannot have been a big surprise.

Figure 5.10 shows how EMFX behaves around the release day (day zero in the charts), where the chart moving up indicates EMFX strength. The period under study is from 2003 to the end of 2018 for the US. The Chinese data are studied starting in 2005 for the PMI and in 2009 for TSF. Most of the initial impact is shown going into day zero, though some components of the EMFX index may be already closed for the day when the release in question comes out. Therefore, the performance after day one is of most interest. Interestingly, NFP is the least reliable indicator in terms of EMFX price action, as there is no strong pattern either for hawkish surprises (where US two-year rates move up by at least one standard deviation) or for dovish surprises (where US two-year rates move down by at least one standard deviation). But for CPI, manufacturing ISM, and FOMC releases, there is some follow-through. Hawkish surprises lead to EMFX weakness over the following 20 trading days, by around 0.7 to 0.8%, even though prices already fell into the release (and it is interesting to note that data releases typically do not change the existing trend). The reaction to the manufacturing ISM is the most interesting here, because it leads to a change in trend (i.e. EMFX is broadly stronger into the release but then turns lower). For dovish surprises, the opposite effect mostly holds, though the impact is slightly smaller and the impact of the manufacturing ISM joins the NFP in having little follow-through (which makes us also slightly more cautious in using the manufacturing ISM on the hawkish side, as well, as there is no obvious reason why the impact should not be symmetric). In addition to these general observations, we also note that it clearly matters where we are in the business cycle. Sometimes the Fed

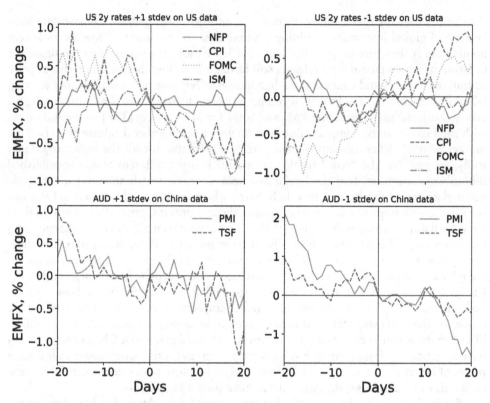

FIGURE 5.10 Forget about NFP: Follow the CPI and the FOMC.
Source: Bloomberg, authors' calculations.

is mostly focused on inflation, and other times on activity. Investors should keep the general pattern we laid out in mind but make adjustments for the current Fed focus, which will be obvious to observers from recent FOMC minutes and speeches.

With respect to the China data, the shorter period under study gives a larger weight to the time when EM were in a bear market. After positive surprises, as measured by AUD performance on the event day, EMFX traded slightly better after PMIs but mostly trod water after the TSF numbers. After 20 days, EMFX was lower, though, probably as the bear market for EMFX took over again. For negative surprises, there was initially some mild follow through for a few days. Then it became more choppy, but 20 days later, EMFX was meaningfully lower for both PMIs and TSF releases. But this was, once more, probably due to the general bear market for EMFX for much of the period under study, rather than the data releases (though the bear market is presumably related to the economic data out of China).

Overall, we conclude that selected data still appear to be tradable after the release. US data still are easier to trade than Chinese data. With respect to the US, price action on NFP release day is mostly noise, while price action for the US CPI, FOMC, and, to a lesser extent, manufacturing ISM can still be chased to some extent. But increased algorithmic trading in FX does pose the risk that price action after those releases also will become less reliable over time, as Stan Druckenmiller believes (Schatzker and Burton 2018).

5.8   SUMMARY

Tradable events in FX space are often driven by policy makers. In particular, policy makers in EM are very sensitive to FX moves (mostly, but not exclusively, on the weak side). FX intervention is often the first measure taken to defend a currency. We find that in the very short term, investors should position with policymakers, as intervention tends to work in the short term, especially for large or rare interventions. Emergency rate hikes are the next weapon in the arsenal of policy makers. Those hikes have much better odds of working than FX intervention, unless they are employed too early in the game, and investors should trade currencies from the long side after such rate hikes, if they are cheap. IMF programmes are the last resort and tend to also be currency supportive, if not necessarily immediately. Severe capital controls are rare and are mostly untradable from a directional trading point of view.

Another class of major events for EMFX is driven by local politics. Elections in EM follow a very predictable pattern where currencies tend to sell off around four months ahead of an election, only to peak shortly before the election. The election is then typically followed by a relief rally.

In terms of trading economic data, the focus has to be on global data, rather than local data. While some data releases (and in particular the US NFP) have much less follow through than they used to, the US CPI, FOMC meetings, and, to a lesser extent, US manufacturing ISM still often lead to follow through. Chinese data are less reliable as a short-term trading tool.

CHAPTER 6

How to Trade Emerging Market Rates: The Cycle

Generating alpha from EM rates is of rising significance to investors. Interest rate cycles in DM have been a major source of alpha for investors broadly and for leveraged investors in particular. With rates across the developed world close to zero, this source of alpha has largely disappeared in recent years, which may have contributed to the weaker performance of the global macro hedge funds after the 2008–2009 financial crisis. While the Fed was able to move away from the zero bound, as of late 2019 it looks like it is reversing its hiking cycle. Looking further into the future, US hiking cycles may remain shallow. After all, leverage in the economy remains high and will likely limit the extent to which the economy can live with higher rates. While it is possible that EM rates also move close to the lower bound, they are likely to stay there for shorter periods of time, given more latent inflation risks, partly on the back of weak currencies. It therefore has become even more important for investors to trade EM rates to substitute for this significantly reduced source of alpha in G10 rates. This chapter outlines how to do that.

6.1 EMERGING MARKETS: A DEFINITION FOR RATES TRADERS

Just as we did for FX, we begin with some quick thoughts on what constitutes an emerging market with respect to rates trading. While EM currencies can hardly be distinguished from most G10 currencies, this is not true for rates. It is therefore very important to figure out which EM rates behave like rates of DM and which ones do not.

The distinction between EM and DM for rates becomes the clearest during times of rising risk aversion. During those times, DM rates typically rally. EM currencies sell off as flight to safety pushes the USD higher. Lower yields in DM would tend to be supportive for EM rates. But there are also factors that push EM rates in the opposite direction, making them behave more like credit. In particular, weaker currencies often lead to higher inflation expectations, which in turn undermine rates. Furthermore, rising risk aversion means that credit spreads widen. To the extent that EM rates have a credit component, even in local-currency-denominated-bonds, this is another force that would push EM rates higher during episodes of risk aversion. Finally, whenever currency depreciation becomes extreme, central banks may be forced to hike rates for financial stability reasons, especially if there are high levels of USD-denominated debt on government or corporate balance sheets. Market fears of rate hikes reinforce the link between risk aversion and higher rates in EM.

The behaviour of rates during risk aversion is the litmus test for understanding whether a country is a developed market, and much more so than traditional classifications by GDP per head, for example. We note that correlations between risk aversion and rates are not necessarily stable over time, but they usually (but not always) change slowly.[1]

The long term correlation structure between risk aversion and rates is presented in Figure 6.1. The y-axis plots the weekly correlation between five-year swap rates and VIX (implied volatility for the S&P 500, an important measure of risk aversion) for the large EM and DM. On the x-axis we have GDP per capita. The chart shows that the US has the strongest negative correlation between risk aversion and rates (meaning higher risk aversion leads to lower interest rates). It is also the wealthiest country in the sample. Not a single emerging market has as large a negative correlation between rates and risk aversion as the US. However, a few (mostly relatively wealthy) EM also have negative correlations. Examples include Israel, South Korea, Taiwan, Czech Republic, and Chile, but also a few poorer countries like China, India, Thailand, and the Philippines. These negative correlations suggest that the market believes those countries may be able to carry out counter-cyclical monetary policies, just like their counterparts in the developed world and that the implicit credit component is small relative to the rates component. At the other end of the spectrum are the countries with the highest positive correlation

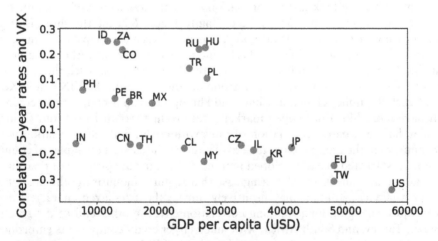

FIGURE 6.1 Only a Few, Mostly Rich, EM Trade like G3 Rates.
Source: Bloomberg, authors' calculations.

---

[1]At some point during the Greek debt crisis, the credit component in Greek government bonds surged. Such a sharp change in bond trading behaviour caught some traders off guard during the Greek crisis, but the credit aspect of bonds would have been quite familiar to EM rates traders.

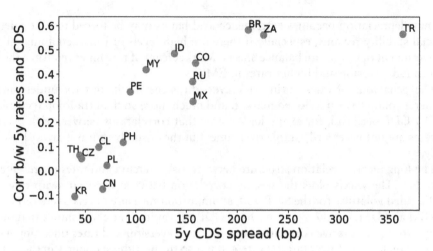

FIGURE 6.2   Most EM Rates Still Have a Credit Component.
Note: Correlation for 2010–2018, weekly changes. Five-year CDS as of end of 2018.
Source: Bloomberg, authors' calculations.

between rates and VIX: Colombia, South Africa, Turkey, Indonesia, Russia, and Brazil. Those countries are among the poorer EM.

Of course, VIX is a somewhat US-centric measure of risk. It may therefore also be of interest to analyse the issue from a country risk perspective. We find that a similar picture emerges if we look at the correlation of local rates with credit default swaps (CDS) written on the same country. According to Figure 6.2, the threshold is around 100 bp in five-year CDS spreads (although this just presents a snapshot at the end of 2018, and the cut off for the CDS level is bound to be time-variant). Above that level of credit risk, local rates are highly correlated with CDS; below that level, the correlation drops very fast. Rates for a very similar group of countries as in the VIX study (Korea, China, Czech Republic, Thailand, Chile, and Philippines) can decouple from credit risk and behave more like a developed market rates product. South Korea and China, in particular, have a negative correlation of rates with credit, and the correlation for the other countries in the group is close to zero. Those are the clearest examples of countries that should be treated like a developed market, at least for the purpose of this chapter. But we note that Chile is an interesting case that requires monitoring: the push in late 2019 for a new constitution may negatively impact the safe-haven characteristics of Chilean rates, changing long-standing correlations. At the other end of the spectrum are Brazil, Turkey, and South Africa, with much larger credit components embedded in their local rates. They have to be analysed as classical EM.

6.2   THE STRUCTURAL EM TRADE IS DEAD; LONG LIVE THE CYCLE

Now that we have put some thought into what constitutes an emerging market from a rates perspective, it is time to think about how to trade them. There are two aspects of trading EM rates: there is the structural compression trade relative to G3 rates and the business cycle trade. The structural trade is, at this stage, limited to a few countries, often found among the frontier EM. For many of the large EM included in the key EM benchmarks, there is no obvious sign of a long-term structural trade. This chapter therefore deals mostly with trading the business cycle. For readers who need more convincing, we list a few reasons for taking this approach.

First, we note that the spread of EM 10-year rates over the G3, as shown in Figure 6.3, does not display an obvious sign that there is a structural ongoing trend in place. Instead, the spread steadily moves in a band from 250 bp to 600 bp. It could be argued that during episodes of stress, emerging market spreads are making lower and lower highs. This is probably correct, and we would expect that during the next crisis, spreads will top out at a lower level than those reached in 2009. But there are no signs of lower lows during the days of strong capital inflows into EM, which would be required to establish a structural downward trend.

Second, even if there were a compelling structural story, it is dangerous for your financial health to ignore the business cycle. The average peak-to-trough move in EM rates over the business cycle has been more than 135 bp, compared to an average structural fall of 7 bp per year over the last 12 years. This can make it very expensive to focus just on the structural story. With instant gratification in high demand, more and more traders are going to focus on the business cycle rather than the structural trade.

Finally, for someone writing a chapter about how to trade EM rates with an approach of backtesting trading rules, it is much more satisfying to focus on the business cycle, as that is where the plentiful data are. For investors willing to ignore the business cycle and aiming to position for a structural trade, there is not much advice to offer other than to go long. Yes, there is the question of which countries to focus on, and we try to answer that in Chapter 9. To make a long story short, in rates space, investors should focus on countries that have abnormally high real yields relative to their peers and debt dynamics that keep default risk at bay. While this is relatively

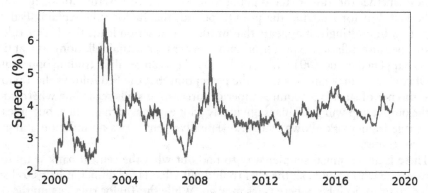

FIGURE 6.3 No Sign of a Structural Compression Trade.
Note: Spread of simple average of 10-year IRS of benchmark EM (5-year for Brazil) over average for G3 10-year swaps.
Source: Bloomberg.

straightforward, it also involves a fair amount of praying to the market gods that the structural story stays structural.

Switching to a business cycle perspective for emerging market rates, the starting point has to be the US rates cycle. After all, one of the main factors that makes trading interest rate cycles in EM different from the G3 is that developments in core rates have a major influence on EM. Everything begins, and sometimes ends, with the Fed. As we shall see later in this chapter, the impact of such global factors on EM rates cycles offers both complications and opportunities.

6.3   US LESSONS FOR EM RATES: TURNING POINTS

We start with the basic rules of how to trade US rates. We study mostly the "good old days" from 1990 until 2009, i.e. the time before rates hit the zero bound, when the living was easy and the median leveraged investor produced outsized returns. We focus on that time period as the relevant monetary policy framework for EM is mostly still one of positive nominal rates. However, we will also add a brief investigation of how to trade core rates in the brave new world of quantitative easing (QE). This is going to help us to understand what to expect from US rates going forward and the impact on EM rates. It will also help us to understand how to trade EM rates if the zero bound becomes binding for more EM.

The starting point for the exploration of how to trade US rates through the cycle is to take the Fed at its word (or rather, at Congress' edict) and believe it follows some sort of Taylor rule in line with its dual mandate. Figure 6.4, from a Brookings paper by former Fed chairman Bernanke, is supportive of the claim that the Fed has been guided by the Taylor rule, at least prior to the 2008–2009 financial crisis (Bernanke 2015). This is especially the case when the original Taylor rule is modified by using core personal consumption expenditure (PCE) inflation instead of the consumer price index (CPI) and by giving greater weight to the output gap relative to inflation. The rule broke down for obvious reasons when the zero bound was hit. And currently, it is an open question whether the Taylor rule is going to become a more useful tool again over time for the Fed. But for studying the pre-QE period, the Taylor rule explains Fed policy adequately. Interestingly, it appears that at times, Fed action leads the Taylor rule (presumably because inflation expectations move faster than actual inflation), and at times it lags, as happened in the 2001 easing cycle. Such lags can result in trading opportunities.

Of course, to make money from the perception that the Fed follows the Taylor rule in the absence of such lags requires superior forecasting skills regarding where inflation and the output gap will go. This is obviously a lot easier said than done, but at least the Taylor rule framework allows us to translate divergent views on inflation and growth into rates trades.

There is also a much simpler way to find out what the central bank is up to. Just like someone who would ask the chef to find out what is for dinner, it helps to listen to the Fed chair to decipher where rates may go. While the Taylor rule sets up the overall direction, there is a lot of uncertainty surrounding the timing, magnitude, and extent of a potential next move. Just how much data is needed to sway the FOMC to go from dovish to hawkish, and vice versa, is known only by the members of the FOMC.

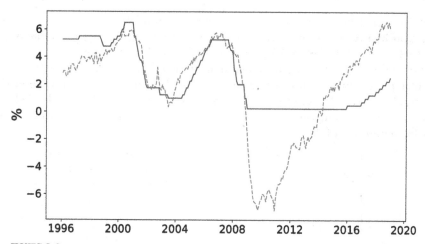

FIGURE 6.4 Taylor Rule as a Good Starting Point.
Note: Rule based on core PCE, unemployment gap (NAIRU less unemployment rate), output gap coefficient of 1.0.
Source: Federal Reserve System, Philadelphia Fed, Bureau of Labor Statistics.

Therefore, speeches by FOMC members, and in particular by the Fed chair, can be major turning points in the rate cycle. Under chair Yellen, the FOMC was arguably more collegiate, making it harder to understand which speeches mattered. But under the leadership of Greenspan, Bernanke, and probably Powell, the Fed's stance could easily be understood by focusing on speeches by the chair. The same is true for many emerging market central banks.

THE MAESTRO RINGS THE BELL

"No one rings the bell when the market peaks," or so the saying goes. This may well be true for equity markets. But bond markets have the advantage that often the bell is rung by the central bank. One example of this is how former Fed chair Alan Greenspan formally announced the end of the bond rally in early 1996. The Fed had started to ease monetary policy in mid-1995 and accelerated the cutting cycle in late 1995 and early 1996. In the aftermath of the January 1996 cut, two-year US rates traded well below Fed funds, indicating that the market was looking for more cuts. Then, on 20 February 1996, the Maestro rang the bell. In his bi-annual testimony to Congress (called the Humphrey-Hawkins testimony at that time), he remarked that "a number of fundamentals point to an economy on track for sustained growth, so any weakness is likely to be temporary". As can be seen in Figure 6.5, 10-year swaps sold off 17 bp on the day, closing the day at 6.35%. Rates subsequently sold off for another five months, to peak at 7.44% in mid-July, as shown in Figure 6.5. The next move by the Fed was a hike in March

(Continued)

1997. Greenspan's speech marked the trough for bond yields. Of course, communication by the Fed is more frequent these days and diminishes the value of any given speech. With the US 10-year yielding below 2%, a 17 bp move in a single day is unheard of. But the principle that markets are unable to adjust to a sea change in information in just one day remains the same. In many EM countries, central banks still deliver information on a less continuous basis than the Fed does it these days, offering opportunities to generate alpha. And 17 bp moves are also far from unheard of.

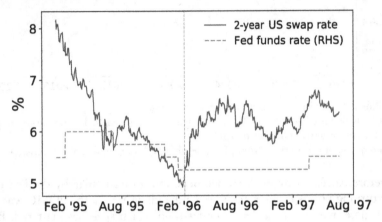

FIGURE 6.5   Greenspan Marks the Low for Yields.
Source: Bloomberg.

The Taylor rule and central bank speeches are helpful for identifying turning points. If everything fails, it pays to trust the market. Typically, when one-year US swaps fall below Fed funds from above, the rate cycle changes direction, and receivers tend to work. Similarly, when one-year rates break above Fed funds from below, payers tend to work. These crossover points are typically good entry points, as by construction they don't suffer from large negative carry. Figure 6.6 illustrates that these trades work quite well. Of course, no rule as simple as the one described is perfect. But this rule caught the coming rate cuts in the 1998 and 2001 easing cycles. In the 2008 easing cycle, it was only on the third attempt that the signal "worked," but the losses from the false signals (mostly slippage on entry and exit) were likely minimal relative to the eventual gain. The latest signal, in May 2019 (not in chart below), also worked very well the first time around. To our mind, this rule usually keeps investors on the right side of the market. At the very least, strong and differentiated beliefs about the economic outlook are needed to go against this rule.

On the paying side, the signal does not work quite as well, largely because positive risk premium in the curve adds to the profit of receivers and detracts from payers. We modify the rule and pay rates only when the last cut of the cycle is already behind us. While this is only fully known in hindsight, central banks typically signal that a cut may

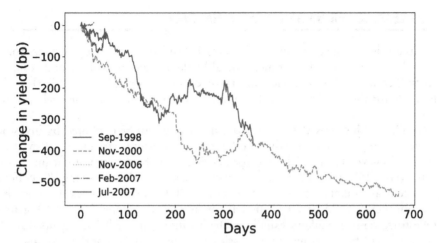

FIGURE 6.6 Receive When One-Year Swaps Break Fed Funds From Above.
Note: The line ends either when the one-year crosses again above the Fed funds
or when the last cut of the easing cycle occurs, whichever is later.
Source: Bloomberg, authors' calculations.

be the last one of the cycle. This simple rule worked reasonably well in 2003 and 2008,
as can be seen in Figure 6.7. Obviously the rule broke down as rates approached the
zero bound. But the zero bound does not apply to most EM and therefore the rule will
remain useful for EM.

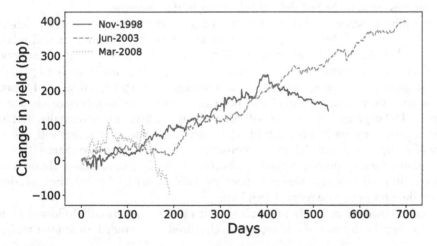

FIGURE 6.7 Pay When One-Year Swaps Break Fed Funds From Below.
Note: The line ends either when the one-year crosses again from above or at the
start of QE for the 2008 episode. For the hiking cycle starting in late 2015 the
one-year had never broken below Fed Funds due to the zero-bound constraint.
Source: Bloomberg, authors' calculations.

6.4 US LESSONS FOR EM RATES: AFTER THE TURN

The simple rules we just described are likely helpful for identifying turning points in rates markets. But most of the time, central banks just get on with it and continue in an existing easing or hiking cycle. And those cycles are long. Since 1987, the average hiking cycle for the Fed has lasted 14 months, and the average easing cycle just under 19 months.

Before analysing how these behavioural patterns can be exploited by investors, it is worth asking why central banks prefer long, consistent, stretched-out cycles over quick and decisive actions. Why did former Fed chair Bernanke not cut interest rates straight from 5.25% to zero, given the size of the calamity that befell the US economy in 2008? If central bankers were prone to cut rates all the way from peak to trough in one fell swoop, there would be very little left for investors to trade the cycle. Fortunately for investors, central bankers usually prefer to move in small increments, largely to avoid the risks of being wrong. In professions where money is not the main motivating force, pride in a job well done often is. Mistakes are therefore something to be avoided, especially as a mistake by a central bank is presumably one of the costlier mistakes that can be made. If central bankers cut rates by 500 bp in one go, only to find out six months later that inflation is out of control and they have to quickly hike rates again, the economic and reputational costs would be enormous. Therefore, risk aversion justifiably runs high inside central banks. Such thinking was highlighted by a famous 2015 incident when Jon Hilsenrath, back then the *Wall Street Journal*'s Fed watcher, tweeted prior to a Fed decision that chair Yellen likes to arrive at an airport three hours before the plane leaves, suggesting that this evidence of high risk aversion would mean the Fed was unlikely to hike without preparing the market first. This was a market-moving tweet, and, needless to say, the Fed did not hike rates in that meeting.

In addition, some form of confirmation bias is also at play. Almost by definition, when a central bank hikes for the last time in a cycle, the economy is still relatively strong. Otherwise, the central bank would not have hiked at all. A central bank which just hiked because decision makers believe in a strong economy is likely to play down the first signs of weakness, especially in a committee setting. Even if signs of weakness persist after some time, it would still not cause committee members to change their views by 180 degrees. Their views will often change at first only marginally. To change a view by 180 degrees in a context of incomplete information is a rare skill, possessed more often by a lone trader than by a committee of career central bankers.[2] Therefore, at economic turning points, central banks tend to be slow in assessing changes to the outlook, and only slight easing measures are implemented initially. After all, there is always the option to ease more if required.

Central bankers certainly understand that rate cuts are usually followed by more rate cuts. But the mistake of adding too much stimulus is avoided, or at least mitigated,

---

[2]Having said that, there clearly are exceptions. After a slow start, Bernanke certainly deserves praise for acting decisively and also aggressively in implementing untested policies such as QE.

by going slowly and constantly looking over the shoulder to see if the data confirm the previous actions. For hiking cycles, the hurdles are even higher for drastic action. Everybody wants to be liked; hiking rates typically doesn't win many friends. This is especially true in EM where in some countries, the Minister of Finance has a seat at the table at rate-setting meetings. Yes, this is the same Minister of Finance who has to pay higher rates on newly issued bonds after each rate hike.

The fact that central bank cycles are long and drawn out is not necessarily a sufficient condition for traders to make money. After all, the market could price large easing cycles perfectly, even if the central bank does not implement such cuts immediately. But this is not typically the case, either. In 2008–2009, the market did not immediately foresee rates reaching zero. Forecasting ability decays quickly with lengthening time horizons. This is an issue not just for markets, but for most problems in life. For example, it is common knowledge that weather report accuracy degrades very quickly if meteorologists try to look beyond three days. If the market were faced with the possibility of the Fed cutting 500 bp in the next meeting in one swoop, it would price a meaningful probability of this happening. But if the market is faced with the probability that the Fed will cut 500 bp over a period of more than one year, it will price a smaller probability of this event happening, because many things can change over a year. An alternative explanation is that the market is correct in forecasting a 500 bp cut over a one-year period but requires a risk premium that rises over time, just in case it is wrong. This theory would also explain why the market initially prices an insufficient number of cuts. This debate about whether the market is a good forecaster requiring a lot of risk premium or simply a bad forecaster is really just semantics, from a trading point of view. If an investor correctly forecasts that a 500 bp cut is coming, they could either make money because the market is wrong and does not price enough cuts or earn the risk premium over time even if the market is correct. The combination of drawn-out central bank cycles and a relatively slow market reaction is what generates profitable trading rules around central bank actions.

6.5   THE POWER OF PATIENCE: RECEIVE AROUND THE LAST HIKE UNTIL THE LAST CUT IS CLOSE

Figure 6.8 shows the P&L of receivers of one-year US swaps over time around the last hikes for the last three cycles, where the last hike is set to day zero. Typically, by the time the last hike happens, the curve is inverted. This results in negative carry, which Figure 6.8 takes into account. The chart demonstrates that on average, the right time to start receiving in past Fed cycles has been around the last hike. Until then, the right trade was to keep paying rates. Receivers remain the correct position until the last cut is close. While there are admittedly not very many observations, given how few Fed cycles there were, we will find a similar pattern for many EM, making us more confident that this rule is sensible to use in trading. Our findings demonstrate that the market is not overly forward looking, maybe due to the reasons alluded to in the previous section. Our rule is

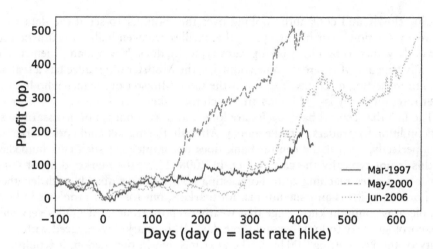

FIGURE 6.8   Stay Received in Easing Cycles Until the Last Cut is Close.
Note: P&L of receiving one-year swaps, carry adjusted, from the last hike on day 0 to the last cut, since 1996.
Source: Bloomberg, authors' calculations.

straightforward, but nevertheless, rate traders often do not follow it. Sometimes traders try to be too smart for their own good. A trader might argue along the following lines: "The market is pricing four hikes, but I believe that only three hikes will materialize. So let me receive right now and be smart and forward looking." While this trader might still come out ahead, it is more often than not a fairly painful way to make money. The market is more likely to price more and more hikes as the tightening goes on. Rates will keep going up more than initially priced. Only when the cycle appears to be drawing to a close will rates start to fall. Patience can be powerful.

But how do we know that there is only one rate hike left? The simple answer is that we don't. And this is exactly why this rule continues to work. If the rule could be sufficiently specific to trade on auto-pilot, it would probably start to fail very fast. However, as described, we can get clues from the Taylor rule and central bank speeches or rely on the market by receiving rates when the one-year rate falls through Fed funds. This is not perfect, but it makes sure investors don't miss a major rate-cutting cycle when it happens.

6.6   MORE ON PATIENCE: PAY INTO THE FIRST HIKE UNTIL THE LAST HIKE IS CLOSE

The same rule works for hiking cycles. Investors should, on average, stay received until there is only one cut left. The period right after the last cut is usually a tricky one to trade. Payers, on average, only come into their own around three months or so ahead of the first hike, as illustrated by Figure 6.9. But then they mostly work until the last hike. Just like at the end of a hiking cycle, investors often try to front run the end of

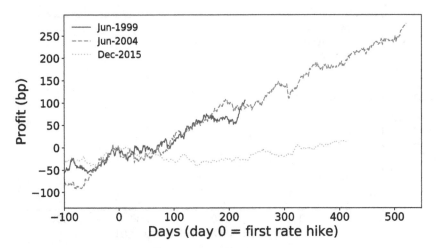

FIGURE 6.9 Keep Paying in Hiking Cycles Until the Last Hike is Close.
Note: P&L of paying one-year swaps, carry adjusted, from the last cut on day 0 to the last hike, since 1996.
Source: Bloomberg, authors' calculations.

the easing cycle. They either take profits in receivers or initiate payers too early. When comparing Figure 6.8 and Figure 6.9, it is noteworthy that the receiving part of the rule is more profitable than the paying part. This is true for three reasons. First, easing cycles are typically larger and longer than hiking cycles and therefore generate more profits. Second, the time period under study is, in the big picture, a fixed-income bull market. Finally, as mentioned earlier, it is plausible that there is usually a positive risk premium, which means that on average, receivers are subsidized relative to payers even outside of fixed-income bull markets. The case for a positive risk premium is even stronger in EM, where the risk of emergency rate hikes is much larger than that of emergency rate cuts.

6.7 STEEPENERS: RECEIVERS FOR CHICKENS

It turns out that the shape of the curve also generally follows the Fed cycles. Figure 6.10 analyses the P&L of a 2s/10s DV01 neutral steepener going into the first cut . It suggests that steepeners start to work well several months ahead of the first cut. This is not too different from Figure 6.8, which suggests that receivers start to generate profits after the last hike. Curve steepeners are very similar to receivers. But the Sharpe ratio can be higher, especially in EM where rising risk aversion often leads to steeper curves. Steepeners are therefore receivers for chickens. This would suggest a bias to go for steepeners over receivers, at least in a well-behaved easing cycle. Less negative carry will also make it easier to hold on to the trade, even after adjusting for the larger notional size needed to generate the same dollar gains. For investors who prefer directional trades

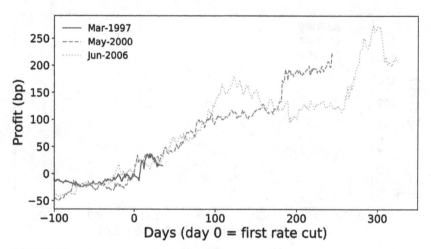

FIGURE 6.10 Steepeners Work Well into the First Fed Cut.
Note: P&L of 2s/10s curve steepener adjusted for carry, from the last hike to the last cut, since 1996.
Source: Bloomberg, authors' calculations.

to curve trades, this finding suggests that in an easing cycle, the best place to receive is usually the front end of the curve.

We analysed 2s/10s in the previous section, partly because many emerging market curves do not go out much more than for 10 years. But, as an increasing number of EM issue ever longer maturities, we also analyse the very back end. For 30-year bonds, it could easily be argued that the Fed cycle should be close to irrelevant, since their yields should be based on the average Fed funds rate over 30 years plus risk premium. But in practice, it appears that even the very long end of the rates curves is usually reactive to the interest rate cycle. Therefore, the steepening in a rates-cutting cycle does not come from the fact that the front end moves and the back end stays steady. It usually happens that the front end moves lower and the back end also moves lower, just by less, i.e. curves bull-steepen. This implies that for cash-constrained investors, there is a legitimate question of whether it is more profitable to go for the long end to have more duration, even if yields at the long end typically move by less. Figure 6.11 shows the return of the 10-year US rates minus that of 1-year rates for the same cash investment. The long end typically outperforms. For cash-constrained investors, it is therefore advisable to add duration at the long end of the curve in spite of the expected curve steepening.

While the steepening pattern is very similar across different segments of the curve, we note that the very front end of the curve behaves differently. 1s/2s typically flatten after the last hike, as can be seen in Figure 6.12. This is the case because the average time between the last hike and the first cut for the Fed is around 10 months (ranging from 3 to 18 months). Even a quick turn by the Fed would therefore not benefit one-year receivers much, as by the time the cut arrives, there is little DV01 left in the one-year receiver. Therefore 1s/2s tend to flatten, and curves invert.

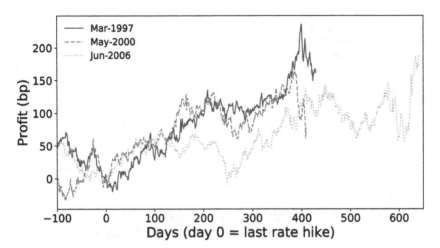

FIGURE 6.11   10-Year US Rates Outperform 1-Year Rates in Easing Cycles.
Note: P&L of receiving 10-year swaps less paying 1-year swaps, cash neutral, from last hike to last cut.
Source: Bloomberg, authors' calculations

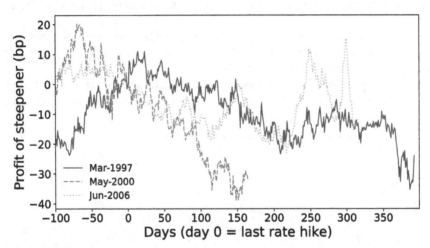

FIGURE 6.12   The 1s/2s Flatten After the Last Fed Hike and Until the Day Before First Cut.
Note: P&L of 1s/2s curve steepener, carry adjusted, daily duration adjusted.
Source: Bloomberg, authors' calculations.

6.8   FLATTENERS: PAYERS FOR CHICKENS

Just as steepeners are chicken receivers, flatteners are chicken payers. In what is a pleasingly symmetric result, flatteners tend to work well going into the first hike, as illustrated in Figure 6.13. And again, the front end does most of the work. But just as outright

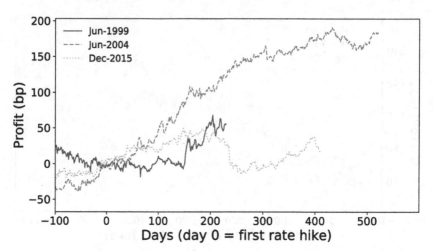

FIGURE 6.13   2s/10s Flatten into the First Rate Hike by the Fed.
Source: Bloomberg, authors' calculations.

payers are not working as well as outright receivers, flatteners are not working as well as steepeners.

For 1s/2s, the same rule also holds in reverse. 1s/2s tend to steepen after the last cut, again because it takes too long for the Fed to turn for 1s to benefit much from the first hikes. This is illustrated in Figure 6.14.

Does this mean that bear steepeners or bull flatteners never occur during hiking/easing cycles, respectively? Of course markets are not that easy. Bull flattening

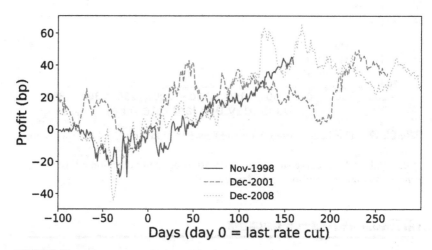

FIGURE 6.14   The 1s/2s Curve Steepens from the Last Rate Cut to the First Hike.
Note: 2008 episode ends after 300 days with the implementation of QE.
Source: Bloomberg, authors' calculations.

happens, for example, if it is driven by a sudden spike in risk aversion at a time when high inflation makes it unlikely that the Fed can react by cutting rates. Bear steepening can happen when the central bank loses credibility and the market hikes for the Fed. We think that during times when the zero bound is not binding, the odds are in favour of bull steepeners or bear flatteners. But the odds are more well balanced than seems theoretically likely. During periods where we have a well-defined traditional monetary policy (1990 to 2009), and using monthly data, 27% of times we observe bull steepening, 22% of the time bear flattening, only 21% of the time bull flattening, 15% of the time bear steepening, and 15% of the time a mix of bull and bear curve moves. This means bull steepening is 29% more likely than bear steepening, and bear flattening is 40% more likely than bull flattening.

6.9　HOW TO TRADE QE

Before modifying these basic rules for EM a quick word is in order about the zero bound for nominal rates. In the G3, interest rates are or were or will be close to or even below zero. Even though the Fed has made progress in moving away from the zero bound, we imagine that the zero constraint will become binding again in the next downturn. In the Eurozone, policy rates have even been pushed below zero. But we note that such rates are not significantly below zero and can easily be interpreted as a storage fee rather than a removal of the zero constraint. Furthermore, after some initial enthusiasm for negative rates in 2015 and early 2016, policy makers have become more worried about the impact of negative rates on the banking system. For practical purposes, we therefore still think that values just below zero are a binding constraint for nominal rates, and it would take a move to a fully cashless society for this to change.

The implication of the zero bound is that we cannot expect any more easing cycles similar to the ones we discussed earlier while rates are close to zero. Furthermore, to the extent that the equilibrium interest rate fell below zero, hiking cycles are impacted as well. Central banks will have to wait patiently until the required rate rises above zero again before rate hikes can begin. This leads to rates sitting at zero for a protracted period and also to short hiking cycles, given that the cutting cycles stopped well before equilibrium rates were reached. This means trading short-term interest rates in G3 has become much less rewarding.

Of course, central banks in G3 have not stood still. The main tool in the absence of rate cuts has been asset purchases, i.e. QE programmes. Initially, these programmes offered good alpha opportunities for investors. The easy rule was "buy what central banks buy" – only faster. Just like "front-running" central banks on policy rates, investors switched to front-running central banks on asset purchases. The rule of thumb for trading those QE programmes was to buy US Treasuries while the measures were being discussed and then take profit upon implementation. Actual implementation often led to rates sell-offs, as the market started to believe that bond buying could actually work and lead to reflation. The trouble with QE programmes is that they work less and less well over time, not just in terms of economic outcomes but also in

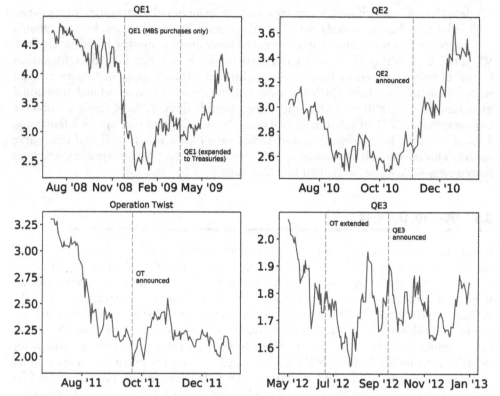

FIGURE 6.15 UST Rallies into QE Announcements and Sells Off After.
Note: Yield of 10-year UST around QE dates.
Source: Bloomberg.

terms of their impact on asset prices. This can be seen for the various QE versions in the US in Figure 6.15, where QE3 did not have a strong impact on US rates.

When QE programmes are unwound, the opposite behaviour is likely. Rates move higher into the announcements of stimulus removal, only to rally when, eventually, the removal of QE negatively impacts risky assets and/or the economy. This will have important consequences for EM rates as well, as they will then face crosscurrents from lower US rates on the one hand but lower risky assets and weaker EMFX on the other.

HAS QE KILLED THE PROFITABILITY OF MACRO HEDGE FUNDS?

To our mind, rates trades at the short end of the curve are among the highest alpha trades for global macro funds. The fact that the zero bound had become binding in many of the liquid front-end markets has to some extent removed these trades from the opportunity set. While initially, QE programmes substituted for lost P&L, Sharpe ratios of trading back ends are often lower than for front ends.

(Continued)

This is because at the front end, asset prices are more anchored due to central banks. The substitution of these high alpha trades by low alpha back-end trades may be one reason the performance of global macro funds has deteriorated in recent years. It is also an additional reason to look for rates alpha in EM, where the zero constraint typically does not bind.

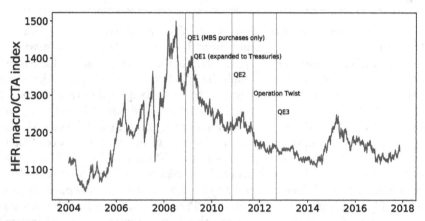

FIGURE 6.16   Macro Hedge Fund Profitability Deteriorated at the Zero Bound.
Source: Bloomberg.

6.10   IT IS TOUGH TO BE AN EM CENTRAL BANKER

In spite of the significant differences between EM and the G3 in terms of how rates react to risk aversion, luckily the trading framework for EM rates is very similar to the one for G3 rates. Once we have a good sense of when the last rate hike is going to take place, we can apply trading rules that are almost identical to those established for US rates. However, to forecast when the last hike will take place is somewhat different in EM. In particular, the Taylor rule used by central banks in EM is often more complex than what G3 central banks follow. We therefore need to spend some time analysing how to adapt the Taylor rule framework for EM.

The first point to note is that the weights in the Taylor rule for CPI and output gap are typically different. In general, EM central banks put a larger weight on inflation, because from a legal perspective they typically don't have a dual mandate. Furthermore, they often have less credibility and therefore are less able to look through transitory higher inflation outcomes. For this reason, most EM central banks have an inflation target, which can be thought of as a Taylor rule with a very small weight on the output gap. The weight put on output is unlikely to be zero only to the extent that the output gap typically has an impact on inflation forecasts.

But further modifications of the Taylor rule for EM are necessary, given another key difference between G3 and EM: global trends matter more to EM than to G3, where domestic conditions typically (but not always) dominate. Given a stronger focus on inflation than on output, the key to investigate is how global drivers impact EM inflation.

6.11 EMFX AS AN UNPLEASANT CONSTRAINT ON EM CENTRAL BANKERS

While the public perception of the omnipotent G3 central banker is very misleading, their EM colleagues have it even more difficult. In particular, the FX market keeps many EM central bankers awake at night. After all, the global impact on local monetary policy is transmitted most clearly through the FX channel. To our mind, the sensitivity of inflation to FX, i.e. the pass-through, is the single biggest difference between EM and G10 fundamentals when it comes to rates trading. Reasons FX matters more to inflation in EM than in DM are manifold. First of all, EM are often small and relatively open economies where import shares are higher than in the often more closed DM. Therefore, the weights of imported goods in the CPIs are higher in EM than in the G3. Furthermore, lower GDP per head implies a higher weight of food (and, for some regions, energy) in the CPI basket. Food and energy are often at least partially priced in USD. This adds to increased pass-through. In Peru, for example, food has a weight of close to 30% in its CPI. In the G3, on the other hand, services, where FX matters the least, are much more important. Figure 6.17 illustrates this fact for the different regions.

Second, because in the 1990s many EM governments used their currencies as a macro anchor to stabilize inflation, the FX rate often plays a large psychological role when EM citizens assess the outlook for the macro stability of the country, including the outlook for inflation. Inflation expectations, in turn, are an important determinant for actual inflation outcomes. And finally, EMFX tends to be more volatile, at least during crisis periods, than G10 FX, which increases the impact of FX on inflation, especially during such crisis periods. As a result, pass-through from FX to inflation is meaningfully higher in EM than in the G3. This is illustrated in Figure 6.18. While it is plausible that pass-through has fallen further since this study was undertaken, we believe that at least relative to DM, pass-through will remain higher due to the reasons discussed above.

If FX impacts rates mostly by impacting inflation expectations and, ultimately, inflation, then this fits very neatly into the Taylor rule framework without requiring us to change the overall methodology of the Taylor rule for EM. Having said that, empirically, it can help to include FX as an additional and separate explanatory variable in the Taylor rule estimations. This is especially the case to the extent that FX can also be a financial stability issue rather than a more narrowly defined inflation issue. Some studies found a separate FX term to be significant, but typically only for a subset of countries.[3]

Similar to the discussion of risk aversion and EM rates, the beta of EM rates to their own EMFX varies across countries. The overlap with the earlier study of risk aversion

---

[3]In Turkey, for example, FX is significant, even though some FX pressure is likely captured in the inflation variable. See Çatık et al. (2018).

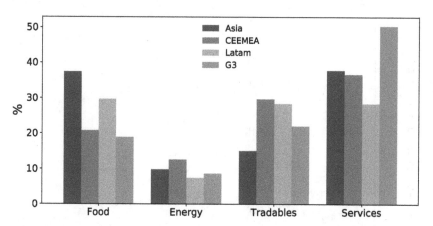

FIGURE 6.17 Smaller Weights for Services in EM Create a Larger FX Impact on Inflation.
Note: Percentage point weights in headline CPIs.
Source: Various statistical agencies.

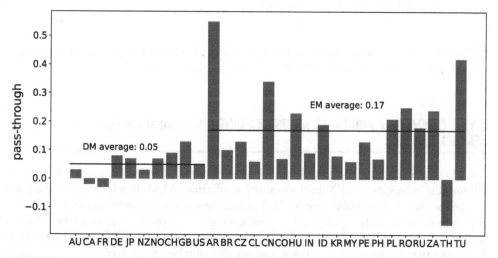

FIGURE 6.18 FX Pass-Through to Inflation in EM is Much Higher Than in DM.
Source: Carrière-Swallow et al. (2016).

and EM rates is, reassuringly, very high. The countries where rates move meaningfully higher when risk aversion rises are also the ones that are sensitive to their own FX depreciating, as illustrated in Figure 6.19. For those countries, it is important to keep in mind that it is not consistent to be bullish on the interest rate of a country and bearish on the FX. More likely than not, they will be positive correlated (i.e. higher USD-EMFX, meaning higher EM rates). Interestingly, this is even the case in some countries where

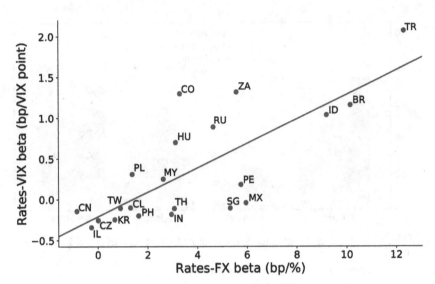

FIGURE 6.19 FX Dominates Rates in Countries Where Risk Aversion Pushes Rates Up.
Source: Bloomberg, authors' calculations.

VIX does not have a meaningful impact on rates, probably because the shocks measured by VIX are more US-centric, while the FX shocks are EM-centric and country-specific.

6.12 COMMODITY PRICES AS AN UNPLEASANT CONSTRAINT ON EM CENTRAL BANKERS

The other main channel for global conditions to impact EM rates very quickly is through commodity prices. Just as FX matters more for inflation in EM than in the G10, the same is true for global commodity prices. And again, there is not much the central banks can do about it. We already highlighted the lower weight of the service sector in the inflation basket and the correspondingly higher weight of commodity-linked prices for most EM. It follows that food and energy prices impact inflation more severely.

Furthermore, institutionally, EM central banks typically have a target for headline CPI, rather than for core. This is largely driven by the fact that many EM have a history of high inflation, and the population is therefore often circumspect of policy makers picking an inflation target based on underlying "true" inflation, rather than on prices that are in line with their daily inflation experience. And the poorer the country, the larger food tends to be as a percentage of the consumption basket, and the harder it is for policy makers to exclude items like food from the monetary policy target. Of course, institutional setups are different across countries, and some countries at least aim to smooth the impact of rising global commodity prices on local prices. Nevertheless, we usually do find that local food and energy prices are impacted by global

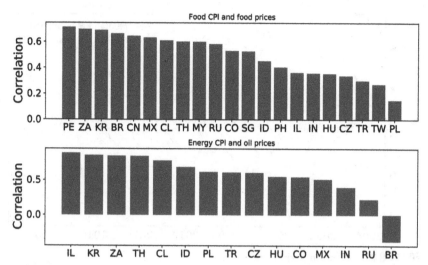

FIGURE 6.20　Global Commodity Prices Impact Local Food and Energy Prices.
Note: Correlation of food and energy CPI versus global prices denominated in local currency (with various lead times).
Source: Bloomberg, authors' calculations.

commodity prices, translated to local currencies. This is shown in Figure 6.20. Here we kept things simple by choosing one fixed lag for each country: the lag resulting in the highest correlation. In reality, the lag structure is likely more complicated, and analysts should run a vector autoregression (VAR) analysis, which will suggest higher cumulative impacts of global food shocks on local inflation, but we think our approach is a close enough approximation.[4]

Figure 6.21 illustrates, that the nature of inflation is global. The underlying reason for the high correlation between inflation in EM and the G3 is the significant impact of volatile commodity prices on headline inflation around the world. When running a principle components analysis (PCA) comparing inflation across the globe, we find that 83% of inflation in emerging Asia, 61% of inflation in CEEMEA, and 55% of inflation in Latin America is driven by the first principal component, i.e. by a global factor. This global factor is highly correlated with global commodity prices.

But there is more to it than just saying commodity prices matter. While on average, higher commodity prices mean higher global inflation and higher EM inflation, there is a subset of EM where higher commodity prices lead on average to *lower* inflation. This is true for most commodity producers among EM. To be precise, factor loadings for a PCA of the first factor for inflation are negative for Brazil, Chile, Colombia, Peru, Russia, South Africa, Indonesia, and Malaysia, i.e. precisely the subset of countries that export commodities.

---

[4]We note that there are fewer energy CPIs available than food CPIs. Also, the negative correlation for Brazil is driven by a large spike of the energy CPI subindex in 2015 driven by electricity prices on the back of water shortages for hydro generation.

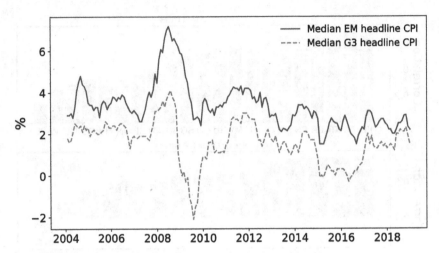

FIGURE 6.21   Inflation Trends are Global.
Source: Bloomberg.

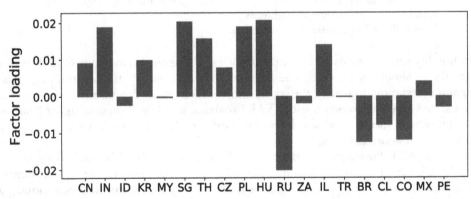

FIGURE 6.22   Inflation Falls for Commodity Producers When Commodities Move Up.
Note: Factor loadings for the first principal component of inflation, 2010–2016.
Source: Citi, Bloomberg, authors' calculations.

The logic is the following: when commodities move higher, EMFX of commodity producers outperform. Large moves by the FX of commodity producers then pushes inflation of tradable goods (and often of commodities, in local currency terms) lower, more than offsetting the move up in USD prices of commodities. This leads to interesting relative value opportunities, where receivers in commodity producers work well at a time when the world overall is worried about inflation. Colombia in the following box is a good example, but the same held true for other commodity exporters, including Brazil, Chile, and Peru.[5]

---

[5]For a more in-depth discussion, see Lam and Willer (2017).

BANREP AT THE MERCY OF OPEC

In Q4 2015, oil prices collapsed by 45% as a result of OPEC refusing to cede market share to US shale producers. Colombia (along with Russia) was one of the key victims of this development, given that at the time, energy exports amounted to 40% of Colombia's exports, the second highest in the EM world. Consequently, GDP growth in Colombia slowed from 3.1% in 2015 to 2.0% in 2016, compared to trend growth estimates sitting at the time at around 4.5%. The size of the terms of trade shock would have typically led a DM central bank to cut rates, partially preemptively, to prevent a recession. However, at the same time, the COP depreciated by 46% between mid-2014 and early 2016. This led to inflation shooting up. Colombia also was unlucky that the El Niño pattern drove food inflation higher. The result was an aggressive hiking cycle where the central bank target rate was raised 3.25% to 7.75%, which drove central bank rates well into restrictive territory, just as the terms of the trade shock slowly worked its way through the system.

Furthermore, and importantly for relative value trading opportunities, at the same time when a hawkish Banrep accelerated its hikes, the rest of the world was fearing deflation again, thanks to collapsing oil prices. But in 2016, the tables turned. Oil bottomed in February 2016, and USD-COP peaked at a similar time – and the whole process went into reverse. Banrep was able to implement a major easing cycle starting in late December 2016, just as the world talked about the grand reflation trade.

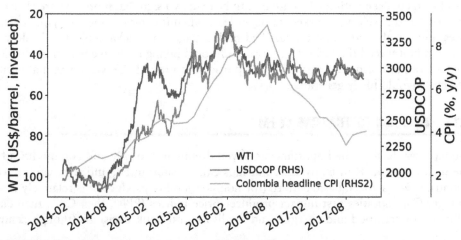

FIGURE 6.23 Inflation in Colombia Shoots Up with Falling Oil.
Source: Bloomberg.

6.13   THE FED AS AN UNPLEASANT CONSTRAINT ON EM CENTRAL BANKERS

There is also a debate about whether the Fed has a direct impact on the behaviour of EM central banks.[6] In particular, there is a question of whether easing cycles in EM can gain traction at time when the Fed hikes, and vice versa. To our mind, the links are very real, but the impact is only indirect, mostly working through the currency channel. If a Fed hiking cycle leads to weaker EMFX, which happened during the last hiking cycle, then the Fed will implicitly be taken into account by a basic Taylor rule framework for EM as inflation expectations will be impacted. This can lead, once more, to the EM central bank having to hike rates irrespective of local conditions if the FX weakens by enough. Another way the link can work is that both the Fed and EM central banks react to some other variable: most frequently, either very weak or very strong global growth. In that case, it may appear that the Fed is part of the reaction function of EM central banks, even though in reality it is not, and therefore there is no need to add the Fed action explicitly to EM Taylor rules.

In reality, EM easing cycles during Fed hiking cycles are somewhat rare. To us, the key reason is the one we have hinted at: when the Fed hikes, global growth conditions are usually (but not always) relatively strong, suggesting that local conditions should not be supportive of easing. And second, many EM central banks prefer to play it safe during Fed hiking cycles, as there always is the latent fear that EMFX may sell off hard during such cycles. And EM central banks will try to avoid adding another reason for investors to sell their currencies by being overly dovish. Still, a very benign hiking cycle by the Fed in terms of its impact on US rates and the USD can coexist with EM easing cycles. Table 6.1 shows a list of such cycles. The fact that more and more central banks are able to cut even with the Fed hiking can be read as a sign that more EM are closer to graduating to developed market status, at least when it comes to monetary policy and rates. But we also note that the last Fed hiking cycle was uncharacteristically slow. If inflation had forced the Fed into a more traditional hiking cycle, we would likely have seen a more uniform monetary policy response, given the EMFX weakness that such a Fed cycle would likely generate.

6.14   INFLATION FORECASTING IN EM

We have established the importance, or even dominance, of FX and commodities for the inflation process in many EM. But lags can be substantial, and they vary across countries. The stylized basic pattern (for non-commodity producers) is relatively clear, though. Commodities first impact producer price indices (PPIs), then CPIs, then core CPIs (excluding food and energy), and finally central bank decisions (though central

---

[6]We focus here on the Fed, as the Fed punches above its weight. Hiking cycles by the ECB or BOJ tend to impact global financial conditions much less than the Fed does. One reason is that Fed hiking cycles often also lead to a stronger USD, which undermines EM together with higher rates. On the other hand, ECB hiking cycles could lead to USD weakness, cushioning the blow.

TABLE 6.1 EM Central Banks Can Cut During Benign US Hiking Cycles.

Jun 99 – May 00	Fed hiking cycles Jun 04 – Aug 06	Dec 15 – Dec 18
ZA	KR[1]	IN
IL	PL[2]	KR
BZ	HU[2]	ID
CO	CZ[2]	MY
	ZA[1]	HU
	IL[1]	RU
	BR[2]	ZA[2]
	CO[1]	BR
		CL[2]
		CO[2]
		PE[2]

Note: [1]Rate cuts followed by hikes. [2]Rate hikes followed by cuts.
Source: Bloomberg, authors' calculations.

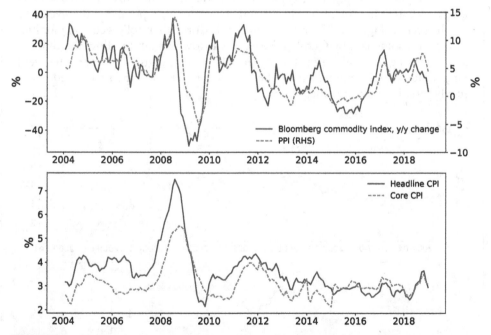

FIGURE 6.24 Commodity Prices Lead PPI Lead Headline CPI Lead Core CPI.
Source: Bloomberg, authors' calculations.

banks sometimes skip the last step and react to headline inflation). This pattern is helpful for forecasting inflation in EM – if only in a directional sense. Trying to come up with point estimates often remains a fool's errand, just like forecasting anything else in life with any precision.

This simple, basic pattern can lead to interesting trading opportunities. If, for example, commodities have clearly turned down, also in local currency terms, the best receivers are in (non-commodity producing) countries that still show some inflation above the central bank's inflation target, maybe just because of longer lags or domestic inflation pressures that will in the end be overcome by global and commodity pressures.

SOUTH KOREA IN THE GLOBAL FINANCIAL CRISIS

The financial crisis in 2008–2009 provides several examples of global factors overpowering local inflation developments. For instance, in the case of Korea, the central bank had been hiking interest rates in 2007 and then implemented an additional hike in early August 2008 because inflation was overshooting its target. However, oil (and many commodities) had already peaked in early July and were falling steeply. Consequently, inflation in South Korea peaked shortly afterward, and July inflation turned out to be the high point for the cycle. As can be seen in Figure 6.25, inflation in South Korea then followed commodities lower with some lag; by October 2008, it was low enough to allow the BOK to start its easing cycle, also egged on by sharply lower growth. One-year rates went largely sideways beginning shortly before the last hike and then collapsed lower just before the first cut came.

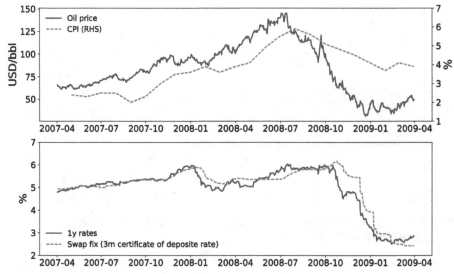

FIGURE 6.25   Global Developments Overcome Local Inflation Developments.
Source: Bloomberg.

Another very simple way to "forecast" EM inflation is to use base effects. Seasonally adjusting EM inflation (or, really, any other EM economic data series) is difficult. Rather than just running the standard X-12-ARIMA procedure, great care needs to be taken to account for shifting local holidays, shifting weekends and trading days, leap years, etc. Seasonal adjustments for EM, where time series tend to have much shorter histories than in the US, and where structural breaks are common, therefore tend to be much less reliable than they are for DM. One simple way to come up with roughly the right answer is to look at year-over-year inflation and see when it started to aggressively take off (or aggressively fall). Often, inflation dynamics begin to change whenever those aggressive inflation moves fall out of the 12-month window used for the yoy calculation. Maybe not much of a forecast, but at least psychologically, the trend of the current headline inflation is important for rates.

More recently, big data techniques have led to many attempts to improve inflation forecasting for EM.[7] These approaches are very promising, even though in the end, any advantage from such an exercise will likely be short-lived. We will discuss this issue further in Chapter 11.

6.15   PEAKS IN INFLATION AS THE HOLY GRAIL

Given our previous exposition, it comes as no surprise that inflection points in inflation (often in yoy terms) are extremely important for central banks in EM, much more so than for their colleagues in DM. One rule of thumb that we have found useful is that it is very rare for EM central banks to continue raising interest rates once annual inflation has turned lower. While this may sound obvious, it is not. After all, inflation can be, and often is, still substantially above target when yoy peaks are materializing. Some would therefore argue that more tightening is needed. But it turns out that even independent central bankers prefer to be liked. They would rather cut rates than hike. This is likely one reason central banks tend to stop hiking at the first signs of hope in the form of peaking headline inflation. This often happens when the market expects more rate hikes. To be precise, on average, EM central banks stop hiking in precisely the same month when inflation peaks, as illustrated in Figure 6.26. This is stunning. To repeat, on average, EM central banks hike exactly until yoy inflation peaks, not a single month less or more. In other words, central banks cannot afford to be very forward-looking. It appears that even for relatively short horizons, inflation estimates are just too uncertain, and costs of stopping too early are too high for central banks to stop hiking before inflation has peaked.

Central banks are willing to look further ahead when considering whether to start an easing cycle, though. On average, rate cuts start when the median CPI is 35 bp lower than where it was when the last hike happened. But by the time of the first cut, median inflation is still 1.3% above the upper end of the respective inflation target. It is good

---

[7]For our attempt, see Willer et al. (2019d).

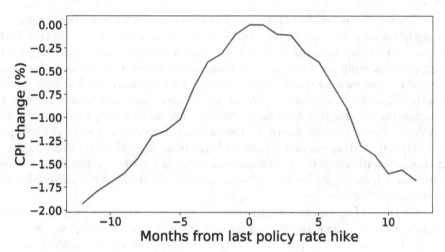

FIGURE 6.26 Central Banks Stop Hiking When Inflation Peaks.
Note: Countries: IN, ID, KR, MY, TH, PL, CZ, HU, TR, ZA, BR, MX, CL, CO.
Source: Bloomberg, authors' calculations.

enough for central banks that yoy inflation is going in the right direction, especially as inflation expectations tend to extrapolate the last set of inflation prints.

It is also noteworthy that this pattern is much less clear for the case of bottoming inflation. Often, central banks are very happy to keep cutting rates even with inflation bottoming, if growth happens to be weak. Even though EM central banks usually are inflation targeters, growth does enter the equation whenever inflation is firmly under control.

In summary, focusing on global factors for inflation, which local investors may be late in internalizing, and focusing on base effects, which many tend to ignore as being too simple, can improve rates trading in EM.

6.18 EM RATES: TRADING THE CYCLE IN THE FRONT

Once we have adapted our Taylor rule to the reality of EM central banking and analysed what a central bank is likely to do, trading the monetary policy cycle is not too different from the rules we laid out earlier for the US. Of course, unlike G3 monetary policy cycles, it does not take as much for global events in the form of rising risk aversion and weaker EMFX to disrupt EM cycles. It is therefore crucial to keep an eye on EMFX. But during "normal" times, "normal" rules apply. In particular, just as in the case we studied for the Fed, for the short-term rate (one year) to cross the monetary policy rate from above is once more a good signal to receive. Following this rule makes sure investors are on the right side of the monetary policy cycle. Of course, there are times when policy makers don't oblige and don't validate the market's view on rates. But on average, the market signal works: if not the first time, then the second time around. While investors smell the end of the hiking cycle before the short end inversion occurs,

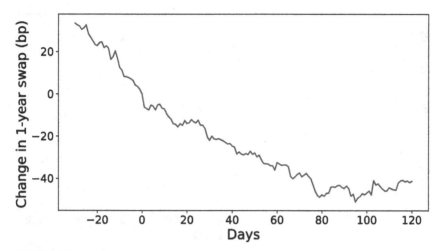

FIGURE 6.27   EM Receivers are Profitable After the One-Year Rate Moves Below the Policy Rate.
Note: One-year swaps after it crosses the policy rate from above (day 0) for Korea, Poland, South Africa, Brazil, and Mexico, Jan 2008–Aug 2017.
Source: Bloomberg, authors' calculations.

an inversion should be a wake-up call to add to receivers, and a dis-inversion a wake-up call to add payers. This is illustrated in Figure 6.27 for the large EM that have liquid swap markets.

For payers, the equivalent rule holds, too. When the one-year rate breaks above the policy rate from below, it is typically a good time for payers. But, just as in the case of the US, it is noteworthy that the P&L for payers is not as smooth as for receivers, likely again due to the fact that there is a positive risk premium in the rates market, which adds to the P&L of receivers but detracts from payers. This is shown in Figure 6.28.

Once the cycle is under way, the same rules as for the US continue to work in EM. In particular, after starting to receive around the last hike, investors on average should stay received until there is only one cut left, positioned at the front end of the curve. The study in Figure 6.29 illustrates the P&L for the case of EM for that strategy. For EM, we have the advantage of many more examples of these cycles than for the US, which makes the results more robust. On the other hand, given that cycles are of various lengths, we can only aggregate behaviours around the first hike and last cut, rather than for the full cycle. But we believe that our findings around last hikes and last cuts generalize for mid-cycle behaviours, too, given that they held for the much more efficient US markets.

For payers, the US results also largely hold. Payers typically lose money into the last cut and have very uneven performance even after the last cut and mostly range-trade. The sweet spot for payers is around 20 trading days before the first hike, and it lasts until around 60 trading days after the first hike, as can be seen in Figure 6.30. Once more, it is much harder to extract money out of payers, and it is much more important to analyse precisely when the first hike will be in the offing.

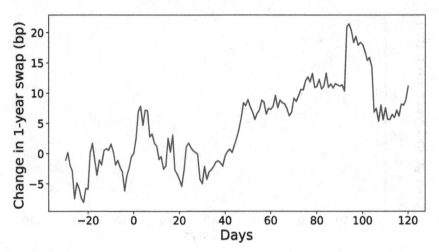

FIGURE 6.28   EM Payers are Profitable After One-Year Rates Move Above the Policy Rate, But Less So.
Note: One-year swaps after it crosses the policy rate from below (day 0) for Korea, Poland, South Africa, Brazil, and Mexico, Jan 2008–Aug 2017.
Source: Bloomberg, authors' calculations.

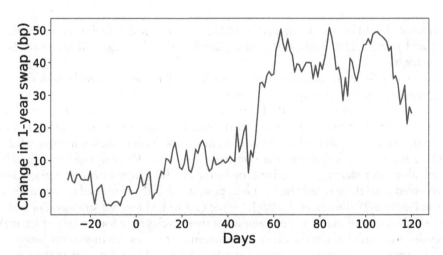

FIGURE 6.29   Receivers Start to Work After the Last Hike.
Note: P&L of receiving rates at the last hike (day 0), including carry and roll-down for Korea, Poland, South Africa, Brazil, and Mexico, Jan 2008–Oct 2017.
Source: Bloomberg, authors' calculations.

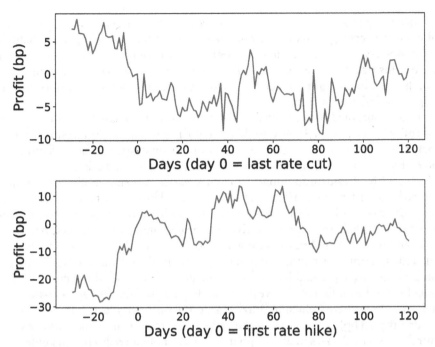

FIGURE 6.30   Pay into the First Hike, Not into the Last Cut.
Note: P&L of paying rates at the last cut / first hike (day 0), including carry and roll-down.
Source: Bloomberg, authors' calculations.

TRADING THE SUGARLOAF

Brazil is a country that is famous for its epic hiking and easing cycles. The average Brazil rates chart looks like Sugarloaf Mountain: straight up, resting for a few moments, and then straight down. Careers have been made (and sometimes destroyed) on the back of moves in Brazil rates. We actually want to describe one of the less epic easing cycles, which started in 2011, just because we feel that it is one of the more regular cycles, not driven by a major crisis. Therefore, hopefully we can learn something from it that is more enduring.

Our story begins in June 2011, when the Brazilian central bank raised its benchmark rate by 25 bp to 12.25% in a unanimous vote, leaving its (short) statement unchanged. The hike itself was not a surprise for markets, given that growth had accelerated and inflation was still moving up, well above the midpoint of the target. However, the market had been looking for a signal that the hiking cycle was in its last innings, given the strong BRL. But the central bank issued a hawkish statement, and rates moved higher. They then peaked in early July, drifting lower into the July meeting. In the July statement, the central bank validated market expectations and hiked another 25 bp with a more dovish statement, cutting the

(Continued)

sentence suggesting more hikes. Rates rallied, and the top was in. One-year rates fell below the central bank target rate on the day of this last hike, also signalling that it was time to receive. Inflation peaked in September at 7.12%, suggesting that on this occasion, the central bank was trusting its lower inflation forecasts once the peak in inflation was relatively close and acted around two months before the peak in inflation was in.

Rates continued to trade well in the aftermath of the last hike, and into the first cut, which came on 31 August 2011. The early timing of the cut surprised the market. The cut was widely seen as premature by analysts, because inflation was still rising and because prior to the cut, President Roussef had asked for monetary easing. For the President to publically call for easier monetary policy to be implemented by an institution that was de facto seen as independent (if not dejure), raised many eyebrows. It led to a perception among analysts that now the central bank would be less likely to cut, irrespective of the economic circumstances, because a cut would be seen as politically motivated, undercutting the credibility of the central bank at a time when inflation had not clearly peaked. Some analysts expected that a premature cut could lead to a sell off in the back end of the curve, and to rising break-even inflation. However, it rarely pays to fight the central bank. The back end of the curve (which in Brazil was at the time five years) only sold off for one day (by 13 bp) before joining the rally at the front end of the curve. Even a central bank like Brazil's in 2011 apparently had enough credibility to guide rates at the back end lower. Of course, this happened in a steepening context, but this is the normal state of affairs in any easing cycle. Breakevens also only sold off for two days before retracing the sell-off and then some within the next month, also suggesting that the credibility of the central bank stayed intact throughout this episode. As can be seen in Figure 6.31, rates then continued to rally for more than a year. It is harder than commonly believed to lose your credibility if you are a central bank.

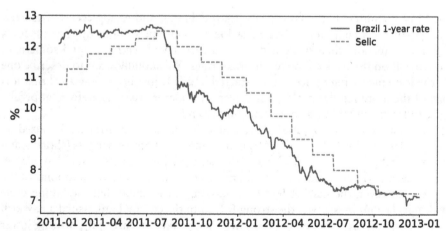

FIGURE 6.31   Staying Received for a Full Cycle in Brazil.
Source: Bloomberg.

6.17   EM RATES: THE IMPACT OF US TREASURIES

One complication for EM rates trading relative to the trading rules we outlined for US rates is that US rates serve as a benchmark for global rates. US Treasuries therefore are important for the back end of emerging market curves, given that risk and reward are assessed relative to what is available in "safe" US Treasuries. When thinking about the impact of US rates on EM rates, we like to distinguish two regimes.

The first regime is when US rates reprice violently, and the second is when moves are less volatile. We have already discussed the cases of a violent repricing of US rates in Table 2.7. If such a repricing is in the offing, all back ends should be paid, irrespective of forecasts of local policy rates for local central banks. Paying US rates as a hedge against EM receivers is also plausible but does not reliably work, as became clear during the taper tantrum in 2013. During those violent times, front-end receivers often also won't work, given rising inflation fears thanks to a sharply weaker FX. Whether the curve steepens or flattens is not always clear during such high-volatility episodes. While steepening is more likely, there are (rare) episodes where the increased FX volatility triggers emergency rate hikes by the respective central bank. Then curves flatten aggressively. The good news is that, as outlined in Chapter 2 such violent repricings in US rates are relatively rare. Furthermore, it is somewhat reassuring that these highly volatile episodes usually happen at only two points in the US rates cycle: around the last cut and leading up to the first hike. Once a smooth hiking cycle is in place, US rates reprice in an overly volatile manner much less frequently.

In low-volatility periods, US rates still impact the back end, and much more so than the front end of EM curves. However, during low-volatility periods investors should not exit receivers that are well supported by views with respect to local central bank easing cycles. Instead, investors should consider US rate payers as hedges for EM back ends. Such hedges tend to work in these environments especially when EMFX is trading in a stable range or is appreciating. Alternatively, a bearish view on US rates would, *ceteris paribus*, support steepeners. This steepening is likely to be less pronounced than during high-volatility periods for US rates, but some steepening is likely nonetheless.

MEXICAN RATES GET TAPERED

Mexican fixed income traded very well in early 2013, starting another leg stronger in a bull market that had begun during the later days of the Great Recession in 2008. For the year, 10-year swap rates had peaked in early January at close to 6% and then started to fall fast. This was mostly driven by lower G3 rates, thanks to the dovish trinity of the Fed, the ECB, and the BoJ, as well as by a stronger MXN. Then, in early April 2013, Banxico restarted its easing cycle, which had been lying dormant since the early crisis response in 2009, with a 50 bp cut in March 2013. This led to an acceleration of the rates rally and to further long positions being

(Continued)

added. After a brief consolidation, rates continued to rally, falling below 5.1%. In other words, positioning was all wrong for what was to come.

Meanwhile, US rates put a bottom in on 3 May, when the NFP print in the US surprised strongly on the upside, leading to an 11 bp sell-off in 10-year US Treasuries. This was the bottom for US rates that held until mid-2015. As an aside, while we demonstrated in Chapter 5 that NFP became somewhat useless for (EM)FX trading, we still think that in the very big picture, major bottoms or tops in US rates coincide with NFP prints more often than seems likely for an indicator past its prime. Be that as it may, starting with NFP day in May 2013, US 10-year swaps moved from 1.80% to a high of 3.18% on 5 September 2013, mostly driven by Fed governor Bernanke's suggestion to taper the existing QE programme. The sell-off only ended when the Fed became more dovish and suggested that the start of the tapering of QE would be pushed out somewhat.

South of the Rio Grande, over the same period, Mexican 10-year swaps moved from 5.25% to 7.21%, as illustrated in Figure 6.32. This means that the beta turned out to be 1.4. However, the move was much more violent in the first part of the sell-off. From 3 May to 25 June, the Mexican rates beta to US swaps was 1.7, and there were days with a beta higher than 3. All this happened with a more hawkish Fed, but with the Mexican central bank staying dovish. While additional rate cuts were put on hold, Banxico did not – publicly, at least – contemplate hikes, and it resumed its easing cycle as soon as the coast was more or less clear, on 6 September 2013.

Many investors tried to use US rates to hedge Mexican rates, given that the relative central bank outlook appeared to make this a sensible proposition. But the crowded positioning in Mexican receivers, coupled with US rates payers that soon also became crowded, was a major headwind. Furthermore, USD-MXN moved straight up from a low of just below 12.00 to 13.50. A higher USD-MXN leads to spread widening between Mexican and US rates making US payers a *Texas hedge*.[8]

Other than illustrating the pitfalls of US rates hedges during high-volatility sell-offs, this episode also illustrates some opportunities in EM rates trading. First, we note that US rates clearly bottomed on 3 May, when WSJ's Hilsenrath tweeted that tapering would come sooner rather than later, while Mexican rates bottomed on 10 May – plenty of time to cut receivers in Mexico. Second, even the front end was not safe, given the USD-MXN move. One-year TIIE (the floating interest rate in Mexican interest rate swaps) sold off by 60 bp – small compared to the back end, but certainly enough to stop out most receivers. Third, rates in the US and Mexico peaked on exactly the same day, i.e. there was no point to revisit receivers in Mexican rates before the US rates sell-off was over. The market only thinks about one or two drivers at a time. When it is set on US rates as the driver,

(Continued)

---

[8] A *Texas hedge* is a hedge that ends up increasing exposure to risk, even though the intent was to reduce it.

nothing else matters. And, finally, another lesson is that when local and external forces happen to align, investors should go all in. As it turns out, 5 September was not only the peak in US rates, but also the start of more cuts from Banxico. Banxico had rung the bell. Mexican rates rallied back to 6.2% by mid-October.

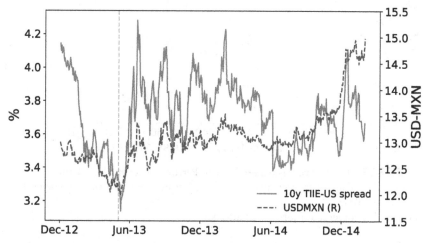

FIGURE 6.32 US Rates Hedges Not Working for TIIE in a Strong USD Environment. *Note:* Vertical line denotes bottom in US rates. *Source:* Bloomberg.

6.18 EM – STEEPED IN RISK

Even with all those caveats related to the impact of US rates, on average, curve trades still behave similar to the US during normal times. The main difference compared to the US is that times are "normal" at a lower frequency, given that there can be volatility spikes unrelated to US rate sell-offs, too. But usually, steepeners start to work shortly before the first cut. This is shown in Figure 6.33.

Just like in the US, the behaviour of 2s/10s is a benchmark for most other curve segments. And also just like in the US, 1s/2s are different. Even in EM, where central banks can turn from hikes to cuts much faster than G3 central banks can, one year is just too short to benefit much from the change of stance by the respective central bank. 1s/2s therefore tend to flatten after the last hike is in, as shown in Figure 6.34.

Similarly, flatteners start working going into the first hike. And just like in the case of the US, flatteners do not appear to work as well as steepeners, partly because they are similar in nature to payers, which work less well than receivers. This is illustrated in Figure 6.35.

And once more, similar to the US, 1s/2s behave differently than most other segments of the curve. Figure 6.36 shows that 1s/2s generate positive P&L for steepeners after the last cut, even though there is no instant gratification. On the one hand, such 1s/2s

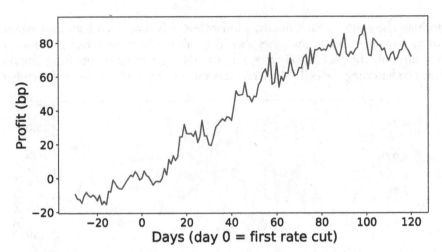

FIGURE 6.33   EM Curve Steepeners Start to Perform After the First Cut.
Note: P&L of a 2s/10s steepener around the last hike (day 0), 2s/5s steepener in the case of Brazil.
Source: Bloomberg, authors' calculations.

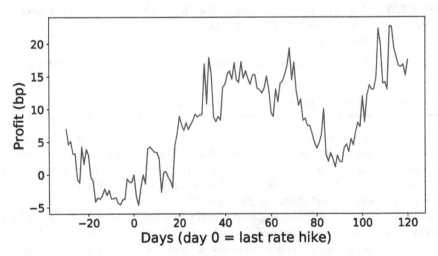

FIGURE 6.34   1s/2s Flatteners Start to Perform After the Last Hike.
Note: P&L of a 1s/2s flattener around the last rate hike (day 0).
Source: Bloomberg, authors' calculations.

steepeners can be attractive because overall, the market is range-trading and there are often few directional trades available. On the other hand, 1s/2s suffer from the fact that 1s roll down the curve very fast, which requires an almost constant re-weighing of the trade.

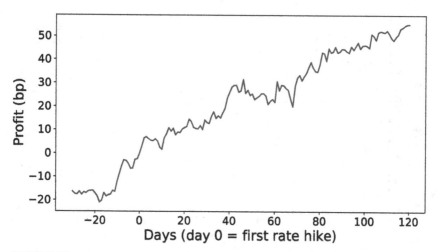

FIGURE 6.35 Curves have a Flattening Bias After the First Hike.
Note: P&L of a 2s/10s flattener around the first rate hike (day 0), 2s/5s flattener in the case of Brazil.
Source: Bloomberg, authors' calculations.

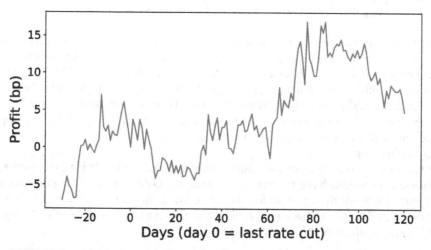

FIGURE 6.36 1s/2s Steepeners Work After the Last Cut.
Note: P&L of a 1s/2s steepener around the last rate cut (day 0).
Source: Bloomberg, authors' calculations.

The stage of the US cycle is also important for EM curve trades. Flatteners work best when, in addition to the local central bank cycle, US rates are also trading well. And the best steepeners are a combination of a local rate-cutting cycle and US Treasuries trading poorly.

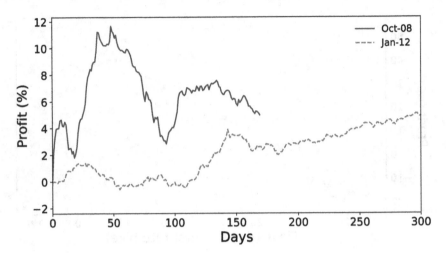

FIGURE 6.37   If Cash Constrained, Position in the Long End During Bull Steepening.
Note: Calculated by taking the difference between five-year subindex and one- to five-year subindex of the FTSE Emerging Market Government Bond Index, 2008–2018.
Source: Bloomberg, London Stock Exchange Group plc and its group undertakings (collectively the "LSE Group"), copyright LSE Group 2019.

For the case of the US, we showed that steepeners are similar to receivers. For EM, there is an added benefit to replacing a receiver with a steepener, which has been illustrated by the case of Mexican rates during tapering. For most EM, risk aversion steepens the yield curve. When FX weakness causes easing cycles to stall, the payer at the back end usually more than offsets losses at the front end, and curves steepen. Of course, if the weakness is severe enough to trigger an emergency rate hike, the opposite is true, and curves flatten aggressively. But emergency rate hikes are very rare, as per our study in Chapter 5.

Of course, favouring front ends during easing cycles does little for cash-constrained investors, who would have to give up meaningful DV01 in order to position at the short end. We think that, just as for the US, cash-constrained investors are better off positioning in the belly to back end, rather than the front end, in spite of the steepening of the curve, as illustrated in Figure 6.37.

6.19   DOES VALUATION WORK?

Readers will wonder if we are ever going to talk about valuation, too. So far, this chapter has mostly discussed strategies that broadly fall into the momentum category, largely omitting valuation. A focus on momentum works well for three- to six-month returns that leveraged investors typically target. However, valuation in bonds is a much more solid concept than in FX, and investors should certainly consider valuation as well, especially to the extent that the focus is on longer-term returns.

The main way to value (nominal) bonds is real rates, i.e. nominal yields adjusted for inflation. But to put this into practice, we first need to clarify which yields and which inflation should be used in order to achieve the best results. On the yield side, the choice is between an outright yield, usually more toward the mid or back of the curve, and a spread relative to G3 rates. On the inflation side, investors usually focus on medium-term inflation expectations and avoid using concurrent inflation. If an inflation spike occurs, in theory, long-term inflation expectations should not react much. After all, inflation spikes tend to revert relatively fast, as central banks take action and as base effects tend to bias inflation lower after the anniversary of the initial price shock. However, in practice, both investors and central banks at times appear to panic, reacting more aggressively to inflation spikes than may be warranted on theoretical grounds. It is therefore worth investigating whether deflating nominal rates with concurrent inflation should be used for valuation-based strategies. Furthermore, 5- or 10-year inflation fore-casts are often not widely available, and if they are, they are often based on long-term averages of past inflation, which are another option to deflate. At other times, inflation expectations can be roughly around where inflation targets happen to be, given that such targets form an attractor for difficult forecasting exercises. Using inflation targets to deflate yields can be a logical choice, given that, presumably, the central bank will succeed in getting – or, rather, try very hard to get – inflation close to the target, at least in the medium term. This frequently makes the inflation target a superior forecast compared to many other approaches. In the end, which inflation measure to use is an empirical question.

To analyse the issue in more detail, we rank the countries by their real yields and receive a basket of rates of countries with the highest real yields and pay a basket of countries with the lowest real yields. This long-short approach has the advantage that it strips out global factors like the movement of US rates. Using a basket mitigates the impact of idiosyncratic country factors. One important question is whether we should normalize real rates by their own history before applying the ranking. If we don't, cer-tain high-yield countries will always show up on the long side of the basket, even if they have low real rates when measured against their own history. We could argue that a valuation strategy is supposed to work because we earn on average higher carry. In this case, there is nothing wrong with always being long certain high-yielding countries with steep curves. On the other hand, it could be the case that whenever rates are low in a time-series sense (even if they are high in a cross-sectional sense), those low rates warn of a coming hiking cycle, as they could be well below neutral for the particular country. In that case, it would be helpful if the country was placed on the short side of the basket. Whether to adjust for the history of real rates for each country is an empirical question.

Here we compare the various ways to calculate real yields by taking the ranking based on each definition, receiving the three swaps with the highest real yield and paying the three swaps with the lowest real yield. We re-balance monthly and use data from 2009 to 2018. The P&L is shown in Figure 6.38. The returns are highest when we generate real rates by using the inflation target midpoints to deflate nominal rates. But the Sharpe ratio is higher if we use five-year average historical inflation to deflate nominal yields. Using concurrent inflation results in lower returns but in a still

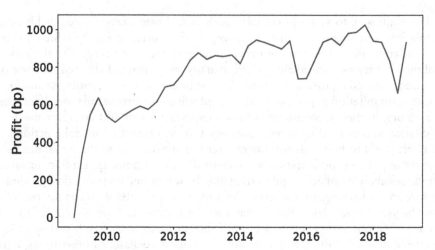

FIGURE 6.38   Valuation Works: Focus on Real Rates.
Note: P&L of receiving five-year swaps of the three highest real yielders against paying the rates of three lowest real yielders. Average inflation for the past five years is used to deflate nominal rates.
Source: Bloomberg, authors' calculations.

reasonably high Sharpe ratio. Results deteriorate significantly if we first express the level of each rate relative to its own history before ranking the countries. It turns out that the market cares about high real rates in an absolute sense, and not about real rates relative to their history.

6.20   TERM PREMIA: USE SPARINGLY

The term premium is the extra yield an investor is paid after allowing for the expected path of the short-end interest rates that are controlled by the central bank. In the past, such term premia were estimated in two different ways. In the first approach, analysts used the assumption that over the long run, markets would "get it right" in terms of forecasting the likely path of central bank rates. Then the term premium could be calculated as the yield investors earned minus the realized path of short-term interest rates. This method is difficult to implement for EM, given how little history is available for local rates. The second approach used surveys to get an estimate of the expected paths of monetary policy. However, typically, surveys do not go out far enough in time to allow for the calculation of term premia at the mid to back end of the curve. Also, it is not clear that asking economists for their expectation of monetary policy rates necessarily results in the same answer as what the market truly believes, as markets tend to move much faster than the median economist whenever there is a meaningful change to the economic environment. As such, a survey-based methodology is also difficult to implement, especially in EM, where not all countries offer such surveys.

Given these practical limitations, analysts have started to use dynamic no-arbitrage models to estimate term premia, popularized in the case of the US by former Fed researchers Adrian, Crump, and Moench (2013). Whether such term premium models work in EM is an empirical question. One hesitation is that often, countries that show a low term premium, which could justify the initiations of payers, are countries where cuts are expected. And countries that show a large term premium, justifying receivers, often are countries where hikes are expected. This has been demonstrated by Kiguel and Willer (2018). At times, upcoming easing cycles require receivers even if term premia optically appear low. But to figure out whether such episodes are frequent enough to invalidate the use of term premia as a valuation anchor, we focus on a more thorough backtest done by Kiguel and Willer (2019). In that piece, it was demonstrated that trading strategies based on an instrument's historical term premia generates alpha. In particular, receiving five-year rates whenever the term premium is more than one standard deviation elevated, when using a three-month rolling window, leads to the best results. The receiving trades of this strategy result in a Sharpe ratio of 1.18, compared to a buy and hold Sharpe ratio of 0.88. Rates in CEEMEA and Latam perform the best (see Figure 6.39).

It is interesting that payers for curves with low risk premia do not work as well as receivers, though Kiguel and Willer provide some evidence that term premia below zero should be paid. Furthermore, using term premia to rank countries does not appear to lead to superior returns. Finally, aggregating term premia for EM overall and versus the US term premium also does not generate alpha. Therefore, we do not advocate relying on term premia either for an assessment of the EM rates asset class or for country rankings as a relative valuation tool. But if a term premium is high relative to its own history, on average it is advisable to receive.

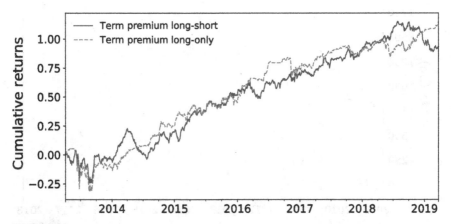

FIGURE 6.39 Term Premia are Most Compelling on the Receiving Side.
Note: Strategy of receiving five-year rates if term premia are extended by more than one standard deviations, long only, as well as long/short.
Source: Citi.

6.21   SLIDING DOWN THE SLOPE

Another way some investors think about valuation is to look at the slope of the curve. The theory is that a steeper curve offers better value, partially because the carry is more attractive. We already outlined that we are not great fans of carry in the context of curves, because we feel that often the time to be long is exactly when curves first invert. We also note that the appropriate slope of the curve must strongly depend on the current stance of monetary policy. A central bank with a tight policy is likely to have a very flat curve, while a central bank with an extremely loose policy must have a very steep curve. Those two points are of course linked. A central bank that has implemented too tight a policy may have inverted the curve and will probably loosen its overly tight stance sooner rather than later, potentially starting an easing cycle. Then receivers are compelling, in spite of (or because of) a very flat curve.

To make slopes a more meaningful measure of valuation, we need to correct for the current stance of monetary policy. We therefore first regress 2s/5s on 2s and then focus on the residuals of that regression. We then rank the curves by residuals each quarter, receive the five steepest curves, and pay the five flattest curves. We adjust for volatility to take the same risk on both sides of this basket. Figure 6.40 suggests that there is indeed some value in curves that are steeper than they should be, given the current stance of monetary policy. But the Sharpe ratio by itself is insufficient to make this valuation measure tradable as a stand-alone measure. It is also noteworthy that ranking countries only after adjusting each steepness for how steep the same curve was in the past weakens the results considerably, just as we found for the real yield valuation exercise.

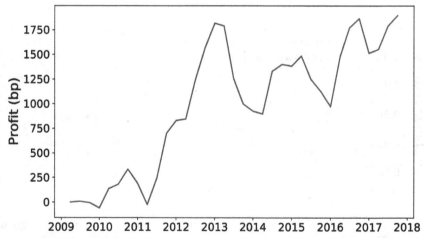

FIGURE 6.40   Curves That are Steeper Than They Should be Need to be Received.
Note: P&L of receiving the five steepest curves adjusted for monetary policy versus paying the five flattest curves, beta adjusted.
Source: Bloomberg, authors' calculations.

6.22 FISCAL: FALLING FLAT

Often, higher real rates and steep curves are there for a reason, in that they compensate investors for certain risks. The most relevant risks for (FX hedged) bondholders are default risks. While it is extremely rare that governments default on local currency paper, it does happen. It is rare because debt in local currency can be more easily inflated away than external debt. But inflating the debt away can also be painful for investors and may also require higher real rates to compensate for that risk. After all, for receivers of swaps, higher inflation would lead to higher central bank rates and negative carry. And for (FX hedged) bondholders, the same is true, assuming a need to roll short-maturity FX hedges relatively frequently – and at higher implied rates. Therefore, the risk of local bonds should also be measured by classic credit quality indicators, and in particular by the level and change of debt/GDP. Inflation is also clearly important. All three indicators are crucial for rating agencies' determination of an issuer's credit rating. We can therefore investigate whether the credit component matters for local rates by using credit ratings as a shortcut. Even better might be to focus on CDS spreads rather than credit ratings, given that rating agencies may be slow in adjusting their ratings.

The simplest way to do this is to plot real rates or residuals from our slope regression against CDS spreads. Figure 6.41 plots those two charts. Interestingly, there is a slight positive correlation between real rates and five-year CDS. However, excluding Turkey and focusing on CDS spreads below 200 bp, it is a weak correlation. There is no correlation between the CDS and the slope of the curve, adjusted for the monetary policy setting. If anything, it may even be negatively correlated. Overall, we conclude that there is a small credit component to real rates that only becomes more sizeable for weak credits, which trade above 200 bp for the five-year CDS. And credit is not overly relevant to the shape of the curve, at least not for maturities of less than 10 years and

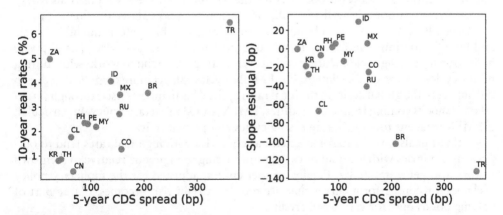

FIGURE 6.41 A Small Credit Component For Locals.
Note: Real rates are 10-year nominal swaps/bonds deflated by current headline inflation (December 2018). Slope residuals are from regression of the 2s/5s swap curve on two-year swaps (2017–2018).
Source: Bloomberg, authors' calculations.

operating in swap space. Bonds may well be more significantly impacted by credit risk, though often bond curves remain anchored by the more liquid swap curves.

A small credit component for real rates is in line with the empirical observation that changes in CDS and changes in local rates are highly correlated, especially for weaker credits. If the CDS moves, real rates move, too, given that some fraction of the real rate is indeed compensating for credit risk, and this part grows whenever the CDS spreads move wider. While credit risk is unlikely to be a major factor for determining cheapness or richness of bonds in a cross-sectional sense, investors should be sensitive to changes in credit risk, as such changes may also impact local rates – at least the ones we discussed as true EM at the beginning of this chapter.

6.23 SUMMARY

A few relatively simple rules go a long way in generating a solid framework for trading EM rates. Our key takeaways from this chapter are the following.

Whether a rates market should be treated like an emerging market depends on the correlation of rates to risk aversion. If rates have a positive correlation with risk aversion, due to the FX channel, they are rates of a true emerging market and should be treated differently from developed market rates.

In DM, we advise using Taylor rules and central bank speeches to determine where we are in the interest rate cycle. For EM, inflation usually has a dominant weight in Taylor rules, given relatively low central bank credibility. To understand where we are in the EM inflation cycle, we focus on commodities and PPIs, as well as on base effects for CPIs.

If all else fails, the market view of where we are in the cycle is valuable. If the one-year rate breaks below the floating rate, the risk reward for receiver positions is very strong. Payer positions do well when the one-year rate breaks above the floating rate.

Generally, the receiving cycle starts when there is one hike left in the hiking cycle and broadly continues until there is only one cut left in the easing cycle. The opposite holds true for paying cycles. During easing cycles, steepeners tend to work; while during hiking cycles, curves tend to flatten. For EM, the cycles can get more complicated due to the impact of the global cycle on the local rates cycle. This manifests itself through (inter-related) shocks coming from commodities, EMFX, or G3 monetary policy. In particular, if EMFX weakens too much, rate-easing cycles end prematurely.

Valuation also works to some extent, as countries with high real rates tend to outperform countries with low real rates over time. Using term premia relative to their own history also generates alpha. Finally, steeper curves, adjusted for the monetary policy cycle, tend to outperform curves that are too flat. Credit risk becomes a large part of valuing bonds only for very weak credits.

CHAPTER 7

Real Rates: Simply Superior

7.1 BUY LINKERS AND SLEEP WELL

The discussion in the previous chapter about inflation risks points to inflation-linked bonds as a good way to avoid sleepless nights. And indeed, linkers are popular instruments in certain EM, especially in the (mostly Latin American) countries with a history of high and variable inflation. Those inflation-linked markets are well developed in several such countries.

Table 7.1 shows the EM that are included in the EMILSI, the EM inflation-linked security index from FTSE. We also list the values for the respective nominal FTSE EM bond index. In aggregate, the market capitalization of linkers is around one-fifth of the market capitalization of nominal bonds when comparing values for both asset classes at the end of 2018. Given lower risks in linkers, it is not surprising that the average life for linkers is more than five years longer than for nominals. The bulk of linkers are issued by Brazil (more than 52% of the index), followed by Mexico. For Brazil and Chile, the market capitalization of the linker market is actually higher than the market cap for nominals – in the case of Brazil, very meaningfully so. In the case of Chile, this is the legacy of a monetary system that was for many years set up in terms of an inflation-linked currency. Even today, linkers are often more liquid than nominal bonds for some tenors in Chile. In the case of Brazil, the extensive universe of inflation-linked bonds is the reaction to a history of violent bursts of inflation. Real-rate bonds were needed to overcome investors' hesitancy to commit to long-duration nominal bonds. The average life of the nominal market in Brazil is therefore correspondingly short.[1] The average life of linkers in Brazil is more than nine years longer. In Mexico and Chile, the average life of linkers is also meaningfully longer than for nominal bonds. This duration mismatch needs to be controlled for when analysing how to switch between real and nominal rates, to not confuse the inflation premium with the impact of differing

---

[1]It is an interesting question whether the existence of the long-duration linker market held back the development of a long-duration nominal bond market. Clearly, having a long-duration linker market in place made it less urgent for both the government as the issuer as well as pension funds and other long-term holders to venture out on the nominal bond curve. The law of unintended consequences may have struck again, but we will never be able to prove it.

TABLE 7.1 Linkers: Deserving Credit.

	Linkers MCap bn USD	in %	Avg life	Real yld duration	Real yld	Nominals MCap bn USD	Ratio to linkers	Avg life	Delta to linkers
EMILSI	460	100%	12.2	8.2	3.93	2502	5.4	7.9	−4.3
Brazil	238	52%	14.0	8.0	4.47	109	0.5	4.8	−9.2
Mexico	74	16%	13.2	9.2	4.18	130	1.8	8.9	−4.3
Chile	40	9%	12.2	10.2	1.59	32	0.8	10.1	−2.1
Turkey	39	8%	5.1	4.2	4.37	49	1.3	4.5	−0.6
SA	37	8%	15.4	10.3	3.17	100	2.7	16.1	0.7
Colombia	30	7%	8.3	6.3	2.62	58	1.9	7.1	−1.2

Source: London Stock Exchange Group plc and its group undertakings (collectively the "LSE Group"), copyright LSE Group 2019, JPMorgan Chase & Co, copyright 2020, as of 31 December 2019.

duration (unless investors want to own very-long-duration bonds, in which case linkers are often the only game in town).

For long-term investors, there are a few interesting points to make. First, cash-constrained investors can get more duration in linkers than in nominal rates, which can be attractive. Second, on a duration-adjusted basis nominal rates usually outperform. Figure 7.1 illustrates this point, plotting performance for the nominal index and the linker index, duration-adjusted. The outperformance of nominals is large and steady. Third, the only times when linkers outperform are during sharp pullbacks for nominal rates. Linkers sell off as well during those periods, but by much less. And during the 2018 sell-off, returns for linkers were flattish. This correlation structure can be useful as linkers lead to outperformance when it is needed the most. Fourth, volatility is lower for linkers than for nominal rates. As highlighted for the case of

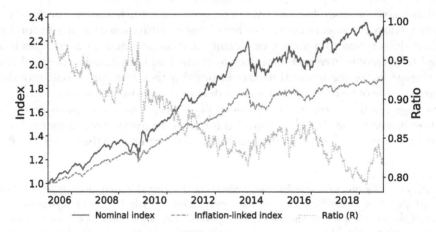

FIGURE 7.1 Real Rates With Less Volatility.
Source: Bloomberg, authors' calculations.

2018, there are sell-off events for nominal rates where real rates do not participate. The logic is that during the pullbacks, EMFX weakens, leading to higher inflation expectations (and inflation outcomes) which is reflected in an outperformance by linkers. This lower volatility leads to higher information ratios for linkers than for nominals. Over the period under study, the IR for nominals was 1.47, compared to the IR for linkers of 1.62. Given that there are good fundamental reasons for lower volatility for real rates, we expect this pattern to continue. Investors should therefore consider leveraging up linkers rather than buying nominal bonds.

7.2 HOW TO SLEEP EVEN BETTER

From a trading perspective, rather than a long-term investment perspective, we can fine-tune the switch between linkers and nominal rates. To do this, we will analyse linkers first from a momentum perspective and subsequently from a valuation perspective. For the purpose of this analysis, we note that we focus on linkers in the belly and long end of the curve, given that the front end is mostly a bet on the next few inflation prints, where trading decisions should largely depend on any potential alpha extracted from big data efforts to improve short-term inflation forecasts. Going further out on the curve also means that we don't have to be as sensitive to the inflation seasonals, which play a very important role at the front end of the curve where the inflation carry is much more relevant given the short duration.

From a momentum point of view, we use a few rules of thumb for trading linkers. First, during easing cycles, nominal rates usually outperform significantly. The reason is that nominal rates are more volatile and outperform in bull markets. Furthermore, easing cycles can only progress if inflation expectations are not rising sharply, also suggesting staying in nominal rates rather than real rates during easing cycles. On the other hand, we expect linkers to outperform during hiking cycles. Going into and during hiking cycles, inflation expectations typically move up, at least early in the cycle. Linkers are a defensive position, which should lead to outperformance during fixed-income bear markets.

As laid out in the previous chapter, for our purposes, the easing cycle starts with the last hike and continues until just before the last cut, and a hiking cycle starts with the last cut and ends just before the last hike. We illustrate the relative performance for nominal rates over linkers after the last hike and after the last cut on a duration-adjusted basis in Figure 7.2. The study covers the large inflation linker markets in the Bloomberg Barclays EM inflation index (Brazil, Israel, Mexico, South Africa, Turkey), as well as Chile, given how well-developed the linker market is in that country. We analyse the period from 2009 to 2018. As we would expect, there is strong outperformance by nominal rates after the last hike, while the performance into the last hike is more mixed (strong in the last days into the last hike, but flat in the last 100 days of the hiking cycle). This confirms our rule of thumb.

After the last cut, nominal rates perform less well with the P&L relative to real rates, going sideways for the first 120 days. However, somewhat surprisingly, nominal rates start to outperform again after 120 days. We would have expected a more pronounced outperformance by real rates during hiking cycles. However, it is worthwhile

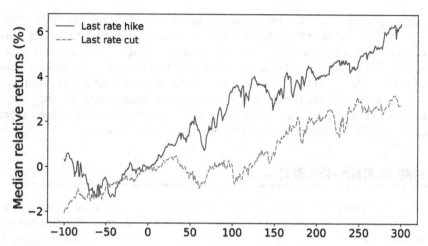

FIGURE 7.2   Nominals Outperform Significantly in Easing Cycles.
Source: Bloomberg, authors' calculations.

to remember that the period under study is one where inflation fell drastically on a structural basis for many EM in the sample. As such, it is not too surprising that nominal rates generally outperform real rates. And, in any case, the results are in line with our prior expectations that nominal rates outperform much more significantly during easing cycles than during hiking cycles. Investors should become more defensive and switch to linkers around the last cut, but should not overstay their welcome.

In addition to easing cycles, the second important factor for favouring nominal rates over real rates is a bull market for UST. This is demonstrated in Figure 7.3, where both the relative performance of nominals over linkers as well as the performance of

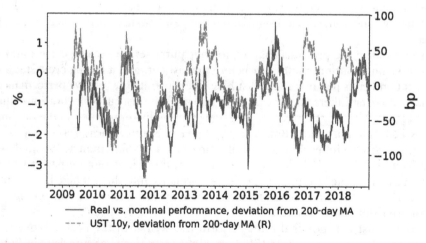

FIGURE 7.3   Nominals Outperform When UST Rally.
Source: Bloomberg, authors' calculations.

US rates are shown as deviation from their 200-day MA in order to detrend both time series. Clearly, the correlation is strong and relatively consistent. There are likely a few factors at play. First, some of the UST rallies are driven by or cause episodes of "grab for yield". Those episodes often happen during deflation fears and frequently are global fears that are supportive for both US nominal rates as well as nominal rates in EM. Second, some of the rallies in UST are driven by Fed easing, either in the form of rate cuts or in the form of QE programmes. Often, Fed easing leads to global easing cycles, which also favour nominal over real yields. While this second explanation is of course linked to the first, they are somewhat separate, as there can be deflation fears even without Fed action, especially to the extent that the zero bound is binding for interest rates in the US.

Given that UST were largely in a bull market during the last decade, it is not surprising that nominal rates performed so well. But even during a US rates bull market, there can be times when investors should favour linkers over nominals. In particular, Figure 7.4 highlights that linkers outperform during commodity bull markets. This is of course not overly surprising, given that linkers reference headline inflation and not core inflation. The fit has been strong other than during 2016 and 2018.

The divergence in 2016 and 2018 was largely driven by moves in EMFX. In particular, 2016 initially saw a strong appreciation of EMFX, which lowered breakevens. In 2018, the opposite happened: a meaningful weakening of EMFX led to wider breakevens. Figure 7.5 illustrates the importance of FX. Especially after 2016, the explanatory power is stronger for EMFX than for commodities. While we do not see a strong case for a structural break in the relationship between the relative performance of nominals over linkers and commodities, given the strong fundamental link, we do believe that FX performance is a more important driver than commodities. After all, FX impacts a larger part of the relevant CPI baskets than commodities, and therefore, a weaker FX can more than offset lower commodity prices. The best environment for linkers is one where commodity prices rise but the local currency does not appreciate,

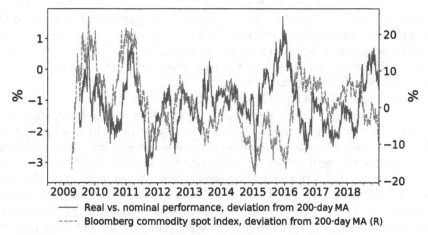

FIGURE 7.4 Linkers Outperform When Commodities Rally.
Source: Bloomberg, authors' calculations.

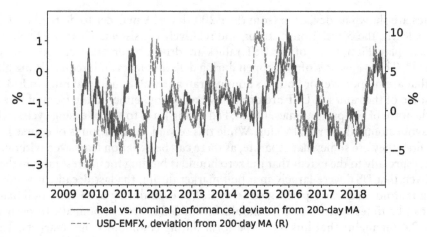

FIGURE 7.5 Linkers Do Well When EMFX Sells-Off.
Source: Bloomberg, authors' calculations.

or when EMFX weakens without commodities selling off too significantly. This will happen more often in the future as the correlation between commodities and the broad USD may have gotten weaker.

7.3 WHAT IS FAIR?

In terms of valuing linkers, we note that the right way to think about them is to start with a view on nominal bonds, largely based on central bank action and the global rates environment. We then generate a view on long-term break-even inflation. This is typically a range on top of the inflation target band used by the central bank. The reason is that over the long term, markets tend to give monetary authorities the benefit of the doubt, which is why long-term inflation rarely diverges much from the target band. But markets do demand some premium to compensate for their trust in the authorities' capabilities. Therefore, breakevens at the back end of the curve typically sit slightly above the upper end of the inflation targets.

For large countries with liquid linkers, we provide some data in Table 7.2. We focus on recent years, starting in 2013, given that many countries saw a trend change lower in inflation, biasing the longer-term averages. The country with the highest inflation in the sample is Brazil, where the median inflation stood at 6.4%. Chile is the low-inflation country in the sample, with median inflation at 2.85%. Colombia and Mexico are in the middle of the pack, with Colombia doing slightly better when focusing on the median. Not surprisingly, the standard deviation of inflation, which can be thought of as a proxy for inflation risk, is also highest in Brazil, in line with its high average inflation. But there is an interesting twist to this very intuitive ranking. The standard deviation of monthly yoy inflation numbers is actually the lowest in Mexico, followed by Colombia. On the other hand, the standard deviation of inflation is quite high in Chile, especially when

TABLE 7.2 Using Current Inflation to Value Breakevens.

	Brazil	Chile	Colombia	Mexico
yoy inflation (2013–2018)				
average	6.17	3.12	4.14	4.05
median	6.29	2.85	3.66	4.02
standard deviation	2.86	2.10	1.78	0.99
Inflation minus target				
average	1.7	0.1	1.1	1.1
median	1.8	−0.2	0.7	1.0
% below target	28%	54%	27%	24%
5-year breakevens (2013–2018)				
average	5.9	2.9	4.0	3.6
median	6.0	2.9	3.9	3.6
standard deviation	1.1	0.2	0.8	0.4
Breakeven minus target				
average	1.4	−0.1	1.0	0.6
median	1.5	−0.1	0.9	0.6
%below target	5%	65%	7%	8%
Breakevens minus inflation				
average	−0.3	−0.2	−0.1	−0.5
median	−0.2	0.1	0.3	−0.3
high	2.5	1.9	1.5	1.4
low	−3.3	−3.0	−3.7	−3.0
Breakeven minus 5-year avg inflation				
average	−0.4	−0.2	0.4	−0.3
median	−0.1	−0.3	0.3	−0.4

Source: Bloomberg, authors' calculations.

taking the relatively low level of inflation into account. The central bank of Chile does a good job of keeping inflation low on average, but there are both major overshoots and major undershoots, which should be reflected in how the market prices inflation risk.

In terms of hitting the inflation target, the ranking is in line with the actual inflation outcomes discussed. We focus here on the midpoint of the inflation target rather than the bands around the target, given that authorities aim for the midpoint. Furthermore, the bands are very similar (+/− 1% for all but Brazil, where the band has been wider than average). As such, we do not lose much when focusing on the midpoint in terms of relative rankings, though we note that this approach leads to a higher percentage of misses compared to the more common definition of a *miss* that requires inflation to be outside of the band, often at year end. On the other hand, we treat outcomes below the target as a win for the central bank, given the history of very high inflation in the countries under study. This is another aspect in which EM are still different from DM, where missing inflation on the downside has become a preoccupation for policy makers.

With this methodology, Brazil misses its target, on average by 1.7%. Inflation is at or below target only 28% of months. Colombia and Mexico are once again in the middle of the pack, also missing the inflation target significantly, by an average of 1.1%. While the magnitude of the miss is less than for Brazil, the likelihood of being at or below target is similarly low, in the mid to high twenties.

Given that inflation targets are more often missed to the upside, it is not surprising that breakevens usually trade above the inflation target and are often closer to actual inflation. When breakevens trade below the midpoint of the target, it has historically been a signal to go long inflation in Brazil, Colombia, and Mexico, as such episodes have been rare and fleeting, occurring only 5% of the time in Brazil, 7% of the time in Colombia, and 8% of the time in Mexico. In Chile, breakevens can stay below target for much longer, though.

We also analyse breakevens versus actual inflation outcomes. We investigate two (somewhat extreme) views of how inflation expectations could be formed. Either the market could put a lot of weight on current inflation outcomes in pricing five-year breakevens, or the market could take a long-run average of inflation outcomes (here proxied with five-year average inflation). We find that, on average, a focus on current inflation does a better job of explaining five-year breakevens than the five-year moving average of realized inflation. The median difference between breakevens and current inflation is quite low: slightly negative in Brazil and Mexico, and slightly positive in Chile and Colombia. This is explained by the fact that inflation is volatile in Chile and Colombia when adjusting for its relatively lower level. The median difference between rolling five-year average inflation and breakevens is, on average, slightly larger. It also is more consistently negative, likely because inflation has been trending slightly lower over time. While it is somewhat surprising that current inflation is a better explanatory variable for breakevens than a longer-term moving average, it is not too uncommon for the market to put too high a weight on short-term developments. In conclusion, we would focus on the delta of breakevens versus current inflation to judge whether there is a mispricing in breakevens. The ranges vary slightly by country, but five-year breakevens undershooting current inflation by 3 to 3.5% is as extreme as it gets, and therefore a safe point to buy inflation, while five-year breakevens being 1.5 to 2.5% higher than current inflation is the extreme on the other side, making it safe to sell inflation. Of course, a negative gap between actual inflation and breakevens can also close by inflation consistently moving lower. During periods of falling headline inflation, the gap between realized inflation and breakevens becomes meaningless for trading breakevens. The clearer signal is to buy inflation when five-year breakevens trades below the midpoint of the inflation target.

Figure 7.6 illustrates the findings for Brazil. As can be seen, breakevens are typically lower than current inflation during surges above 6%, which was the upper end of the target range at the time. Still, breakevens tend to follow realized inflation higher, sometimes with some lag as the market tends to fade what could be short-term spikes. Breakevens are also sticky on the downside if inflation breaks below the inflation target. In Brazil, inflation was meaningfully below the target for almost a year, but the

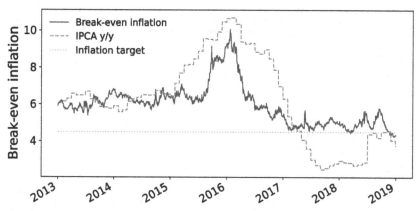

FIGURE 7.6 Brazil Break-Evens Above Target, Below CPI.
Source: Bloomberg, authors' calculations.

five-year breakeven could not break below the then midpoint of the target at 4.5%. Buying breakevens is relatively safe at the inflation target, at least in terms of capital gains. Carry can of course be negative if inflation realizes below the target for a longer period. Another important take-away from Figure 7.6 is that with respect to disinflation periods, breakevens are on average a good leading indicator for falling inflation in the future. This is not necessarily the case on the other side of the spectrum, as break-evens do not necessarily offer a good warning indicator for rising inflation, at least when focusing on the belly of the break-even curve.

Having a view on nominal rates and breakevens results in a view on a fair level of real rates. In our view, this is a more robust approach than trying to come up with a "fair" level of real rates based on fundamentals like credit ratings or CDS levels. Our main evidence for this statement is the chart in the previous chapter that highlights that the explanatory power of CDS for real rates is quite limited for the safer credits (Figure 6.41).

The other approach to think about valuation is to analyse inflation expectations versus break-evens. The problem with this analysis is that we have inflation expectations often only for one year or, at best, two years forward. But there is still some information in this data, even though we would prefer a longer horizon. In particular, we focus on episodes when the spread between market-based inflation measures and survey measures is extreme. Such occurrences often provide entry signals for break-even trades. Figure 7.7 demonstrates this opportunity once more for the case of Brazil. To be precise, we show both the four-year Brazil break-evens and the delta of break-evens and the rolling one-year forward inflation expectations, divided by the level of break-evens to adjust for different rate levels. If this adjusted delta falls below zero, it suggests that the inflation risk premium is too low, and break-evens typically rise shortly afterward. While it would be preferable to use four-year inflation expectations for this exercise, we note that during inflation scares, the whole break-even curve moves sharply higher; as such, it is quite rare, and not sustainable for long, for a country with high and variable

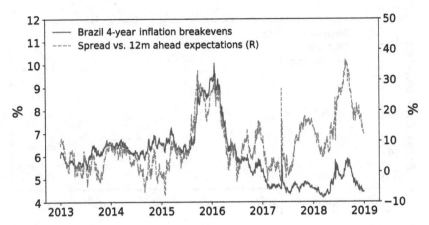

FIGURE 7.7   Buy Break-Evens When They Fall Below Inflation Expectations.
Source: Bloomberg, authors' calculations.

inflation, like Brazil, to have four-year inflation expectations below the one-year survey of economists. On the top side, it is harder to know what level constitutes a tradable overshooting; but in both 2015 and 2018, levels of around 30% for breakevens minus expectations, divided by breakevens, turned out to signal a peak in break-evens.[2]

The best trades happen when valuation and momentum line up: for example, when depressed breakevens coincide with the end of an easing cycle, or extended breakevens with the end of a hiking cycle. Then it is time to go all in.

7.4   OR IS IT STRUCTURAL?

This chapter has been very much in line with the overall focus of this book on business cycles rather than looking out for potential structural trades. But when it comes to inflation, there is a very valid question of whether there has been a structural move toward lower inflation that could continue. If this were the case, then the rules of thumb we listed may still work, as the cyclical aspect can easily more than offset the structural trend at any given point in time. But the bias would have to be strongly in favour of buying nominal bonds rather than buying linkers, and many of our point estimates for what constitutes too little risk premium in linkers would have to be adjusted downward.

---

[2]Having said that, we should note that this discussion of Brazil is designed to explain our general methodology, rather than to come up with point estimates for the case of Brazil. With respect to Brazil, it is important to know that the country is in the process of lowering its inflation target. So far, it has been agreed that the target will be moved from 4.5% in 2018 to 3.75% in 2021, presumably with a goal of eventually arriving at a 3% target. While such a structural change should not impact our methodology, it may impact what level of break-even overshoot constitutes a buying or selling opportunity.

We are sceptics when it comes to the view that inflation has disappeared for good. First, we point to Figure 6.21, which shows average inflation for EM and G3. Our reading is that yes, the inflation range post-Great Recession has shifted lower. Global crisis lead to a sharp fall in inflation. But that fall is temporary. And within the post GFC range post 2010 there is no obvious trend for EM or for the G3. Furthermore, we also note that policy makers in the G10 are trying their hardest to generate inflation, be it through monetary policy, fiscal policy, or, perhaps inadvertently, trade policy. We think they have a good shot at, eventually, achieving their goals and maybe more, presumably when everyone has fully given up on a return of inflation. For EM, we are more open to the idea that there is a slow moving trend toward lower inflation, largely as wealthier countries change consumption patterns and consume more services and fewer commodities, which will eventually be reflected in the relevant CPI indexes. And a few countries, like Brazil, are using the current disinflationary environment intelligently to lower inflation targets. On the other hand, many EM are still vulnerable to EMFX spikes creating inflation. As such, we are confident that the structural move lower in inflation will remain slow when compared to the inflation cycle surrounding it.

7.5 SUMMARY

Linkers are an important way to outperform the index. For accounts that can leverage, real rates are attractive, as information ratios are often higher for linkers than for nominals. As a rule of thumb, times to prefer nominals over linkers are during easing cycles and during rallies in UST. Times to prefer linkers, on the other hand, are during commodity bull markets, during EMFX sell-offs, and, to a lesser extent, during hiking cycles. Valuation also matters. A key valuation indicator is the spread of break-evens to current inflation, given that current inflation is very important for the formation of inflation expectations even in the medium term. Another important valuation indicator is how break-evens behave relative to the inflation target, which also serves as an anchor for long-term inflation expectations. As breakevens are inherently mean-reverting under credible central banking, investors should fade extremes in valuation. In particular, we show that for the case of Brazil, four-year breakevens falling below one-year surveys of inflation expectations are opportunities to pay inflation.

CHAPTER 8

How to Trade EM Rates: Event Guide

Having laid out the general principles for trading EM rates in the previous chapters, we now go into the weeds and explore the trading rules that we find useful for idiosyncratic events.

8.1 TRADING DATA

In line with our earlier findings that local factors matter more for rates than FX, it is not surprising that there are more compelling rules for trading local rates based on domestic data than was the case in FX land. Given that most central banks target headline inflation, inflation releases become the natural data points to focus on. Here, we show the median trading behaviour after positive and negative inflation surprises. We measure surprises by price action on the release date, rather than by Bloomberg consensus estimates, as the estimates lag the "true" market consensus. Furthermore, sometimes it is the core inflation figure that surprises the market, and consensus estimates are not available in many countries.

We select instances where the two-year swap rate reacts by more than 2 standard deviations on an inflation release. We find that on average, there is follow-through even after the initial reaction. Figure 8.1 shows that the two-year local rates trade wider for another 1.5 standard deviations over the next 20 trading days after inflation surprises on the high side. On the flip side, rates fall by another 1 standard deviation over the next 25 days after an initial negative reaction. Nimble investors can benefit from short-term trading on inflation releases, although liquidity on inflation release days may be somewhat limited.

A priori, there is no reason to believe that this rule should apply to every country. After all, the quality of inflation forecasting as well as central banks' reaction functions differ by country. We therefore also show the move in 2-year rates 10 days after the surprise (excluding the initial reaction on inflation release day) by country and separately for positive and negative inflation surprises (Figure 8.2). For the high-inflation surprises, the most significant follow-through occurs in Mexico, Hungary, Russia, and India. In Taiwan, the price action is in the wrong direction, and this market should be avoided for this strategy. Negative surprises in CPIs do not work quite as well. Chile, Hungary, Peru, and Turkey work the best, while price action in China and Poland goes

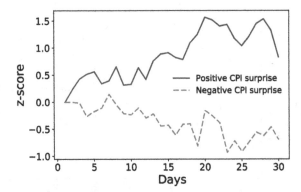

FIGURE 8.1 Inflation Surprises have Follow-Through.
Note: z-score of EM rate changes after data release on day 0.
Source: Bloomberg, authors' calculations.

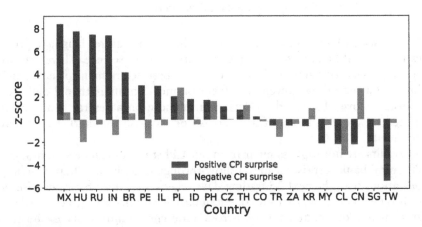

FIGURE 8.2 But Not All Inflation Surprises are Equal.
Note: z-score of EM rate change 10 days after data release on day 0, excluding event day.
Source: Bloomberg, authors' calculations.

meaningfully in the wrong direction. Needless to say, these markets should be avoided for this strategy.

The other key releases are central bank meetings. Once more, we define a surprise as a as a meaningful move by two-year interest rate swaps on the day of the central bank meeting. This definition makes sense because most of the time, central banks do not surprise the market with an actual change in the policy rate. Rather, they surprise investors with a statement that is more or less hawkish than was expected. Such surprises cannot be simply judged against some readily available consensus number. They require a thorough analysis of the statement and a detailed comparison to market participants' expectations. There are attempts to quantify central bank statements as

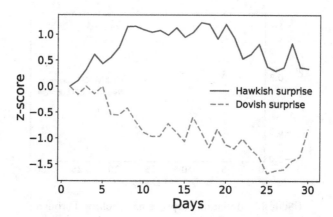

FIGURE 8.3   Central Bank Meetings Also "Work".
Note: z-score of EM rate changes after a CB meeting on day 0.
Source: Bloomberg, authors' calculations.

dovish or hawkish based on word counts or the use of natural language processing. But reading central bank statements is still more art than science. Therefore, we once again go with the price action on the day as the best determinant of hawkishness or dovishness of a central bank event and focus on moves of more than 2 daily standard deviations. A move of 2 standard deviation or more on a central bank day tells us all we need to know in terms of how dovish or hawkish the market considered the announcement.

The results are not too dissimilar from our CPI study, as can be seen in Figure 8.3. Dovish central bank surprises lead to follow-through of a bit more than 1.5 daily standard deviations over the next 25 trading days. Hawkish central bank surprises lead to follow-through in rates of just above one standard deviation over the next 20 days or so.

Once again, the patterns vary across different countries, as is illustrated in Figure 8.4. On the dovish side, the best follow-through is observed in Thailand, Israel, Colombia, Chile, the Czech Republic, and South Korea. On the hawkish side, the best follow-through is to be found in Hungary, Indonesia, the Czech Republic, and Thailand. Argentina and Russia work the least well, as they have the opposite sign. We are not overly concerned by the fact that the strategy does not work for all central banks. After all, different central banks have different ways to communicate with markets. For some, the central bank meetings may be of lesser importance as part of their overall communication strategy. And for the case of Argentina, it is clearly a different situation, since interest rates in many time periods trade much more like a credit than like a rates product.

Emergency rate hikes are a special case. As mentioned before, emergency rate hikes are only "approved" by policy makers with the understanding that extremely high rates are necessary only for a short period of time. Policy makers expect emergency hikes to be followed by cuts in short order. Figure 8.5 illustrates that this expectation is only half right. The median policy rate peaks at around 50 trading days after an emergency

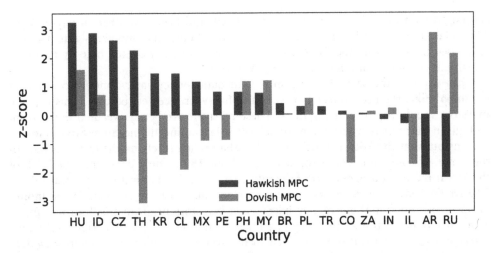

FIGURE 8.4 But Pick Your Countries Carefully.
Note: z-score of EM rate changes 10 days after a CB meeting on day 0, excluding event day.
Source: Bloomberg, authors' calculations.

hike. Rate cuts start on average at around 75 trading days (or more than 3 months) after an emergency rate hike. As we laid out earlier, on average, emergency rate hikes stabilize the currency, though not on day 1, and only for cheap currencies. For rates, the picture is similar. Figure 8.5 illustrates this by showing the P&L of five-year and two-year receivers. Obviously, receiving either into or on the day of the emergency rate hike is a major money loser. After the event, there is some follow-through, and investors

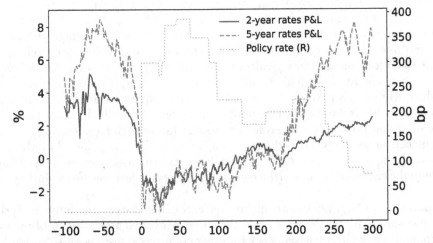

FIGURE 8.5 Fade Emergency Rate Hikes – But not on Day 1.
Note: P&L of receiving two- and five-year IRS around emergency hikes on day 0.
Source: Bloomberg, authors' calculations.

should go with the price action on the event day and keep a short-term paying bias. This is because on day 1, the jury is still out as to whether the emergency rate hike has succeeded in stabilizing the FX market. The front end (represented here by two-year rates) sells off more than the belly (five-year rates).

Just prior to the second leg up in the (median) policy rate, a month or so after the initial hike, the P&L of the two-year and five-year receivers bottom. This is when investors should begin receiving rates. These receivers are better executed in the front end, given that this is where the prior sell-off is larger and the negative carry is lower. It turns out that the P&L is much smoother than when receiving the five-year part of the curve. It's only much later (on average, about 180 trading days) that the P&L of the 5-year receiver outpaces that of the two-year point. It takes just under a year (about 220 trading days) for receivers to return to pre-hike levels if we include the month or so before the initial emergency hike, when investors begin to smell an imminent, aggressive policy action. The policy rate takes even longer to make it back to pre-hike levels. Emergency rate hikes are not easy or fast to unwind, which is an interesting data point for policy makers in EM.

8.2   LEARN TO LOVE NEGATIVE CARRY

In the preceding chapters, we discussed how to trade the shape of the curve and how to use an inversion at the front end of the curve as a trading tool. We have not said much about the long end of the curve, but it is important. More often than not, investors look at the shape of the curve to determine value. A steeper curve is seen as offering more value than a flat curve. While we found some evidence for this approach in Chapter 6, we also believe that inverted curves should not be feared. After all, an inversion can suggest an upcoming recession, which in turn may trigger a large easing cycle.

We study all the 2s/10s swap curve inversions for individual EM countries from 2009 to 2018. Using only every first inversion on a rolling 40-day window results in 28 events. We also distinguish between low yielders and high yielders. The low yielders invert due to the market smelling an eventual easing cycle, while the high yielders can also invert due to an emergency rate hike. Figure 8.6 shows the P&L of receiving the 10-year swap for high and low yielders separately, where day 0 is the day, when the 2s/10s invert. For the low yielders, inversions are rare (only six sample points), and the subsequent P&L is positive. Just as in DM, a curve inversion signals that monetary policy is too tight for the existing economic environment. Typically the central bank gets the message and starts to cut interest rates sooner rather than later, leading to strong performance for receivers across the curve, including the 10-year point. The only caveat is that our sample starts post-2008. During 2008, extreme risk aversion played havoc even with the curves of the low yielders, making the results less conclusive during times of stress.

Inversions for high yielders are highly concentrated in Turkey and India. In Turkey, curve inversion is almost the status quo: the curve is inverted around 60% of the time. This compares to an average frequency for other countries at just above 10%. For high yielders, the P&L going into day 0 falls sharply, suggesting that on average, the inversion is due to aggressive rate hikes. The P&L subsequently stays negative for another 40

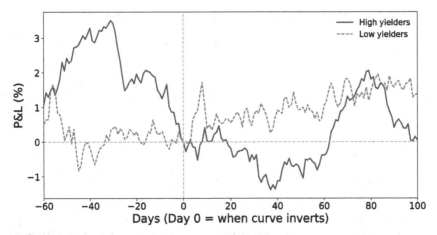

FIGURE 8.6 Curve Inversion is a Good Thing!
Note: P&L of 10-year receivers.
Source: Bloomberg, authors' calculations.

trading days before rebounding and moving strongly into positive territory. So even for the high yielders, curve inversion eventually "works," but investors have to be much more patient, and the gains are less consistent.

8.3   BEING INCLUSIVE PAYS OFF NICELY

Index inclusion trades have been an important trade for equity markets for quite some time. Of course, in equity markets, the times are long gone when an index inclusion trade could be put on after the inclusion announcement. At this stage, equity investors run screens to determine which equities may be included; they then go long those baskets against the overall market in the hope that the basket contains enough equities that get included to compensate for the losers. The outperformance on average ends on the day of the inclusion announcement, even though the actual inclusion typically happens later.

In EM fixed income, things are still somewhat easier. Just as in equities, correctly guessing potential candidates for inclusion creates attractive returns. But in EM fixed income, the added advantage is that the number of potential candidates for inclusion is relatively small. As such, the uncertainty is more with respect to the timing of the inclusion rather than whether a country gets included. But more importantly, buying the respective bonds and currencies even after the inclusion announcement still makes money going into the actual inclusion: i.e. it is not just one day of out-performance, but can be a few months. In our study, we focus on index inclusions into the World Government Bond Index (WGBI), now owned by the FTSE Russell, as one of the key cross-over indices; and on the JPMorgan EM Government Bond Index (Global Diversified), the main dedicated EM fixed-income index. Figure 8.7 shows the (absolute) performance around the inclusion announcement as well as around actual inclusion. As can be seen, bonds perform very well post inclusion announcement, and

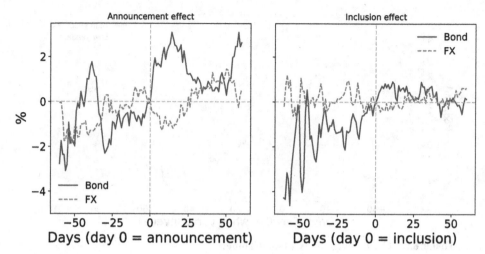

FIGURE 8.7 Index Inclusion: Buy the News, Sell the Fact.
Note: P&L of 10-year bond and long relevant EMFX versus USD.
Source: Bloomberg, authors' calculations.

it is clearly more than just a one-day impact. FX, on the other hand, is not impacted much by inclusion. On average, FX is even slightly weaker following the inclusion announcement. Going into the actual inclusion, bonds also trade very well (though in a volatile fashion), while FX mostly trades sideways. The strong performance of bonds on average ends a few days after the actual inclusion. Post inclusion, bonds consolidate with a weaker bias. The main reason the effect is much larger for bonds than for FX has to do with the buying pressure (defined as the value of bonds the indexers need to purchase divided by the average daily trading volume). Given that liquidity is typically much better for FX than for bond markets, buying pressure is usually much higher for bonds than for FX.

The best strategy for investors is to have an off-index position in likely inclusion candidates. But investors should also add to bond positions after the inclusion announcement. The bonds then should be held until actual inclusion. Profits need to be taken right around the actual index inclusion. We also note that for larger index inclusions, the dates can be staggered. For the sake of our analysis, we took the date when the first batch of bonds was included. But we note that in the case of staggered inclusions, it is unlikely that bonds will start to underperform before at least 50% of the total amounts to be included have actually been included. For staggered inclusions, we therefore would not take profits after the first inclusion date, but would hold on to those bonds longer.

At the time of writing, the index inclusion is going to be especially relevant for China. At this stage, an inclusion of China is being phased in for the JPMorgan EM benchmark, as well as for the Barclays Global Aggregate index. The main index that may still include China in the future is the WGBI, followed by around USD 2 trillion of assets under management. Including China in the WGBI would have to be phased in slowly over a long time, given the tremendous size of the Chinese market. The market impact is unlikely to be a major positive for the prices of Chinese bonds, given that the initial weight of China would remain constrained. We think the main response will be a negative impact on the countries that are already in the index (and below the cap). Those countries will be crowded out by China, but given the slow phasing in of the inclusion the size of this negative impact is unclear.

8.4 TRADING DOMESTIC DISASTERS

Given the sheer number of EM, it is sadly relatively common for a natural disaster to occur in a given country that is of a sufficient scale to impact the local macroeconomy. Such disasters are always upsetting events, and the first order of affairs is to mourn any human losses or misery. For policy makers, there is a question of how to react. Humanitarian aid is always required and almost always provided. But should there also be a reaction by monetary policy makers, for example? From the point of view of interest rate markets, there is a relatively clear pattern. The rule of thumb is that the macroeconomic effects are likely fleeting and that in the medium term, markets tend to fade the impact. One major reason is that most EM are relatively small and often relatively open economies, where global macro forces are much more relevant than local short-term shocks. Having said that, in the short term, there can be trading opportunities, as central banks at times overreact to these local shocks. As such, it often is observed that local central banks either pause in an ongoing hiking cycle or, rarely, even ease when a natural disaster strikes. Central bankers do this because they either truly fear that the impact of the disaster in terms of lost output and secondary effects on confidence requires a more supportive monetary policy, or implicitly yield to political pressure, irrespective of whether a looser monetary policy is justified. Be that as it may, when natural disasters strike, there can be an initial receiving opportunity, which is typically followed by a paying opportunity, as the impact of the disaster quickly fades.

Between 2000 and 2018 we found seven natural disasters with damage of more than 1% of GDP (including small open G10 economies). The largest damage was 12% of GDP in the case of the 2011 floods in Thailand. Markets usually move in response to such disasters. Figure 8.8 shows the typical behaviour of two-year rates after disaster strikes. As can be seen, two-year rates initially rally, as the market expects fewer hikes or additional cuts in order to protect the economy from the shock. How long the rally lasts depends on whether the central bank judges that the disaster is a big enough threat to the economy that it should ease financial conditions. In our sample of seven events, only two central banks eased shortly afterward, and one of those two instances could be seen as part of an ongoing easing cycle. In most cases, the central banks did not change course, and the rally subsequently reverted. In the median case, the receiving trade has run its course 20 days after the disaster hit.

The curve usually steepens, as can be seen in Figure 8.9. This is first due to the expectations of a more dovish central bank, but also because the subsequent rebuilding effort is likely to be inflationary and will also impact fiscal balances. The steepener peaks out in the median case at 10 bp around 40 days after disaster struck. It is interesting to

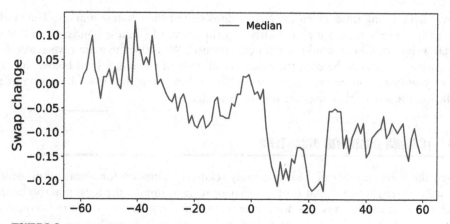

FIGURE 8.8   Central Banks Show Mercy – Briefly.
Note: Change in two-year swap rates around disasters on day 0.
Source: Bloomberg, authors' calculations.

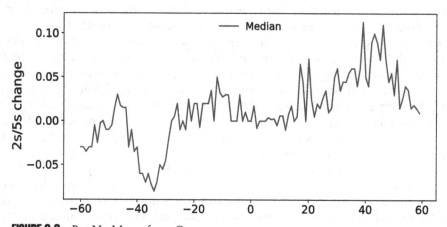

FIGURE 8.9   But No Mercy from Curves.
Note: Change in 2s/5s slope around disasters on day 0.
Source: Bloomberg, authors' calculations.

note that whenever a disaster causes rates to sell off due to extreme FX weakness, as in the case of the Chilean protests in late 2019, curve steepeners again work quite well.

8.5 SUMMARY

In summary, both local CPI and central bank meetings are often tradable – at least in small size, given liquidity issues – in that they often offer follow-through after the event day. This strategy works better in some countries than in others. Emergency rate hikes are special: they also offer first opportunities for short-term payers, as some follow-through is likely. But after a month or so, the peak of rates is in, and rates should be received.

Curve inversion in the 2s/10s space is usually a good short-term signal to receive 10-year rates for the low yielders. The next one to two months on average offer strong returns to receivers. Valuation only catches up with the trade afterward, making inversion a good trend signal in the short term. But for high yielders, much more patience is required, as inversion may be the result of an emergency rate hike. Index inclusions are also an important source of alpha. The rule of thumb is to receive after the announcement and to stay received until shortly after the actual index inclusion. This trade works better in rates than in FX. Finally, when it comes to localized natural disasters, there is a case for short-term receivers at the front end of the curve, but in the bigger picture, the rallies after disasters are paying opportunities. Curve steepeners may be preferable.

CHAPTER 9

How to Trade EM Credit

9.1 THE STRUCTURAL TRADE IS DEAD: LONG LIVE THE CYCLE

Just as for other EM asset classes, we don't think that there is a structural trade left in EM credit, at least in the sense that we do not expect a structural spread compression on an index level for EM HY. This is somewhat counter-intuitive. The overall investment appeal for EM is based on the notion that EM structurally grow faster than DM until their GDP per head has mostly caught up. This should over time structurally lower the credit risk and lead to spread compression. However, any growth catch-up over the last 10 years has not been reflected in EM sovereign HY spreads. While the spreads of close to 1500 bp in the late 1990s have not been seen since, progress stopped around the Great Recession. The all-time-low spread was reached in 2007. Post crisis, the range has been a very stable 250 bp to 500 bp. And this happened during a period where global credit (outside of the 2008 crisis) traded generally well, suggesting a positive global environment prone to lead to further spread compression for EM. Given that spread compression for EM has largely been missing in action in spite of a favourable environment, it stands to reason that the structural trade for spread compression when focusing only on the EM HY sub-index is at best progressing extremely slowly, and possibly stalling.

When going into relative value space and comparing EM HY to US HY, there is also no structural trade in sight, even though EM GDP has grown by an average of 5.3% since 2007 while DM averaged only 1.5% of GDP growth over the same period. But abstracting from the 2008 crisis, when EM HY unsurprisingly traded at much tighter spreads than US HY, there is no visible trend toward tighter EM spreads relative to US HY, in spite of the superior growth performance. This is illustrated in Figure 9.1.

This discussion has focused on the HY component of the EM index, largely to make it more comparable to the US corporate HY index. But the benchmark EMBI index includes both IG and HY issuers. And there has been strong ratings migration in EM, as a strong upgrade cycle has led to a rising ratio of IG-rated constituents in the EMBI. The share of IG-rated issuers increased almost monotonically starting in the early 1990s and until 2014. Interestingly, even the Great Recession in 2008–2009 did not make a major dent in this upgrade cycle (see Figure 9.2).

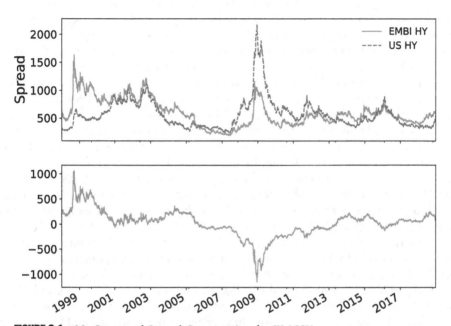

FIGURE 9.1 No Structural Spread Compression for EM HY.
Note: Option adjusted spreads (OAS) for US HY and EM HY; difference in the lower panel.
Source: Bloomberg, authors' calculations. Index data courtesy of J.P. Morgan Chase & Co., copyright 2020, as of 31 December 2018.

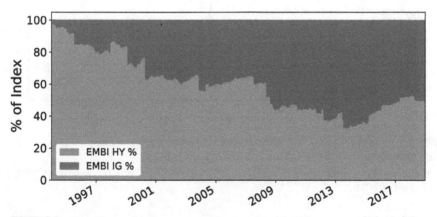

FIGURE 9.2 The Share of IG Issues in EMBI Rose Until 2015.
Source: Bloomberg, authors' calculations. Index data courtesy of J.P. Morgan Chase & Co., copyright 2020, as of 31 December 2018.

Remarkably, even this strong upgrade cycle has not resulted in a trend spread tightening for the EMBI index, as can be seen in Figure 9.3. Furthermore, it appears that the upgrade cycle peaked out in 2014 as global growth weakened, leading to some important index components suffering downgrades. In summary, it is not clear that there is going to be significant spread compression going forward for EM credit.

So far, so sobering. However, we would like to point out that even with stable spreads, we have a structural long bias for EM sovereigns over US corporates. The reason is that default probabilities for EM sovereigns have been generally lower than default probabilities for US corporates, while recovery values have been higher. The default probability for sovereign credits below investment grade was 2.5% for the period from 1983 to 2016. During the same time, the default probability for US HY was 4.2%. Over the same period, the recovery value was on average 65% for sovereigns (and 45% if weighted by value), but only 37% for US HY. We don't see a reason for those long-term averages to move against EM going forward, at least in relative terms. On a total return basis, EM sovereign HY should therefore outperform US HY.[1]

Furthermore, there are still structural EM credit trades available on a country level; one reason this is not showing up on the index level is that such positive country stories are offset by other countries going in the opposite direction. An alternative explanation, for which we have a lot of sympathy, is that by the time a country enters an index, the bulk of the structural catch-up trade is already behind it. Be that as it may, we think the lesson from the last decade is that for alpha generation, the focus should be on trading the credit cycle as opposed to a structural long EM trade.

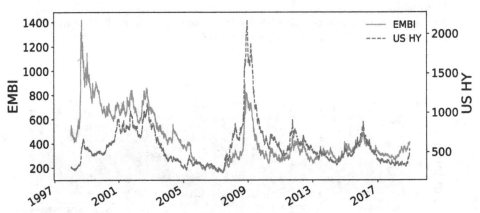

FIGURE 9.3   EMBI Driven by US HY Spreads.
Note: OASs in bp.
Source: Bloomberg. Index data courtesy of J.P. Morgan Chase & Co., copyright 2020, as of 31 December 2018.

---

[1]There is of course a question why this is not recognized by the market, leading to tighter spreads for EM. This answer is likely that home bias, which characterizes investor behaviours in many asset classes, also impacts EM credit. But home bias is likely to become less pronounced over time, which opens the door for long-term spread conversion, slow as it may be.

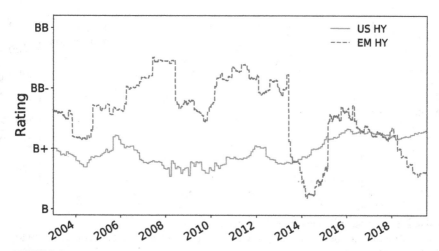

FIGURE 9.4 EM Ratings Cycle Lagging US HY Ratings.
Source: Citi.

Figure 9.3 also illustrates that the cyclical aspect of the EM credit trade is largely driven by the global credit cycle, as the correlation between US credit spreads and EM sovereign credit spreads is extremely high. This phenomenon is driven not just by a repricing of EM risk based on the cost of US credit, but also by a spillover of fundamentals from G3 into EM, as can be seen by the positive correlation of rating changes. When the US corporate rating cycle turns down, the EM rating cycle follows with a lag, as shown in Figure 9.4. This is in line with the discussion in Chapter 2 that suggested that US recessions often trigger recessions in EM.

Trading the global credit cycle well largely depends on predicting US recessions, which lead to the largest drawdowns in returns of credit markets. And when it comes to forecasting US recessions, we largely rely on the power of the US yield curve. The warning signal the market has focused on in the past has been an inversion of the UST curve, though at times it turns out that the following disinversion is more dangerous for risky assets like credit than the inversion itself. Figure 9.5 illustrates that there were several episodes of inversions of 2s/5s in the US in 1998, 2000, 2006–2007, and 2018. In 1998, EM credit spreads widened very early on, and staying long credit until the subsequent disinversion of the US rates curve occurred would have been a mistake. The reason is that the 1998 inversion was driven by an EM crisis, which then spilled over into LTCM, which in turn forced the Fed to cut. As such, it is only natural that EM credit traded poorly already when the curve inverted. But the inversions of the UST curve in 2001 and 2006 were very early. In those two episodes, it would have been advantageous to wait for the subsequent curve disinversion before getting more negative on EM credit. Both 2001 and 2006 were much more classical US recessions, driven by domestic US issues and not by an EM crisis. The inversion in late 2018 has at the time of writing not disinverted, and neither is it clear if a US recession is indeed going to materialize or not. Our rule of thumb is therefore to be long EM credit most of the time but to cut positions upon disinversion of the UST curve if the issue appears to be a US problem,

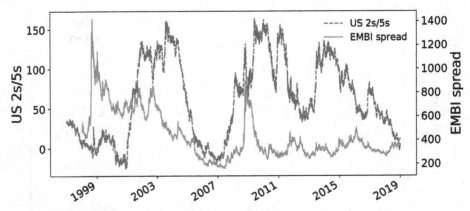

FIGURE 9.5 Get Scared When the US Curve Disinverts.
Source: Bloomberg. Index data courtesy of J.P. Morgan Chase & Co., copyright 2020, as of 31 December 2018.

and to cut positions earlier on actual curve inversion, if an EM issue appears to be the driver for the likely Fed cuts.

9.2 CARRIED AWAY BY MOMENTUM

In Chapter 4, on EMFX, we saw that simple carry strategies performed well for a long time – but they have underperformed ever since the onset of tapering in 2013. In EM credit, on the other hand, carry is still alive and well. The easiest way to see how carry performs in EM credit is to chart the EM HY index relative to the IG index on a cash-neutral basis. As is illustrated in Figure 9.6, the HY index handily outperforms the IG index for both the sovereign and corporate universe.[2] Drawdowns are relatively contained, other than during the 2008 crisis. Simple carry strategies still work in EM credit. One hypothesis explaining the difference *vis-à-vis* EMFX is that global credit has been in a bull market, while EMFX has been in a bear market. Carry just does not work well in bear markets.

Other than overweighting high yielders, another popular carry strategy is to replace sovereigns with quasi-sovereigns, which is an alternate form of earning the carry. While we have not run the backtest to prove this point, casual observation suggests that this carry strategy also adds to returns without adding much to volatility. This is more than just a bull market strategy. While the strategy got hurt in 2008, it performed well in several other drawdown periods for the EM credit benchmark. The strategy has an oil component, given that many quasis are state-controlled oil companies, and as such a view on oil could be used to improve further on this simple strategy.

---

[2]As an aside, we also note that the corporate and sovereign carry indexes look almost identical. But sometimes there are leads and lags that can create opportunities. Sovereign credit is often leading, such as in late 2015. Such a pronounced lag offered a clear opportunity to buy EM corporate credit.

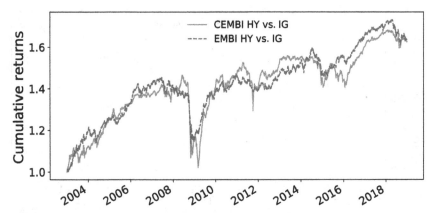

FIGURE 9.6 Carry Still Works in EM Credit.
Source: Bloomberg, authors' calculations. Index data courtesy of J.P. Morgan Chase & Co., copyright 2020, as of 31 December 2018.

Next we show how the carry trade works when moving from the index level to the country level. Given that there are many more countries in the EMBI than in the GBI-EM, we double the number of credits in both the long and short baskets, compared to our FX study, to eight countries on each side. Again we use volatility adjustments twice: once to find the best volatility-adjusted carry and again to make sure each credit in the basket adds the same risk to the portfolio. Figure 9.7 shows the excess returns for that strategy. Prior to the 2008 crisis, returns were largely in line with the EMBI index.

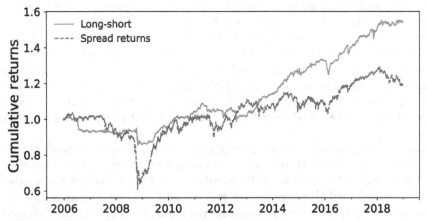

FIGURE 9.7 Carry Works Even Better on a Country Level.
Note: Performance of top eight versus bottom eight yielders, volatility-adjusted.
Source: Bloomberg, authors' calculations. Index data courtesy of J.P. Morgan Chase & Co., copyright 2020, as of 31 December 2019.

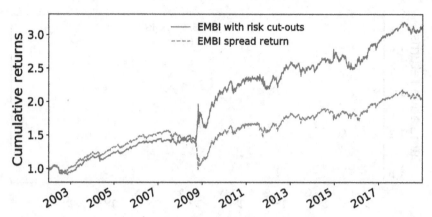

FIGURE 9.8 Applying our Currency Risk Indicator to EM Credit.
Note: EMBI with risk cut-outs based om FX risk indicator.
Source: Bloomberg, authors' calculations. Index data courtesy of J.P. Morgan Chase & Co., copyright 2020, as of 31 December 2018.

But the strategy suffered a much smaller drawdown in 2008 than either the index or the simpler HY versus IG carry strategy. And post crisis, performance continues to be very strong. This reinforces the earlier point that carry still works in credit.

Of course, it would have been nice to avoid the 2008 blowup completely, as well as a few other, smaller drawdowns. But given that EM credit has much fewer drawdowns than local markets, the worry is that any risk indicator is overly fitted to avoid long credit exposure during the all-important 2008 episode. We therefore refrain from creating a credit-specific risk index but apply our risk indicator introduced in Chapter 4 (see Figure 4.8) to EM credit. This approach has the added benefit that using our indicator for EM credit serves as an out-of-sample test of sorts for our EMFX risk indicator. As it turns out, just as in EMFX, our risk indicator based on the maximum of rising volatilities for various asset classes works well. As can be seen in Figure 9.8, the underperformance from 2002 to 2008 is relatively small, the outperformance in 2008–2009 is large, and using the indicator generates further outperformance after 2008. The IR for spread returns from 2002 to 2018 is 0.53, while the IR using the risk indicator rises to 0.85.

Alternatively, momentum also works quite well. A simple momentum rule similar to the one that we used for EMFX also avoids the 2008 problem. For credit, we use a longer look-back window of 12 months (while for FX, we did a more thorough investigation and settled on one-month momentum). Once more, we volatility-adjust on two levels. First, the return to calculate the momentum is volatility-adjusted. And second, the weights of the eight top- and bottom-ranked credits that are added to the long-short momentum basket are also volatility-adjusted. We reweigh on a monthly basis. Figure 9.9 illustrates the resulting P&L. This strategy generates an IR of 0.7 from 2004–2018, compared to an IR of 0.4 for the spread return of the EMBI index.

FIGURE 9.9 Momentum Strategies Avoid the 2008 Bust-Up.
Note: Long-short, top/bottom eight credits ranked by 12-month volatility-adjusted momentum.
Source: Bloomberg, authors' calculations. Index data courtesy of J.P. Morgan Chase & Co., copyright 2020, as of 31 December 2018.

9.3 FINDING YOUR SWEET SPOT

There are two ways to pick up carry versus the index. First, investors can go down in quality and overweight riskier, higher-yielding credits. Alternatively, investors can increase duration *vis-à-vis* the index. Given that credit curves are usually upward sloping, increasing duration is also a way to pick up carry. Table 9.1 shows that since 2011 (when the subindexes became more reliable as the number of constituents increased), the sweet spot on an IR basis in terms of ratings has been BBs. As and Bs also still generate respectable IRs, while for BBB, performance has been much worse. For duration, the sweet spot has been the front end, and in particular anything below five years. The worst performance occurred in the sector with the longest duration (>10 years), partly because the roll-down is typically worse.

TABLE 9.1 The Sweet Spot: Three- to Five-Year BBs.

Rating	IR	Duration	IR
B	0.72	>10yr	0.45
BB	0.89	7–10yr	0.66
BBB	0.46	5–7yr	0.97
A	0.70	3–5yr	1.32
		1–3yr	1.28

Source: Bloomberg, authors' calculations. Index data courtesy of J.P. Morgan Chase & Co., copyright 2020, as of 31 December 2018.

9.4 THE WARREN BUFFETT TRADE IN EM CREDIT

Warren Buffett famously focuses on safe companies, as levering up portfolios of safe companies tends to result in higher IRs than taking the same amount of risk in risky companies. Given the sweet spots indicated in Table 9.1, it is no surprise that the Warren Buffett trade works in credit, too. Leveraging up the short-duration part of the EMBI index results in higher IRs than owning the riskier, long end of the index. We demonstrate this in Figure 9.10 by using six months of rolling volatility to calculate the right ratio to lever up the short end. We operate here in excess return space, i.e. we implicitly charge Libor for the additional notional needed for bonds on the short end of the curve. Since 2012, when our index data starts, excess performance has been impressive. Investors do not get paid to venture out on the long end of the credit curve.

Of course, if there is an actual default, the back end outperforms, as every bond starts to trade at a very similar USD price. The strategy that focuses on the short end of the curve is basically selling jump to default risk. While defaults of countries are obviously very rare, this argument would suggest that this strategy should be used mostly for IG or highly rated high-yield issuers, as IG issues rarely default overnight.

When taking credit risk rather than duration risk, the Warren Buffett rule needs to be slightly modified. Figure 9.11 applies the same methodology to credit ratings that we applied to duration buckets and shows the volatility-adjusted performance of the various rating buckets. As per the Buffett principle A-rated credits outperform BBB-rated ones. However, BB- and B-rated credits perform even better. Another way to look at it is that in each rating category (HY and IG), the better-rated credits perform better. BB outperforms B in HY, and A outperforms BBB in IG. The Buffett trade works for each rating bucket, but it does not work across buckets. After all, levered-up A and BBB-rated credits do not beat the returns of HY. There clearly is an excess premium for HY.

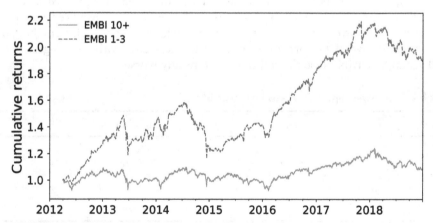

FIGURE 9.10 Front Ends Outperform.
Note: Short-duration indexed leveraged up using six-month trailing volatility.
Source: Bloomberg, authors' calculations. Index data courtesy of J.P. Morgan Chase & Co., copyright 2020, as of 31 December 2018.

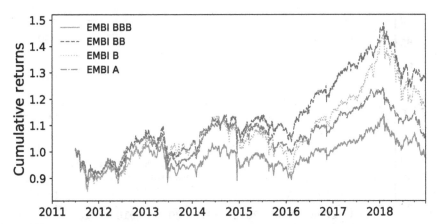

FIGURE 9.11   Higher-Rated Credits Outperform – in Each Bucket.
Source: Bloomberg. Index data courtesy of J.P. Morgan Chase & Co., copyright 2020, as of 31 December 2018.

One reason for the poor performance of BBB is that there has been a downgrade cycle during the period under study, and the worst market impact of a downgrade is when IG is lost: i.e. when ratings move from BBB to BB. These downgrades dragged down BBB performance and have helped BBs. BBBs should especially be avoided during weak growth cycles. We will discuss this issue in more detail later in this chapter.

9.5   IMPROVING ON BUFFETT

Using the business cycle, we should be able to improve on the simple Buffett rule to always lever up high-quality credits at the short end of the curve. After all, spreads of HY issuers tend to widen by more than spreads of investment-grade issuers whenever the US business cycle turns down. Carry is rarely enough to offset this spread widening during such downturns, and as a result, HY underperforms. The opposite is true during upturns, where the best-performing positions are weaker credits, which were previously hit the hardest by rising default risks. Such spreads then normalize early in the cycle as default fears subside post-recession. This is illustrated in Figure 9.12, which shows the relative performance of HY against IG as a deviation from the 200-day MA, used here to detrend the return series, next to the US manufacturing ISM. The problem is, of course, that relative returns often lead the ISM and, in the last instance, by a considerable amount of time. The best way to use this chart is therefore to position for HY underperformance and IG outperformance whenever the manufacturing ISM hits the high 50s.

The other question related to the business cycle is what to do with duration exposure across the cycle. Figure 9.13 shows that on an index level, spreads at the short end often do worse than spreads at the back end of the curve when the ISM is falling. This happens as default probabilities rise for the near term; but it also has an index

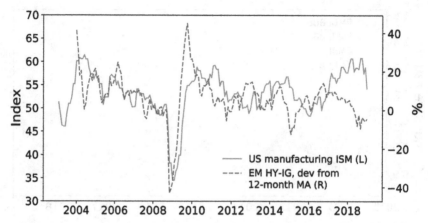

FIGURE 9.12   Switch to IG When ISM is Too High.
Source: Bloomberg, authors' calculations. Index data courtesy of J.P. Morgan Chase & Co., copyright 2020, as of 31 December 2018.

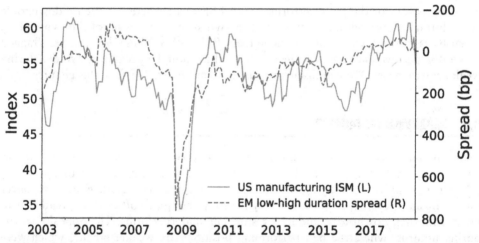

FIGURE 9.13   Leveraged Investors Benefit from Curve Inversion During Downturns.
Source: Bloomberg, authors' calculations. Index data courtesy of J.P. Morgan Chase & Co., copyright 2020, as of 31 December 2018.

composition component, given that the ratio of IG to HY constituents is higher at the back end than at the front end of the curve because IG is longer duration than HY. The opposite is true during business cycle upturns, when spreads at the short end fall faster. To position for an inversion during times of a toppy ISM index is mostly a leveraged money trade, as it would have to be put on in a duration-neutral manner.

But the duration question is difficult to analyse on an index level as the composition across ratings at the front end and back end is so different. We therefore move from the index level to the country level. In particular, we are interested in the question of whether long duration can outperform short duration during downturns, given that the

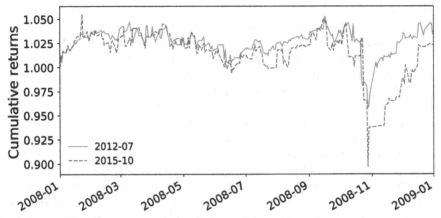

FIGURE 9.14   The Case of Poland: The Front End is Where it is Safe.
Note: Cumulative returns of 2012 and 2015 Polish bonds.
Source: Bloomberg, authors' calculations.

UST component should be more supportive for the back end of the curve. As the UST component is most meaningful for highly rated bonds, we analyse the case of Poland, one of the safest EM during the 2008 crisis. But as shown in Figure 9.14, even for a country as safe as Poland, the front-end bonds (we use 2012s) outperform 2015s (back then, the longest bond on offer). As such, we would conclude that when the ISM peaks, real money investors should not only move out of HY and into IG but also reduce duration even for the safest curves – and even if the bonds are held without a UST hedge, at least for severe downturns. The only clean way to benefit from falling US rates is to buy UST!

9.6   CREDIT SELECTION ACCORDING TO RAY DALIO

Of course, there is more to trading EM credit than just deciding how to best take risk from a top-down perspective. Investors spend a significant amount of time getting individual country calls right. There is a great deal of literature on which economic indicators to analyse to do that. The classic indicators that credit investors as well as the rating agencies follow are based on the external position of a country and government finances (both flows), as well as debt levels (the stock). In particular, popular indicators are the current account balances, fiscal balances, debt levels, and inflation. Typical warning signals are current account deficits in excess of 3–4%, fiscal deficit in excess of 7–8%, external debt of more than 45%, and inflation above 20%. We are not sure that these widely watched indicators will lead to major advantages in trading EM credit. If credits seem mispriced compared to current credit fundamentals, as picked up by such numbers, it is more likely that the market is already pricing future changes of such variables than that the market offers a trading opportunity to investors. A better approach would be to forecast changes in the variables we listed. To our mind, there are two approaches to this.

First, investors should focus on commodity exporters. For commodity producers, forecasting changes in the relevant numbers is often as easy or hard as forecasting the relevant commodity. For commodity producers, the current account balance is usually highly impacted by the relevant commodity price, as are parts of the capital account (including FDI, but also portfolio investments). Depending on the regime under which the commodity producers operate, the fiscal balances are also highly sensitive to the relevant commodity price. This may be the case because the government takes a large share of the profits directly from commodity producers though licenses and royalties. In extremis, the company may be state owned, when 100% of the profits accrue to the government. Alternatively, the effect can be mostly indirect, to the extent that the commodity cycle dominates the business cycle of a country and therefore influences the tax take. Of course, the credit of commodity producers moves in a coincident fashion with the relevant commodity, which then requires a credible forecast for the relevant commodity price in order to profitably trade the credit. Forecasting commodity pricing is about as difficult as forecasting credit spreads, but there can be divergences from time to time, as can be seen in Figure 9.15. For example, in 2007, commodity credits showed poor relative strength versus commodity markets, which was followed by a sharp downturn. Similarly, commodity credits showed significant relative strength in 2015, which was followed by a strong upturn. A solid bottom-up analysis of supply and demand in commodity markets may turn out to be more helpful than such technical patterns, though.

A second way to forecast credit fundamentals is for investors to be on the lookout for signs of major exuberance with respect to asset markets as well as flows, which often go hand in hand with imbalances in current accounts and fiscal accounts. We propose to use the analysis of Ray Dalio from his excellent book on credit cycles as a guide (Dalio 2018), which we implemented for EM (Willer et al. 2019a). We focus on the extent of equity performance over the last few years (Dalio suggests that an equity rally of more

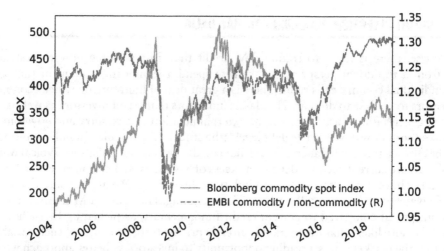

FIGURE 9.15 Commodity Credits Can Lag Commodities.
Source: Bloomberg, authors' calculations. Index data courtesy of J.P. Morgan Chase & Co., copyright 2020, as of 31 December 2018.

than 25% cumulative over three years is a warning signal), on the extent of capital inflows (where inflows of more than 12% of GDP cumulative over 3 years serve as a warning signal), and on the extent of the appreciation of the real exchange rate (values more than 10% cumulative over 3 years are problematic). Furthermore, growth above potential is also a warning sign, and a positive output gap of more than 2.5% or more suggests severe overheating according to Dalio. During these phases of market exuberance, investors often do not focus on large current account deficits, given how easily they seemingly can be financed. The artificially high growth numbers also suggest that the fiscal numbers do not deteriorate much. Therefore, focusing on the indicators of exuberance leads to alarm bells ringing quite early. This means using such signs of exuberance for credit selection is very difficult, as it often takes a trigger to end the market's love affair with the country in question. We suggest two different ways to overcome the timing issue. First, we keep a list of countries at risk. But we only short the credit of countries that are hit by a negative shock, which changes the consensus narrative: for example, a fall in commodity prices, a bout of USD strength, or a political change. Second, given how hard it is to ascertain that a given shock is of sufficient size to end exuberance, we also use technicals. A technical break in an uptrend (for example, the 200-dma) for a country on our list for major exuberance may be a good entry point for a short.

ARGENTINA: TICKING ALL THE BOXES – AGAIN !

One recent example illustrating the power of the Dalio approach has been Argentina, starting in 2017. Interestingly, Argentina fit the bust framework almost perfectly; but in spite of this, almost no one saw the bust coming, partly because the narrative was focused on the positive political changes taking place in the country.

The seeds for the problem were laid by the election of President Macri in November of 2015. The election of the market-friendly Macri was seen as a major victory for economic orthodoxy. And the contrast to the previous president, Ms. Kirchner, could not have been bigger. Under Kirchner, the country had largely insulated itself from the world economy by implementing severe capital controls, massaging economic statistics, and breaking off relationships with the IMF and international creditors. It had also resorted to large central bank financing of government deficits, and subsequently artificially suppressed inflation with price controls.

This insulation resulted in one important advantage, though: President Macri inherited an economy with very low levels of credit. Debt over GDP in 2015 stood at only 26% of GDP. Given Macri's somewhat tenuous hold over the Argentine parliament, and given the nascent love affair of global markets with the returning prodigal son, Argentina, Macri decided to use the low leverage in his favour. He implemented a very slow fiscal adjustment, financed by foreign investors who embraced the new Argentina. Between 2015 and 2017, the fiscal

(Continued)

deficit rose from −5.1% of GDP in 2015 to −6% in 2017, in spite of a (gradual) adjustment to subsidies for utilities. And external debt grew rapidly from 26% of GDP in 2015 to 37% of GDP in 2017. Given large capital inflows, the currency remained artificially strong, resulting in the current account deficit rising from −2.7% of GDP in 2015 to −5.8% of GDP in 2017.

However, the market was not concerned with these statistics. The narrative at the time was that President Macri would eventually bring down the fiscal deficit, possibly after his hand in parliament was strengthened by the midterm election. The current account deficit was seen as financing, to a large extent, investment goods needed to push the trade balances into more positive territory, while the consumption part of the current account deficit was thought to be catch-up consumption that would fade away when Argentines made the purchases that they had been unable to make during the capital controls of the Kirchner years. Growth dipped in 2016 as a result of the initial adjustment of the FX but then rebounded strongly in 2017 to 2.9%. Financial markets were buoyant: at its peak in February 2018, the equity market was up 83% in USD terms over three years, the real exchange rate remained very overvalued, only 20% weaker than the all-time strongest level reached before the devaluation in 2001 and around 50% stronger than at its weakest level, seen after 2001. That 2017 was a good year for EM assets also helped, as it made it easier for Argentina to finance its external deficit. This combination of weak fundamental indicators and bubbly financial markets meant that the table was set for a major crisis. By late 2017, both the economic and market indicators were therefore in line with levels that typically precede a severe debt crisis, as illustrated in Figure 9.16.

FIGURE 9.16   The Old Classic: Exuberant Equity Markets and a Large CA Deficit.
Source: Bloomberg.

(*Continued*)

The beginning of the crisis came when, in December 2017, the central bank was forced by the administration to give up on its inflation target – after insisting for many months that the inflation target was crucial as the nominal anchor of the system. The central bank claimed – with some justification – that the inflation target was merely adjusted, as it had become clear to everyone in the market that it could not be met, irrespective of central bank policies. But the revision of the inflation target was a shock to investor confidence that led to outflows and to a sharp correction in Argentine asset prices. The narrative had changed, and investor focus shifted decisively from a positive political narrative to macro fundamentals, making Argentina susceptible to a sudden stop of capital flows. Argentina tried to stem the tide with emergency rate hikes, but they came too early and before the peso cheapened sufficiently. In what must be an all-time speed record in terms of going from boom to an IMF bailout, Argentina signed a bail-out agreement on 7 June 2018, which subsequently had to be increased in size on 26 September 2018. This second attempt managed to stabilize the situation into late 2018, until election uncertainties started to take their toll. And the rest is history (repeating itself).

9.7 PEGS MAKE IT WORSE

In the past, pegged exchange rates were seen as instrumental to bring down inflation. Nowadays, policy makers understand that using exchange rates to anchor inflation and inflation expectations is a very dangerous game to play. More often than not, such arrangements lead to overvalued exchange rates, especially during strong USD cycles, and subsequent sharp devaluations. Given these risks, many of the large EM have moved in recent decades from pegged to free-floating, or at least dirty-floating, exchange rates. And it is plausible that the prevalence of flexible exchange rate regimes has led to less severe EM crises in the last decade when compared to the 1990s. However, we point out that some countries still use pegged exchange rates, especially in the Gulf. For commodity producers, a pegged exchange rate is especially ill-designed to cope with the manifold external shocks that being a commodity producer entails. This is illustrated in Figure 9.17, which shows the three pegged oil credits (Bolivia, Iraq, and Oman) underperforming the EM commodity credit basket during the last three major episodes of falling oil prices. While Saudi Arabia had not yet issued external debt by the end of the study at the end of 2018, we advise adding Saudi to the basket of the pegged currency credits to be worst hit during oil downturns. When bearish oil, the oil producers with a pegged FX are the best shorts.

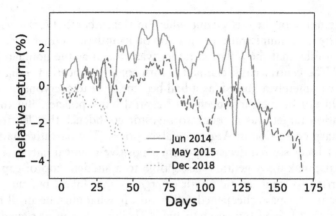

FIGURE 9.17 Oil and Pegs Don't Mix!
Note: Relative performance of pegged oil credits against
non-pegged commodity credits during three episodes of oil
bear markets.
Source: Bloomberg, authors' calculations.

9.8 IMF: WHAT IS IT GOOD FOR?

Exuberance is usually followed by a bust. How the bust unfolds varies considerably. EM tend to have inflationary busts, rather than deflationary busts, largely because FX tends to adjust very significantly, leading to high inflation. EM have the advantage that the vast majority of them are relatively small in terms of global GDP. It is therefore theoretically feasible for institutions like the IMF to bail them out, which is not the case for large developed countries. Access to IMF credit lines at times when markets no longer offer a country credit can be very helpful in mitigating, or at least stretching out, a painful adjustment. It is therefore not surprising that an IMF package is usually part of the end game for a country in crisis. Of course, the IMF monies come with strings attached: the *conditionality*, as the IMF outlines performance criteria that need to be met to obtain each following tranche. Those criteria usually demand a tighter fiscal policy and often structural reforms as well. More recently, social criteria have been added. With respect to its advice, the IMF often plays a role similar to McKinsey in the corporate world. Usually, the incumbent management knows very well what needs to be done; but hiring an outsider like McKinsey to spell it out offers a way to allocate the blame for the harsh medicine to be administered to someone else. This strategy works especially well if that outsider has a very strong reputation for having the relevant expertise. The IMF packages therefore end up providing both the benefit of access to credit as well as the benefit of a having a scapegoat for the required adjustment. While there are examples where countries, for political reasons, choose not to go to the IMF, such examples are rare and tend not to last forever. Attempts to adjust without IMF help are usually even more painful, as doing so requires an external imbalance to correct in a very short period of time. Such sharp adjustments often lead to a change of government, and the new government then often quickly proceeds to knock at the IMF's door.

While there are many studies of whether IMF programmes work, such studies are mostly focused on macroeconomic or socioeconomic outcomes. Here we are interested whether IMF packages work in a trading sense. We studied this question first at Citi Research, where we analysed all IMF packages since 2001 and investigated whether the announcement of an IMF package led to subsequent outperformance by the credit in question (Willer and Guarino 2018). There were 32 IMF packages. Figure 9.18 shows that spreads widen significantly two months prior to the IMF announcement, by an average of 130 bp and with a median of 45 bp. Spreads stabilize around 15 days before the announcement. This is likely the case because there are typically rumours of an IMF deal ahead of the announcement. Such rumours are very hard to avoid because the number of officials involved in these negotiations is fairly large. Furthermore, the officials from the countries under attack have an incentive to leak some good news to stabilize highly volatile markets, and they may also attempt to force the IMF's hand to some extent. Be that as it may, clearly good news travels fast.

The IMF announcement stabilizes the spread, but during the initial 20 to 30 days after the announcement, the spreads on average still move higher by 50 bp (and 18 bp for the median case). This is surprising to us, as the IMF package meaningfully improves the credit outlook for the country in question. But clearly, markets remain sceptical at first, and some investors use the IMF package to cut exposures. This tends to be a mistake. Median spreads subsequently move sharply lower: 150 trading days after the announcement, the median spread is more than 100 bp tighter than just before the IMF announcement. Furthermore, as also noted in the Citi report, there is no strong relationship between the size of the programme, expressed as a percent of the country's GDP, and the trading behaviour of the bonds. This is also counterintuitive, but perhaps

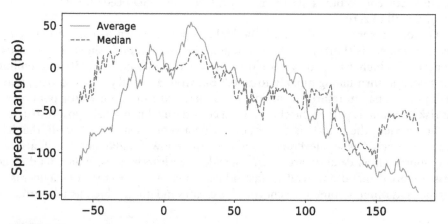

FIGURE 9.18 IMF Packages Work – With a Delay
Note: Spread changes around IMF announcement dates (day 0).
Source: Citi.

it is the result of the IMF accurately assessing the required size of the package. For us, the way to trade IMF packages is to go long the credit post announcement, but it is interesting to observe that there is no need to rush. The best strategy, on average, is to wait for the first pullback post IMF announcement before buying the credit.

9.9 EMBRACE DEFAULTS

Of course, not all governments choose to go to the IMF. And, equally, not all IMF packages are able to prevent a default. Still, as outlined in the introduction to this chapter, overall, the default ratios on sovereign emerging market debt is low when compared to default ratios for US corporates. The problem for investors is, of course, that defaults are highly correlated, as they are often driven by a global slowdown or recession and falling commodity prices. But the same is true for US HY issuers.

There is some reason to believe that the default ratio could rise over time for EM, largely because in recent years, the IMF has started to consider private debt restructurings as part of a bailout, most famously in the case of Greece. In the past, the IMF was too worried that a default would shut a country out of capital markets for a very significant time, holding back the recovery. But such fears were never relevant in practice. On the contrary, it is somewhat surprising just how short the memory of the market is when it comes to defaults. Academic treatments of the question suggest that the period during which a sovereign remained in default was only around four years for post-1991 defaults. And since 1998, this has dropped further, with only one of the well-known debt restructurings taking longer than two years to resolve. Once the restructuring is concluded, sovereigns can generally borrow again quite quickly.[3] Two years without external borrowing is usually easy for a sovereign to survive, given that as a result of the crisis, current accounts are often in surpluses and USD needs for debt repayments obviously fall to zero.

Of course, spreads will initially be higher upon a return to capital markets. But even that impact is short-lived. Borensztein and Panizza (2008) show that spreads are about 400 bp higher than they should be in year one, falling to a 250 bp premium in year two, and then falling quickly to zero.[4] But from a country point of view, that is a small price to pay in return for major debt relief; and from an investor point of view, this risk premium is part of the charm when considering buying debt post restructuring.

In our view, the market is correct in having a short memory. After all, the default creates a situation where leverage is suddenly quite low. Fundamentals will also likely have improved, as defaults are often coincident with recessions, which tend to compress import demand and lead to fast adjustments of the balance of payments. The currency has often become very cheap. This creates inflation, which usually erodes real

---

[3]See Panizza et al. (2009), who also note that the global credit cycle is more important than the default history to judge how quickly a country can borrow again post restructuring.

[4]See Borensztein and Panizza (2008). There is also some evidence that the cost to a borrower is higher, the more extreme the haircuts (Cruces and Trebesch 2013).

wages and makes countries more competitive. Often, old governments fall, generating hope that economic management will improve. But investors, still shocked by the recent default, require very high risk premia to be tempted back into the market. As such, a default creates the very best circumstances for investors to invest in bonds of the relevant country.

We study that issue in Table 9.2. The table lists the defaults post 1995 that were for more than USD 1 billion and for which we found bond prices after the restructuring. The table also includes the *haircut* (NPV of old bonds over NPV of new bonds at the exit yield, using data from Cruces and Trebesch 2013). We then add the one-year return of a country subindex post restructuring to the table (using monthly data). We find that returns are very strong. The median one-year return is 16%, for an excess return over the index of 11%. This explains why markets are very willing to let a country back into the credit market after a default. This in turn keeps the cost of a default, in terms of lost market access and risk premium, quite low for the borrower, increasing the frequency of defaults – time consistency is difficult to achieve for investors or issuers.

In spite of this finding, anecdotal evidence is that governments fight tooth and nail to avoid defaults, even when giving up the fight earlier may be better economic policy. After all, digging in for a fight to the bitter end means that FX reserves are depleted to sometimes shockingly low levels, making the subsequent recovery harder to finance. Of course, it also means there is less money for a bond restructuring, leading to higher haircuts. The reason for holding out is very simple and can be seen in Table 9.2. Defaults

TABLE 9.2 Embrace Defaults.

Country	Amount USD bn	Date of exchange	Haircut NPV/NPV	Regime chg (y/n)	Return 1 yr	Excess
Argentina	43.7	Jun-05	77%	y	28%	21%
Cote d'Ivoire	6.5	Mar-98	63%	n	−18%	−10%
Cote d'Ivoire	2.9	Apr-10	55%	y	−13%	−21%
Cote d'Ivoire	2.7	Oct-12	6%	n	8%	14%
DomRep	1.1	May-05	5%	n	18%	7%
Ecuador	6.7	Aug-00	38%	y	20%	11%
Ecuador	3.2	Jun-09	68%	n	36%	19%
Greece	261.4	Mar-12	65%	y	133%	124%
Iraq	17.7	Jan-06	89%	y	2%	-7%
Panama	3.9	Apr-96	35%	n	63%	36%
Peru	10.6	Mar-97	64%	n	13%	2%
Russia	31.9	Aug-00	51%	y	21%	12%
Serbia	2.7	Apr-05	71%	y	11%	−3%
Ukraine	1.6	Apr-00	18%	n	32%	20%
Ukraine	18	Nov-15	25%	n	14%	1%
Uruguay	3.1	May-03	10%	n	13%	11%
Median	5.2		53%		16%	11%
Average	26.1		46%		24%	15%

Source: Cruces and Trebesch (2013), Bloomberg, authors' calculations.

significantly increase the probability of a change in government. In our sample, the government changed in more than 40% of cases, significantly higher than the norm.[5] And some of the changes have been quite violent, where Presidents are forced to leave by helicopter or in the middle of the night (or both). While capital markets are very forgiving, the populace is not.

One open question is whether bond returns are better if new governments come into office post default. Our data are not conclusive on this question. Median returns are the same post restructuring with and without government change, though average (as opposed to median) returns are higher in cases with a change. Investigating the events in Table 9.2 more closely suggests some episodes where post default a more market-friendly government takes over, but also events where the opposite happens and a market-friendly government gets the boot. As such, it is not too surprising that there is no conclusive evidence. More surprisingly, there is also no conclusive evidence that larger haircuts lead to stronger performance post restructuring. This is a hypothesis that we would have thought makes sense, but it is not borne out in the data. In summary, investors should buy the bonds when governments come to market after a default and not worry too much about whether regimes changed.

But what is the right trade going into the default? Investors follow two strategies. When defaults are looming but are not seen as imminent, investors hide in the very front end of the curve to clip coupons. Clipping coupons can be rewarding at a time when bond prices are already relatively low, such that every coupon that gets paid makes a big difference. However, when the actual default is very close, the credit curve flattens aggressively, mostly by the front end selling off. The reason is that restructurings usually pay the same USD price to all bonds on the curve, implying a highly inverted curve (though it is not fully obvious why every bond should be paid the same price). Bearish investors often position for such an inversion as the default gets closer.

But correctly timing the switch from owning the front end to positioning for a flatter curve is very difficult. Generally speaking, investors should be biased to clip coupons at the short end, as defaults almost always take longer than expected. One interesting statistic is the following: of the 16 events when the country-level ESBI index average price traded below 50 cents to the dollar at month end between 1996 and 2018, there were 10 defaults and 6 false alarms. Only three of the defaults happened within six months, and four took longer than two years. That is a lot of coupons to clip. It is therefore no surprise that on average, bonds perform well after having fallen below 50 cents, as demonstrated in Willer and Guarino (2019). This paper shows that this strong average return is driven by the countries that end up not defaulting, where prices recover very quickly after they fall below 50 cents. Countries that subsequently, but not immediately, default also contribute to the positive performance, as prices tend to recover before a second leg lower – which happens, on average, three months before the actual default. Prices then bottom one month after the default. The process of defaulting takes a long time.

---

[5]Borenztein and Panizza (2008) find that in a wider sample, the likelihood of a change of president or prime minister in the year of default or the following year is 50%, about double the probability during normal times.

TABLE 9.3 50 Cents Says: So What?

Defaults	Number
Within 6 months	3
Within 1 year	6
Total defaults	10
False alarms	6

Note: Monthly data from 1996 to 2018. Event triggers if the ESBI country index trades below 50c. A new event can trigger after a rally above 70c.
Source: Bloomberg, authors' calculations.

But how can we time the default better? When do we flip to a curve-inversion strategy? While it is tempting to watch FX reserves as an indicator of how close we are to default, it is much harder than it seems. Ernest Hemingway famously quipped about the two ways of going bankrupt: "Gradually. Then suddenly." The same processes are reflected in FX reserve levels. FX reserve losses can accelerate impressively in a very short time and may not provide much of a heads up. In the end, investors will probably be late in making the switch and may give back some of the coupons they clipped when the default comes close.

9.10   OF CREDIT CURVES

The curves of relatively good credits steepen as the credits get riskier. The idea is that a credit probably will not default in the short term, but if the current deterioration in credit quality lasts long enough, default risks will clearly rise. However, there is a point of deterioration in credit quality where the short end of the curve starts to reprice more as the risk of an imminent default moves up significantly.

Figure 9.19 illustrates this by showing the relationship between the slope of the curve (1s/10s on the y-axis) and a proxy for the default probability (one-year CDS) on the x-axis. We focus on four large EM where one-year CDS spreads moved above 500 bp during the 2008 episode: Argentina, Brazil, Turkey, and Venezuela. As can be seen, the level of one-year CDS where inversion took place was not the same. For Brazil, CDS spreads moved to above 600 bp, and the curve did not invert. But in Turkey, the curve inverted even when the one-year CDS was trading below 500 bp. Both Venezuela and Argentina inverted much closer to 1000 bp. The reason is that the slope is not just driven by default probabilities: it also has a risk premium component. If it is not a rise in the default probability, but a rise in the required risk premium, that causes the CDS spreads to widen, the curve is under less pressure to invert, because the risk premium at the longer end is presumably also going up – possibly by more than at the short end of the curve. Brazil in 2008 was an example of this. With little external debt and high FX reserves, Brazil was very unlikely to default within a year, and the spread widening was likely driven by extreme risk aversion in the midst of the Great Recession. From

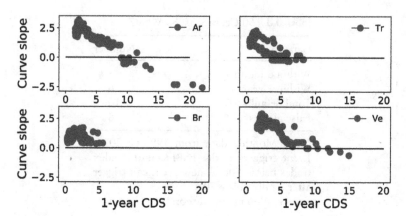

FIGURE 9.19 The Art of Curve Inversion.
Note: One-year CDS versus 1s/10s slope, both in percent.
Source: Bloomberg, authors' calculations.

a trading perspective, it is important to understand that a steepener is a bearish trade when the one-year CDS trades below 200 to 300 bp but flips to a bullish trade when spreads widen beyond 300 bp. We note that the threshold isn't precise, making curve inversion trades an art rather than a science.

The other question from a trading perspective is whether inversion is a warning signal that should be heeded. Just as an inverted IRS curve signals an impending easing cycle, an inverted credit cycle may warn of an impending default. However, to short a credit on an inversion is not a profitable rule. Defaults are simply too rare for this rule to work. Turkey did not default in 2008, for example. The similarity of the CDS curve to the IRS curve breaks down. An explanation is that central banks generally have no qualms about cutting rates and do so at the slightest provocation, whereas governments don't like to default and work extremely hard to avoid it. Having said that, defaults in the absence of an inversion are even rarer. As such, Brazil credit was an easier buy than Turkey back in 2008, as it never inverted. The Brazil one-year CDS trading above 500 bp likely reflected risk aversion rather than rising default risks. While it is impossible to compare the "true" default probabilities for Turkey and Brazil in 2008, we would be biased to sell CDS protection after spikes for countries that do not have an inverted curve.

9.11 EVALUATING VALUE

On an asset class level, the main way to find value in EM credit is relative to US credit, comparing HY with HY and IG with IG. However, as Figure 9.1 showed earlier in this chapter, the spread of EM HY over US HY is anything but easily tradable. In the late 1990s, the spread was very positive, driven by the EM crisis at the time; but then it narrowed over many years, falling into negative territory before accelerating even lower during the Great (US-centric) Recession. It then started to rise strongly back into positive territory, mostly as the US market recovered. This resulted in a very wide trading range indeed, and there is no quick mean-reversion in sight. Yes, spreads of >1000 are very cheap, and spreads of <-1000 are very expensive, but that range is too wide to be helpful. And it is very difficult, if not impossible, to true up ratings and duration for HY and EM over time, given how few EM sovereigns are traded, which means every single downgrade in EM leads to a major discontinuity in the spread. This is even before taking into account the changing industry composition of the US HY index. For example, during the oil bust in 2015, the fact that the oil component in the US HY index had previously increased sharply, made itself felt. US HY underperformed again, just because of this compositional change in the index.

The only obvious rule is to try to forecast the EM-US growth differential or, at least, distinguish between US and EM recessions, and overweight EM HY over US HY whenever EM growth improves *vis-à-vis* the US and vice versa. This is illustrated in Figure 9.20, which shows very clearly how to position in the big picture – if investors have any confidence in their forecasts of growth differentials in EM versus the US. Using Citi's EM and US economic surprise indexes and EM and US data change indexes offers a promising avenue for further research in our view.

Moving to the country level, the simplest way to think about valuation is to assume that the credit rating of a country captures all the relevant fundamentals. We can then compare the spread of countries with the same ranking to each other. However, given how few countries are in each rating bracket, EM investors tend to estimate a curve by translating credit rating to spread. Countries with a wider spread than this estimated curve are deemed to be cheap, and vice versa. The estimated curve is exponential, as the relationship between default probabilities and spreads to compensate for the case of default is exponential in nature, too. Figure 9.21 illustrates this exponential nature of spreads and ratings as of early 2019. Every dot represents the spread of a sovereign

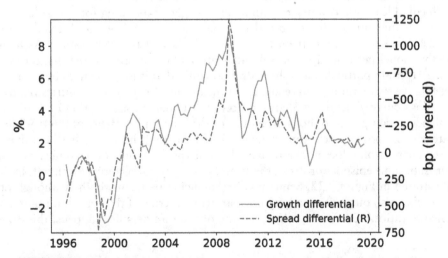

FIGURE 9.20 Spread of EM Versus US HY, Largely Driven by Growth Prospects.
Note: GDP growth of EM minus US versus spread EM HY – US HY.
Source: Bloomberg, authors' calculations. Index data courtesy of J.P. Morgan Chase & Co., copyright 2020, as of 31 December 2018.

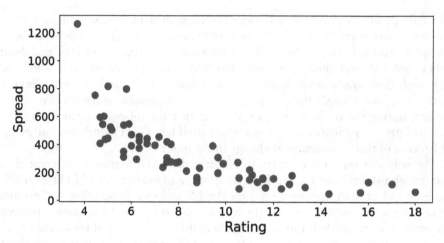

FIGURE 9.21   Ratings Summarize Fundamentals.
Note: The x-axis is the average credit rating, where positive and negative outlooks are half steps. Spreads are for country indexes in the 7- to 10-year maturity bucket as of 3 April 2019.
Source: Bloomberg, authors' calculations.

country's external bond index in the 7- to 10-year maturity bucket. There are half steps between each rating, too, to allow for positive or negative outlooks by rating agencies.

Ex ante, it is not obvious whether a country that screens as cheap against an estimated curve does so because the market is making a mistake, maybe driven by large flows, or whether the market foresees a change in rating. Alternatively, it could be that credit rating agencies do not capture all the pertinent fundamentals sufficiently well, which could lead to a country remaining cheap against its rating for a very long time. To see whether this rating vs spread methodology is useful, we backtested a simple model based on deviations from fair value as indicated by credit rating. As it turns out, the model performed quite well, alleviating our concerns on the margin (Willer et al. 2019b). In particular, a cash-neutral portfolio that is long the five cheapest countries relative to the ratings curve and short the five most expensive countries relative to the ratings curve generates a Sharpe ratio of 0.9 under the assumption of semiannual rebalancing, compared to the Sharpe ratio of the long-only strategy of 0.64. While the strategy has a positive beta (on average 0.7), as the longs have a higher beta than the shorts, the portfolio does not systematically underperform in periods of negative index returns. In some episodes of stress, the strategy actually outperforms meaningfully. This is illustrated in Figure 9.22. Semiannual rebalancing performs the best, though other time frames also outperform a long-only strategy in terms of returns – but not in terms of Sharpe ratios.[6] Of course, whenever one of the rare defaults happens, the strategy

---

[6]It is not fully obvious that we should compare a cash-neutral long-short strategy with index performance. After all, cash needs are much lower for our long-short strategy. We make the comparison because the strategy has a positive and relatively high beta; but often the benchmark for long-short strategies is Libor.

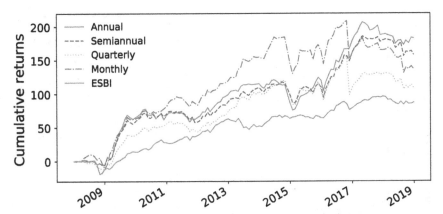

FIGURE 9.22 Valuation as a Basis for a Long-Short Strategy in EM Credit.
Note: Strategy returns of a cash-neutral portfolio that is long the five cheapest
countries relative to the ratings curve, and vice versa.
Source: Citi.

is likely to suffer. The good Sharpe ratio in the backtest really just highlights how rare
defaults have become and we would need some out-of-sample performance during the
negative part of a credit cycle before becoming fully comfortable with this strategy.

9.12 RATING AGENCIES: LATE, BUT MARKET MOVING

A related question is how to think more broadly about rating agencies. Rating agencies
are famous for reacting very slowly to changes in fundamentals. This is by design, since
their aim is to get the long-term credit cycle right rather than the short-term business
cycle. However, this also means rating agencies will only downgrade when the situation
is already relatively dire, which is at a time when markets have already priced in a
fair amount of the worsening fundamentals. In spite of this institutional latency, rating
agencies can be market moving. The reason is that many investors are highly ratings
conscious and may, for example, have mandates that are purely investment grade. This
is not as arbitrary a threshold as it seems. Since 1975, there has not been a single default
by a sovereign that was ranked IG one year prior to the default by S&P.[7] Given the
importance of the IG denomination, we first discuss ratings broadly and then focus in
more depth on rating moves that straddle the IG/HY divide.

We studied credit ratings at Citi using rating changes from January 2003 to December 2018 for 59 EM countries, and reproduce the key charts and findings from that study
here (Willer 2019). Figure 9.23 shows the median z-score of the spread change going
into an upgrade/downgrade on day 0. In the 60 days before day 0, spreads tighten into

---

[7]However, the history of ratings for structured products should give us some pause on betting
too strongly on the impossibility of defaults in IG space.

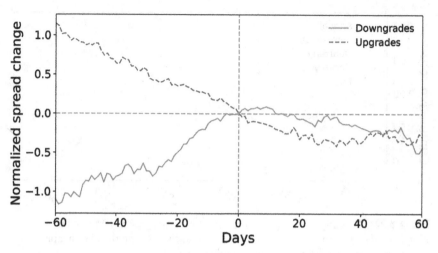

FIGURE 9.23   Ratings Follow the Price Action.
Source: Citi.

upgrades and widen into downgrades. Spreads then stabilize after the event. Downgrades have larger moves into the event than upgrades. This is in line with typical market behaviour: up on the staircase and down in the elevator. It is, of course, not clear whether the spreads move in anticipation of ratings action, or whether both ratings action and spread tightening are driven by the same (improving) underlying fundamentals, or whether rating agencies (subconsciously) become bullish due to euphoric price action. In any case, by the time the rating action occurs, the party is over, especially for downgrades. For upgrades, there is a modest follow-through, but probably not enough to position for it post event. This is in line with the common complaint from market participants that rating agencies just lag market developments. We also find that the impact of a laggard rating agency (most frequently Moody's, least frequently S&P) is less than the impact of the first mover. Doing the same analysis for outlook changes, which we would have expected to be more leading, gives very similar results. Overall, the findings suggest that investors should not react to ratings changes. It is too late.

For credits that lose IG, the moves are much larger – on average, 2.5 times as large, as illustrated in Figure 9.24. The second IG loss usually leads to a smaller sell-off than the first one. And, again, the overall pattern is very similar, in that spreads stabilize shortly after the event.

While the sell-off eventually resumes after the first IG loss, on average spreads stabilize first. These stabilizations are good entry points to short the credit again. The reason is that rating agencies display a herding behaviour similar to investors (though it is admittedly a tiny herd). For the 12 downgrades below IG since 2008 in sovereign EM credit, there was only one case where the second downgrade below IG did not occur within six months, as per Table 9.4. The sole exception was Bulgaria, where the split rating has been in place since December 2014. But on average, investors should position for a second downgrade in relatively short order.

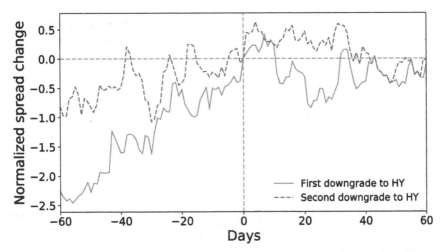

FIGURE 9.24 Buy When Passive Money Sold.
Source: Citi.

TABLE 9.4 Credit Rating Agencies Also Display Herding.

2nd downgrade below IG	No	perc
<1m	5	42%
<3m	8	67%
<6m	11	92%
<1yr	11	92%
Not at all (so far)	1	8%

Note: Percentage of issues downgraded below IG after the first downgrade below IG.
Source: Bloomberg, authors' calculations.

The second downgrade below IG is often the peak in negativity, even though it may take a few days for prices to truly bottom because a relevant subgroup of investors is benchmarked to an IG-only benchmark. This means such investors are forced to sell bonds upon the downgrade below IG (i.e. bonds of the "fallen angels"). EM sovereigns are less sensitive to this effect than EM corporates, which explains why the price action shown in Figure 9.24 is not more extreme for second downgrades. The reason is that EM-dedicated investors benchmarked to the J.P. Morgan EMBI index can hold both IG and non-IG paper in the same fund. Only cross-over investors may be forced out of an EM sovereign upon the loss of IG. EM corporates, on the other hand, have a higher share of cross-over holders.[8] Still, the same trading rule works for EM sovereigns and

---

[8]For US credit, the fallen-angel effect is actually much stronger because most investors are unable to hold both IG and HY paper. Therefore, one portfolio manager needs to sell, and another one subsequently needs to buy, which leads to increased downside price pressure.

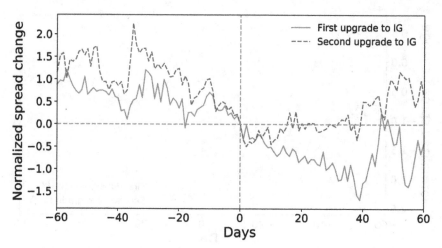

FIGURE 9.25   An Upgrade to IG is More Boring Than a Loss of IG.
Source: Citi.

EM corporates: on average, we give it two or three days after the second loss of IG, and then we buy the credit. Alternatively, investors can wait until the forced selling is done, which is typically the case at the end of the month following the second downgrade (which explains why the spread chart in Figure 9.25 revisits the wides for the second downgrade). This is another case where investors should be patient. Frontrunning this second downgrade can be deadly.

With respect to upgrades, a very similar dynamic unfolds. But once more, the bullish move into an upgrade to IG is not as sharp as the bearish move into an IG loss. Furthermore, there is strong follow-through on the bullish side, but only after the first upgrade to IG. On average, it pays to still go long after the first upgrade to IG. The second upgrade is usually peak bullishness, as can be seen in Figure 9.25.

In summary, we think traders should not react to most upgrades or downgrades. By the time they (upgrades or downgrades) happen, the market has already fully priced it. But a loss of IG is special. While the first rating agency downgrading below IG also leads to a pullback first, investors should use the pullback to position for the second downgrade below IG. The second downgrade is often peak negativity. Investors should buy a credit a few days after the second downgrade below IG. However, the effect is more pronounced for EM corporates than for sovereigns. On the upgrade side, the first upgrade to IG has good follow-through on the bullish side, and investors should go long into the second upgrade to IG. The second upgrade is on average the peak in short-term bullishness.

9.13   EXTERNAL VERSUS LOCAL

As we saw in Chapter 1, EM external debt has performed much better than EM local over the last decade. However, this has been largely due to FX. On an FX hedged basis, local EM bonds have had a higher IR than external debt. How should investors think about which asset class to favour?

On an unhedged basis, the decision to be in local or external is really quite simple. Whenever the USD weakens (strengthens), local bonds outperform (underperform). Given how difficult it is to forecast the USD, this is not overly helpful. But given our pointers in Chapter 4, we don't consider it hopeless to choose external versus local debt in line with expected FX moves.

So far, so obvious. But we also want to analyse how to choose between FX hedged local bonds (i.e. EM rates) and EM credit. It turns out that on an index level, EM credit can be relatively well explained by hedged EM local (with a beta of around 1.2) and US HY, as can be seen in Figure 9.26. So again, and not overly surprisingly, the most important factor to overweight external debt over FX hedged local debt is if investors are bullish on US credit. The bottom line is that investors, in the absence of a strong USD call, should favour external debt when bullish on US HY. Furthermore, all else being equal, cash-constrained investors should favour external debt, largely due to its higher beta.

Valuation can also be useful. The best way to compare local and external debt valuation is to use real rates, as has been shown by (Lam and Willer 2018). To arrive at the real rates spread, we use EM credit and deduct the US CPI from it. To approximate real rates for local rates in countries where linkers are not traded with any liquidity, we deduct the current CPI from nominal rates. Plotting the real rate differential between local debt and external debt for a basket of the most important EM suggests that mean reversion is very high. Figure 9.27 shows that the real rate spread peaks at 100–150 bp. On the lower end, there does not appear to be an obvious floor that investors can use to take the other side. Instead, the rule of thumb is that whenever external outperforms local by 4%, beta adjusted, over rolling 12 months, it is time for a reversal. Once

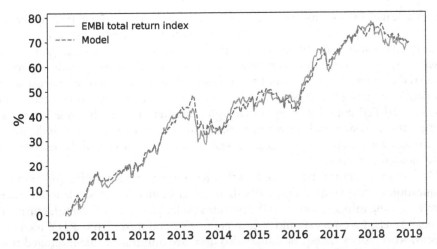

FIGURE 9.26 EM Credit is Mostly Explained by Hedged Local and US HY.
Source: Bloomberg, authors' calculations. Index data courtesy of J.P. Morgan Chase & Co., copyright 2020, as of 31 December 2018.

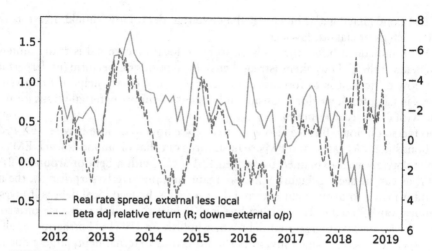

FIGURE 9.27   Real Rate Differentials are Mean-Reverting.
Note: Calculated for Brazil, Mexico, Colombia, South Africa, Turkey, and Indonesia.
Source: Citi, Bloomberg, authors' calculations.

investors have taken the direction of the USD and US HY into account, valuation on a real rates basis as well as beta-adjusted performance differentials should be used to choose between local and external debt.

9.14   SUMMARY

In summary, we note that just as in local markets, the alpha is more in trading the credit cycle, rather than positioning for structural tightening of the asset class. But unlike in FX, carry still works in credit. Given that the key is to avoid credit longs going into US recessions, the time to get out of credit longs in general and the carry trade in particular is when the US curve first inverts and subsequently disinverts. This is the correct strategy for a garden variety US recession, which is mostly driven by US-centric factors. Only in the case of Fed cuts driven by an emerging market crisis is this rule too slow. In that case, the inversion itself serves as a sell signal. Alternatively, the risk indicator that we introduced in Chapter 4 also keeps investors on the right side of the market, as do simple momentum rules.

On a more structural basis, we find that leveraging up safe credits (IG credit, and low-duration bonds) creates higher IRs than riskier bonds. It is possible to improve on this rule by using information from the business cycle. When the US manufacturing ISM is at peak levels, investors should reduce credit risk and move from a HY focus to an IG focus. Real money investors should also decrease duration, while leveraged traders can position for a curve inversion.

On the valuation front, the spread between EM HY and US HY is mostly driven by changes in growth differentials. On an individual credit basis, even simple valuation models, which assume that credit ratings capture all the relevant fundamentals, show some promise in terms of generating alpha. When it comes to credit selection, we build on the methodology of Ray Dalio, which uses a combination of weak fundamentals and exuberant markets to get a head start on the market. Alternatively, a focus on commodity shocks is useful. Pegged commodity producers underperform during oil price declines.

In terms of credit-specific events, we found that IMF packages typically work, though not necessarily on day 1. The first new bond issue coming out of a default is almost always a buy and outperforms the index. In terms of ratings actions, the evidence suggests that by the time a change happens, it is mostly in the price. However, attainment or loss of IG matters: investors should go short on a pull-back after the first IG loss, and go long after the second loss of IG. Investors should also go long after the first upgrade to IG, until the second upgrade happens. The easiest trade is to buy EM corporate credits after the second loss of the IG rating.

On the choice between external and local bonds, it is common sense to choose external whenever a strong USD is expected. On a FX hedged basis, investors should prefer external to the extent that they expect US HY to do well. Valuation, proxied by real rate differentials between local and external bonds of the same country, is highly mean reverting and therefore also shows some promise for alpha generation.

CHAPTER 10

Portfolio Construction

10.1 SMARTER WITH BENCHMARKS

There has been a fair amount of criticism with respect to fixed-income benchmarks in recent years. The main argument is that market capitalization–weighted fixed-income indexes blunt the power of the bond vigilantes. This could be the case, as increased debt issuance goes hand in hand with increased index weights. Higher index weights force indexed investors to add the most money to bonds of countries where debt is rising the fastest. This makes it easier for profligate governments to avoid necessary fiscal adjustments. But, of course, the adjustments are only postponed; and when they finally occur, bondholders own more bonds of that particular country than they arguably should. This may hamper index performance. While the same phenomenon exists in market capitalization–weighted equity indexes, investors don't object to allocating more to successful companies that issue more stock to fund growth, or where the value of the stock goes up due to improved earnings. For debt, it is the other way around. Successful countries could, at least in theory, reduce the debt stock, and investors would therefore hold less of it, while less successful countries' weights would increase.

One obvious way to mitigate how much debt a particular country can sell is to limit the weight of any particular index member, either by introducing a hard ceiling for the weights or by adding enough countries to keep weights for any country relatively low. Both strategies are employed by index providers. The JP Morgan benchmark for local markets, GBI-EM Global Diversified, has a 10% cap for country weights. Furthermore, the number of constituents has been slowly rising, though the index remains quite concentrated. One way to assess whether adding more countries improves performance is to compare the GBI-EM Global Diversified (pre China inclusion) with the GBI-EM Broad, which includes China and India at 10% each. This is an interesting test case, as the sheer size of the Chinese and Indian debt markets is such that even at weights of 10% index-linked assets do not make a major difference to the two issuers. At the same time, weights for smaller countries, where the index-linked assets could make a difference, are much lower. It turns out that the IR of the GBI-EM Broad, at 0.73, is slightly higher than that of the GBI-EM Global Diversified, at 0.68 (for the period from 2003 to 2018).

Of course, the comparison is heavily driven by the performance of India and China. A better way to limit the impact of any given country would be to weight the index

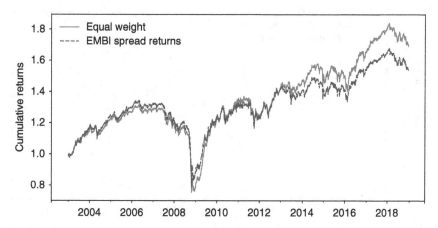

FIGURE 10.1 Equality Rules – in Bull Markets.
Source: Bloomberg, authors' calculations. Index data courtesy of J.P. Morgan
Chase & Co., copyright 2020, as of 31 December 2019.

constituents equally. Focusing on external debt, Figure 10.1 shows the performance of
the EMBI and the equal weighted EMBI. The equal weighted EMBI has clearly outperformed, and very consistently so since the bottom of the 2008 crisis. However, to
essentially go overweight the smaller credits very much looks like a bull market strategy. Going into the 2008 crisis, as well as during the crisis, the equal weighted index
underperformed. The IR over the full sample still puts the equal weighted index ahead,
but not by as much as hoped for. The IR of the equal weighted index in terms of excess
spread returns was 0.49 over the period, while the IR of EMBI came in at 0.38.

In any case, for most funds, it is just not realistic to implement equal weights. Even
relatively small funds would very quickly run into liquidity problems if they aimed
to buy up a sufficient amount of bonds in the less liquid credits. Furthermore, equal
weighting does not protect investors from overleveraged small countries, where equal
weights could actually result in increasing exposures.

Another alternative that has been proposed is to weigh credits by GDP. Doing so
would likely mitigate the problem of excessive weights for over-leveraged smaller countries that equal weights can create. A GDP weighting would create bond indexes that are
closer to equity indexes in spirit, as successful, i.e. faster-growing, economies increase
their index weights, similar to what happens with successful stocks. This approach
would also limit liquidity constraints, as larger countries tend to have more debt outstanding. Sadly, GDP weights do not work in terms of generating improved performance. The reason is that GDP weights are almost the opposite of equal weights. Given
that an equal weighted index outperforms, it is not surprising that a GDP weighted
index underperforms. Small countries tend to outperform, at least during bull markets, probably for reasons similar to why US small cap stocks have outperformed US
large cap stocks in the past. Smaller countries are often less diversified and riskier and
therefore carry a risk premium that, on average, investors should harness. Therefore,
GDP weighted indexes lag the EMBI, whose weights are closer to equal weighting

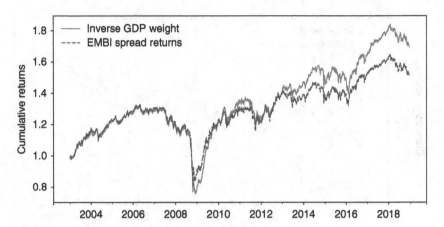

FIGURE 10.2   GDP Weights: Good Idea, Bad Performance.
Source: Bloomberg, authors' calculations. Index data courtesy of J.P. Morgan
Chase & Co., copyright 2020, as of 31 December 2019.

than to GDP weighting. If anything, investors should be biased to inverse GDP weightings. Figure 10.2 shows the EMBI next to an index we constructed with inverse GDP weights.[1] After briefly lagging the EMBI at the bottom of the 2008 crisis, our inverse GDP weighted index has mostly outperformed ever since.

The next step would be to investigate rules for index construction that are smarter than something as simple as a GDP rule. For example, debt/GDP could be used to weight countries, which might theoretically be the best way to get around being too exposed to overleveraged countries. However, we do not have high hopes that such indexes will perform well, either. The same issues that plague the GDP-weighted indexes will likely also hold back indexes with weights based on the soundness of the various countries. Safety only pays during short periods, when markets aggressively re-price to the downside, but not over the medium term. The risk premium that riskier countries carry on average more than compensates for adverse outcomes. This is similar to our finding in Chapter 4. The current account factor, which is to our mind the single most important factor in terms of the "safety" of a currency, typically loses money, too.

Overall, we think the best way to go about this is to move to truly smart indexes, which could be based on some of our rules laid out in the previous chapters. For example, the simple ratings-based valuation tool discussed in Chapter 9 holds some promise in this regard, but some of the more complex rules could also be implemented as an index. Of course, the final result will be the same regardless of whether fund managers use the rules to outperform the index or whether the rules are embedded in a smarter index product.

---

[1]For our exercise, we set the weight for country i, w_i, as follows: $w_i = \dfrac{\ln \frac{1}{gdp_i}}{\sum_{i=1}^{n} \ln \frac{1}{gdp_i}}$, where gdp_i is the GDP of country i in the period prior to the reweighting.

10.2 FRONTIER MARKETS AT THE FRONTIER

Frontier markets refer to the less developed capital markets in the emerging world. These countries do not meet the market microstructure requirements (for example, regular issuance of benchmark bonds) or liquidity requirements to be added to the main EM benchmarks. These markets are also riskier, partly due to this lower liquidity, but often also due to weaker fundamentals. They are included in indexes followed by far fewer assets under management than the main benchmarks. Usually, frontier markets issue external debt, as local issuance is harder to place for weaker credits. One important index for frontier credits is the JPMorgan NEXGEM. The index is roughly composed of 40% credits from Africa, 25% from Latin America, 20% from Asia, 10% from Europe, and 5% from the Middle East. It is mostly B rated. This is very different from the EMBI, where the most common rating is BBB, and where Latam is much more heavily weighted than Africa.

Frontier markets are often used to generate alpha by adding them as off-benchmark positions to the portfolio. The case for increased alpha is twofold. First, over the long run, frontier markets outperform, given that there is a risk premium included in asset prices that can be harvested. Second, whenever a frontier market has developed sufficiently to be added to the EMBI benchmark, investors benefit from a significant index inclusion rally. Figure 10.3 illustrates that NEXGEM has outperformed EMBI very significantly since 2003. However, the index also had a more severe drawdown during the 2008 crisis. NEXGEM is clearly highly correlated with EMBI and may just be a higher-beta version of EMBI. Indeed, the IR is only slightly higher, at 1.42, compared to 1.38 for EMBI. To buy NEXGEM countries for an EMBI benchmark is the ultimate bull market trade.

But the high correlation to the EMBI also has advantages. When it is difficult to sell the NEXGEM due to illiquidity during downturns, the more liquid EMBI can be

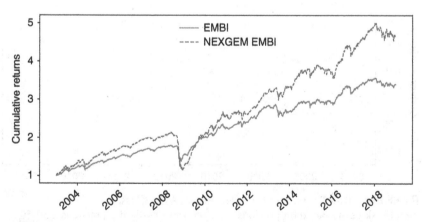

FIGURE 10.3 Fun at the Frontier – While the Music Plays.
Source: Bloomberg. Index data courtesy of J.P. Morgan Chase & Co., copyright 2020, as of 31 December 2019.

used for hedging. This is reassuring, as a common perception is that frontier markets are very difficult to hedge. While that may be true for individual markets, a basket of frontier markets clearly can be hedged quite easily. In addition, NEXGEM at times lags EMBI. For example, in 2009, investors could have bought NEXGEM at the lows at a time when the bottom in EMBI was already in.

10.3   PORTFOLIO ALLOCATION WITHOUT MARKOWITZ

It is well known that the Markowitz mean variance framework does not work overly well in practice. It commonly produces corner solutions that are difficult (and risky) to implement. Even adding constraints to the optimization often leads to suboptimal returns. One of the problems is that return forecasts are extremely unreliable: a problem the Black-Litterman models also suffer from. For these reasons, many practitioners ditch return forecasting and focus mostly on the covariance matrix. The risk-parity framework for portfolio construction is one example of this approach that is currently riding high. In its most basic form, risk parity allocates the same risk to all positions in the portfolio, mostly by leveraging up safer assets. Risk is here mostly measured by volatility of returns. But more recently, returns for risk parity have been sub-par, raising the question of whether it should be applied to EM or not. Figure 10.4 shows returns from applying the risk-parity framework to the GBI-EM and the EMBI, where we weigh each index in line with its realized volatility over the previous three months. While the results are not terrible, we note that a simple 50-50 blend of GBI-EM and EMBI outperforms. The same is true for risk parity more broadly. While the returns for global risk-parity funds have been attractive, a blended portfolio of equities and interest rates

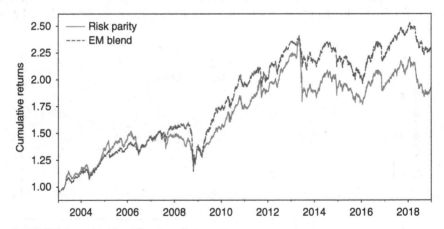

FIGURE 10.4   Risk Parity: Not Up to Par Across Asset Classes.
Note: Risk parity based on previous three months of volatility; blend is a 50-50 mix of EMBI and GBI-EM.
Source: Bloomberg, authors' calculations. Index data courtesy of J.P. Morgan Chase & Co., copyright 2020, as of 31 December 2019.

would have outperformed. It is not that easy to beat the old adage of 60% equities, 40% fixed income, certainly in a bull market. Overall, there are clear benefits from combining local and external debt in one portfolio, but we are not sure that the risk-parity framework is the best way to determine the weights. Instead we point readers to section 9.13 to determine which asset class to overweight.

We next analyse several other contenders for portfolio allocation and apply these techniques to EMFX. We pick EMFX because it is the most liquid of the EM asset classes under consideration, and also one of the more volatile. This allows for an independent currency overlay portfolio sitting on top of the EM portfolio. Figure 10.6 shows the performance of three contenders benchmarked against the GBI-EM currency index. First we apply a simple risk-parity strategy (equal volatility, again using three-month trailing data), second an equal-weighted strategy (each currency with an identical weight), and finally hierarchical risk parity (HRP).

What is HRP? The basic idea is that estimation errors in the variance-covariance matrix can be reduced by putting a structure (hierarchy) on the matrix. As laid out by Marcos López de Prado (2016), this is how it works: The first step involves clustering the assets under consideration into several groups based on their correlation structure. For EMFX, this is done in Figure 10.5. As can be seen, Poland and Hungary are placed together, with Israel close to that group but not quite as close as the former two. Similarly, South Korea and Singapore are grouped together, with Thailand one node removed, etc. The results are quite intuitive in grouping fundamentally similar currencies together. In the next step, the variance-covariance matrix is reorganized so that similar investments are placed together. In the third step, the portfolio allocation is made based on the cluster covariance matrix.

Figure 10.6 shows the result. In return space, HRP outperforms significantly. This is followed by equal weights with roughly similar performance. The benchmark

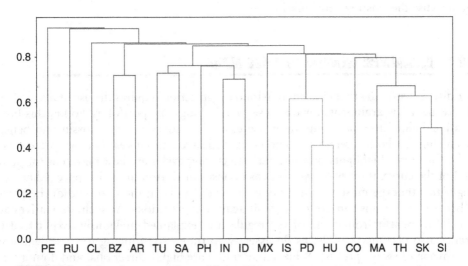

FIGURE 10.5 A Dendogram to Group Them All.
Source: Bloomberg, authors' calculations.

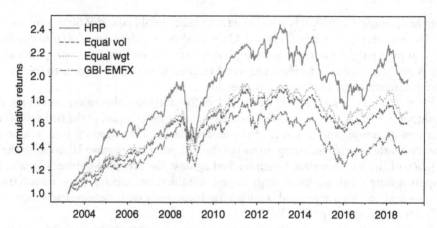

FIGURE 10.6 In EMFX, Risk Parity has the Highest IR.
Source: Bloomberg, authors' calculations. Index data courtesy of J.P. Morgan Chase & Co., copyright 2020, as of 31 December 2019.

GBI-EM currency index performs much worse. In terms of IRs, it turns out that the equal-volatility approach performs the best, with an IR of 1.31, followed by HRP with 1.23 and equal weight with 1.14. The actual GBI-EMFX index has an IR of only 0.61. In currency space, risk parity is therefore rehabilitated. We also note, though, that the three competing strategies have additional currencies added to the universe that are not part of the GBI-EM currency index (as GBI-EM weights are driven by bond markets, not currency markets), demonstrating that more diversification is also beneficial. It is clear to us that there are meaningfully better ways to construct an EMFX portfolio than to use the existing benchmarks.

10.4 DERIVATIVES: WEAPONS OF MASS ALPHA

We also feel strongly that efficient portfolio construction requires the use of derivatives. There are a few arguments for their use even in long-only portfolios. So far, this book has highlighted the most important use case: derivatives make it possible to benefit from shifts in both interest rate curves as well as credit curves. On the interest rate side, Chapter 6 highlights that interest rate cutting cycles are best played at the short end of the curve, if investors are not cash-constrained. And in credit space, Chapter 9 highlights that the most significant opportunities can be at the short end of the curve, whenever sovereigns can avoid a default against expectations. As such, derivatives are crucial to benefit from some of the regularities explained previously. Explicit curve trades also become possible, as do asset swap trades (positioning for a widening or narrowing of swap spreads). While curve trades are highly directional and do not tend to diversify portfolio risk very efficiently, swap spread trades provide a more diversified source of alpha. Asset swap spreads are highly mean reverting and often have a weak directional component. Adding a mostly uncorrelated earnings stream to the portfolio will be beneficial.

In addition, there are a few other benefits. First, derivatives can be more tax efficient. Whenever capital gains or withholding taxes are in place, as there are or have been in Brazil, Colombia, and Indonesia, total return swaps can at times mitigate such tax liabilities. Second, in many markets, derivatives are more liquid than bonds. To the extent that many of our trading rules require more frequent trading than the average long-only account typically engages in, the use of derivatives will be crucial to limit transaction costs. In many cases, it is possible to replicate the behaviour of a given country index, consisting of all of a country's issued bonds with a maturity above one year, with a few interest rate swaps.

The higher liquidity in IRS markets versus bonds also allows for the full separation and independent expression of interest rate and FX views. This can overcome the suboptimal approach where investors are always long bonds and then use FX hedges whenever they turn bearish on EM. While the latter strategy works well either when shocks are big enough (think 2008) or for EM where rates are highly sensitive to FX, they work decidedly less well for the more developed EM where rates can sell off at the same time FX performs well, and vice versa. More and more countries will reach a more developed stage over time, so it is crucial to separate FX and rates bets to a larger extent. While rates will never be as liquid as FX, the use of IRS is a step in the right direction.

10.5 ESG AND EM: NOT FAIR!

ESG investing is defined as investing with environmental, social, and governance (ESG) concerns in mind, at least alongside the traditional financial indicators. ESG investing has become a hot topic in recent years as investors have become more conscious of the negative long-term consequences of only focusing on financial indicators. As of the end of 2018, assets managed with at least some ESG component are thought to have risen to USD 12 trillion in the US alone, or almost 25% of the total assets under management in the US financial industry. It is therefore not surprising that an entire ESG ecosystem has developed. Asset managers are offering ESG funds, index providers have started to provide ESG benchmarks, research firms are providing ESG indicators and rankings for assets, and academics are busy trying to prove that ESG investing is making money – the latter with some success, even though the suspicion must be that supportive results are more keenly reported than negative ones.[2] For what it is worth, in EM, the JPM ESG index is performing very similarly to its non-ESG cousin, as can be seen in Figure 10.7. To us, this is actually good news, as ESG could also have underperformed in an EM context. After all, there could be a trade-off between growth and ESG goals, and EM are famously highly growth-sensitive assets. But it turns out that ESG is not costing investors any money. Investors get a free lunch but do not get paid to eat.

---

[2]For a meta study, see Gunnar et al. (2013).

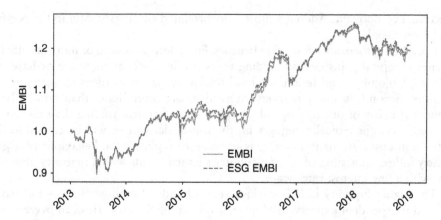

FIGURE 10.7   ESG Index with Identical Performance to Non-ESG.
Source: Bloomberg. Index data courtesy of J.P. Morgan Chase & Co., copyright 2020, as of 31 December 2019.

In terms of asset classes, equities have been leading the charge into the ESG future. This is mostly the case because ESG categories can be better defined for firms than for countries and data availability is better. Furthermore, the opportunity set is less negatively impacted when implementing zero weights in equities than in EM sovereign assets, given that there are more than 100,000 publicly listed equities but fewer than 100 investible countries.

Table 10.1 lists some of the more common criteria, as suggested by the CFA Institute in conjunction with the UN-supported PRI (see Orsagh et al. 2018). While this (and similar) lists are fairly intuitive, there is a question of how investors should weigh the various ESG indicators. The temptation is to go with equal (or unspecified) weightings, partly to avoid thorny ethical questions about the importance of various indicators. But giving all ESG indicators the same weight is unlikely to be optimal, and letting data availability dictate the focus of the ESG effort is also undesirable. Many ESG factors are just proxies for what investors truly care about, and not necessarily great proxies at that. In the end, how to weigh various ESG indicators is highly subjective, and it is unlikely that one size fits all.

But one criterion that does make sense regardless of individual value systems is whether the behaviours involve an externality. An *externality* means the country in question does not fully bear the cost of its behaviours, as some of it is borne by other countries. For example, using cheap but dirty energy resources may boost growth, which the country benefits from; but some of the cost of the resulting pollution is borne by other countries (through climate change), and only part is borne by the local population. CO_2 emissions are a good example where part of the cost of pollution is borne by other countries. If there are no externalities, the hope is that over time, maybe as countries get richer, ESG compliance will improve by itself because the population will want to avoid the environmental cost. But if there are important externalities, incentives will never be in place to fully comply with a stricter ESG regime. It could

TABLE 10.1 ESG: So Many Targets.

Governance issues	Social issues	Environmental issues
Institutional strength	Human rights	Effects of climate change
Corruption	Education and human capital	Water resources and pollution
Regime stability	Health levels	Biodiversity
Rule of law	Political freedoms	Energy resources and mgmt
Security	Demographic change	Ecosystem quality
Regulatory effectiveness	Employment levels	Air pollution
Accounting standards	Social exclusion and poverty	Natural disasters
Freedom of the press	Life expectancy	Natural resources
Political and civil liberties	Trust in society/institutions	
	Crime and safety	
	Food security	

Source: Orsagh et al. (2018).

therefore be argued for investors to put a higher weight on ESG criteria that involve externalities.

Another way around the question of how to best construct an overall ESG score is to just not do it! We have explored that topic in Willer et al. (2019c), on which the following paragraphs are based. In the piece, we argue that focusing on an aggregated score allows some poor ESG behaviours to be hidden behind the averages, and that company management or governments can be more easily incentivized to change behaviours if, for each individual target, there is a clear reward. We therefore propose for ESG funds to focus on a single ESG component. Suppliers could offer a whole suite of single-factor ESG funds. Then the weighting of the ESG factors would be the AUM of the relevant strategy. Another benefit of this approach is that it would increase transparency for investors. After all, some ESG factors lead to positive alpha, while some lead to negative alpha. Using individual ESG factors over time makes it clear just how much an ESG factor costs in terms of performance and allows investors to consider how many private gains they are willing to give up for social gains.

For EM, the ESG wave is somewhat of a mixed blessing. Clearly, EM do not excel at many of the criteria. This is largely the case because earlier stages of development are often characterized by more pollution, worse labour force and product safety conditions, and generally weaker corporate governance. The amount of growth that countries are willing to forego in return for less pollution or increased product safety usually depends on how wealthy the country is. Therefore, high ESG scores are significantly positively correlated with how wealthy a country is.

But applying the standards of a country with a GDP per head of USD 50,000 to a country with a GDP per head of USD 10,000 raises the question of whether it is fair toward the poorer countries. After all, it may lead to capital allocation decisions that favour richer countries, even though investments in poorer countries may be more urgent than in developed countries. This question is even more important as EM, with some justification, complain that the more severe environmental legislation in DM is what drove dirty industries to set up shop in EM in the first place. Part of the loss of US manufacturing jobs to countries like China is presumably a reaction to expenses related to increased worker protection and environmental standards in the US. As such, we feel that the environmental measures used to rank countries along the ESG criteria should be adjusted for where a country is in its development. GDP per head may be the most appropriate measure to do that.

In the Citi piece, we therefore adjusted CO_2 emissions for the stage of development. Figure 10.2 reproduces a ranking of the worst offenders in terms of CO_2 production per USD of GDP, and a ranking by residual when regressing that number on GDP per head, (and GDP per head squared, given that the relationship is not linear: extremely poor countries are presumably not producing much CO_2).

We also show a third ranking. To improve incentives for policy makers, it is likely more efficient to focus on changes rather than levels. This rewards countries that invest enough in clean energy to use less CO_2 for the next unit of GDP than for the previous one. We therefore add a ranking for countries with respect to the change in the residual of our regression. For all three rankings, rank 1 is the country with the highest emissions.

In terms of outright CO_2 per unit of GDP, the median rank of the DM is 51, while the median rank of EM is 36. DM are much cleaner than EM and, unsurprisingly, the 13 most emitting countries are all EM. However, EM rank better than DM when controlling for stages of development. Using the residuals from our regression on GDP per head, the median developed market moves from rank 51 to 19. This indicates that more DM are among the high CO_2 emitters after our adjustment, making the median developed market a heavier emitter than the median emerging market. Interestingly, the US now makes it into the worst 10 countries and scores worse than China. When focusing on improvements, i.e. the change of our regression residual, DM come in at median rank 35, compared to the EM median rank of 42. Interestingly, some of the worst polluters have improved the most, including Ukraine, South Africa, and China. This should be rewarded by ESG-centric funds.

One big problem is the timeliness of the indicators. Lags can be very long. For example, with respect to CO_2 emissions, the data is yearly, and the publication lag for many countries is another year. Countries that perform well may not be immediately rewarded by improved ESG scores. Therefore, a big data approach should be investigated to generate more timely ESG scores. For example, many of the data listed in Table 10.1 could presumably be proxied by intelligent use of natural language processing of the main three or four local newspapers, potentially combined with internet searches.[3] More timely indicators would make it easier for investors to focus on changes in ESG scores, rather than just on levels.

In summary, implementing ESG in EM fixed income, rather than EM equities, has some unique challenges. In Table 10.2, ESG is likely going to be a force that leads to better outcomes, but careful analysis is necessary to make sure that countries most in need of capital are not shut out. From an investor's point of view, more thought

---

[3] See Rink et al. (2019) for an evaluation of some external AI ESG data providers. However, we note that the vendors under study focus much more on equities than sovereigns, and lead to performance enhancements in DM, but not in EM.

TABLE 10.2 EM is Better at ESG When Poverty-Adjusted.

	$CO_2/$ GDP 2017	$CO_2/$ GDP Rank	Res	Chg		$CO_2/$ GDP 2017	$CO_2/$ GDP Rank	Res	Chg
Trinidad	0.96	1	1	17	Turkey	0.21	40	31	2
Mongolia	0.71	2	12	18	Holland	0.21	41	15	50
S Africa	0.67	3	13	78	Azerbdjn	0.21	42	42	76
Kazakh	0.61	4	7	13	Pakistan	0.20	43	69	14
Ukraine	0.61	5	27	79	Gabon	0.20	44	43	70
Bahrain	0.55	6	3	71	Hungary	0.19	45	30	6
China	0.51	7	18	75	Armenia	0.19	46	61	58
Russia	0.49	8	11	34	Croatia	0.19	47	35	60
Uzbek	0.47	9	41	49	Angola	0.18	48	67	77
Oman	0.45	10	6	74	Namibia	0.18	49	57	56
Saudi	0.40	11	5	51	Romania	0.18	50	36	3
Canada	0.38	12	8	32	Spain	0.18	51	25	8
Belarus	0.38	13	29	20	Indonesia	0.17	52	54	16
Vietnam	0.37	14	51	66	Phillip.	0.17	53	63	11
Australia	0.37	15	9	61	Italy	0.17	54	28	27
Kuwait	0.36	16	4	69	El Salv	0.17	55	64	33
Iraq	0.33	17	32	25	Brazil	0.17	56	48	45
Georgia	0.32	18	44	1	Ghana	0.15	57	70	4
Jamaica	0.32	19	49	48	Belize	0.15	58	65	59
Qatar	0.32	20	2	5	DomRep	0.15	59	47	46
Poland	0.31	21	20	29	UK	0.14	60	24	53
Jordan	0.30	22	50	68	Cote d'I	0.14	61	74	12
US	0.29	23	10	55	Peru	0.14	62	55	54
Suriname	0.29	24	39	40	Guatam.	0.14	63	66	57
Lebanon	0.28	25	40	72	Norway	0.14	65	14	10
Bahamas	0.27	26	21	52	Panama	0.13	66	38	22
Bolivia	0.27	27	60	43	France	0.13	67	26	21
Japan	0.27	28	17	36	Kenya	0.13	68	77	31
Egypt	0.25	29	46	63	Camern	0.12	69	76	47
Honduras	0.25	30	68	39	Colombia	0.12	70	56	67
Argentina	0.25	31	34	62	Paraguay	0.11	71	59	15
Senegal	0.25	32	71	7	Sweden	0.11	72	23	44
Morocco	0.23	33	58	23	CostaR	0.11	73	53	28
Mexico	0.23	34	37	65	Uruguay	0.10	74	45	26
Ecuador	0.23	35	52	73	Sri Lanka	0.10	75	62	19
Tajikistan	0.22	36	73	24	Nigeria	0.09	76	72	42
Chile	0.22	37	33	64	Ethiopia	0.08	77	79	9
Germany	0.21	38	16	37	Switzerld	0.08	78	19	35
NZ	0.21	39	22	30	Zambia	0.08	79	78	41

Source: Citi.

needs to be given to how to generate better behaviours while keeping the financial (opportunity) costs as low as possible. Controlling for the stage of development and focusing on changes rather than levels will get us closer.

10.6 SUMMARY

There is a case to improve the indexes that asset managers are benchmarked to. Adding more countries to the index is preferable to fewer index constituents, but as an asset class, frontier markets are just a more volatile version of the existing benchmark. Equal-weighting countries is preferable for small investors, but larger investors will quickly reach liquidity limits, at least in bonds and credit, if not in FX. Smarter index rules are possible, but GDP weighting does not generate alpha. Our (biased) suggestion is to use some of the rules proposed in this book for smart index construction.

Given the difficulty of generating return forecasts, we eschew Black Litterman for risk-parity approaches. We find that a simple 50-50 weighting for external and local debt performs better than risk parity, though. Moving to FX, given more binding liquidity constraints in bonds, we apply HRP as well, and compare it to simple risk parity, equal weights, and the existing benchmark. Here, risk parity outperforms in IR terms, followed by HRP. But all three approaches outperform the benchmark, suggesting that portfolio construction can be instrumental in generating alpha.

We end the chapter advocating for the use of derivatives as tools for alpha generation and for using ESG sensibly when it comes to EM. To us, this means offering single-factor ESG funds that could focus on factors that involve an externality. We also advise adjusting ESG rankings for the stage of development of the constituent countries and focusing on changes in ESG scores rather than levels, in order to improve incentives for policy makers.

CHAPTER 11

The (Near) Future: Big Data, Machine Learning, and What if There Are No Emerging Markets Left

The investment industry is currently in the middle of a gold rush. Big data, machine learning (ML) and artificial intelligence (AI) are the topics du jour, and fund management companies expect salvation from the onslaught of passive investment by investing in big data and ML. Of course, even though the two topics are often used in the same sales pitch, the two concepts are very different. Big data is almost certainly real, but not revolutionary. ML may be revolutionary, but the pitfalls are legendary. Here we discuss the application of these concepts to EM fixed-income investing and where we see the field developing.

Another topic we address is whether one day, all EM will be developed, leading to an extinction event for EM.

11.1 BIG DATA IS COMING TO FIXED INCOME

In our view, big data is largely an arms race where only the first mover earns rents for some time before those rents get competed away. For late movers, all that happens is that they incur additional costs to implement the innovation that the leaders already implemented. And by then, the additional alpha is gone. Of course, not implementing big data solutions may mean deteriorating performance, and our characterization certainly does not mean that organizations can afford to not implement big data solutions. They clearly have to do it, and doing it earlier is better than doing it later, to at least participate in the alpha generation that is available to the early movers. But in steady state, big data is unlikely to be the salvation many seek, especially after taking into account the considerable costs to buy data and reinvent investment processes. The longer-lasting benefit may accrue to the providers of the infrastructure for the big data bonanza, rather than to the investment firms who use those tools. Think selling shovels rather than digging for gold.

Given this backdrop, investment professionals in fixed income have been lucky. Or, to be more precise, organizations that typically do not have it in their DNA to be first movers have been lucky. The reason is that big data has so far been much more impactful for the equity business and much less so for fixed income. After all, at this stage it is much easier to crawl the web to forecast the earnings for a company with a large digital footprint than it is to forecast the NFP number with web crawlers. One reason is that for many firms, everything they do is online – and online is easier to digitally measure than the offline part of the economy. Furthermore, for equities, earnings are presumably doing a relatively good job of describing the underlying fundamentals (though in the world of non-GAAP (generally accepted accounting principles) earnings this is not quite as clear as it should be). Whether most government statistics are a fair characterization of the underlying fundamentals is much less clear. The NFP number, for example, gets heavily adjusted. Not just seasonality adjustments, but also the infamous birth-death adjustment, can lead to very large swings in the published number that would be impossible to pick up by, for example, running a large survey of firms in order to estimate the likely NFP number. And even if someone designed a superior survey to the NFP, it would not matter: the market has been trained to trade the NFP number, not an arguably superior private sector estimate – which is currently already provided by ADP, the largest payroll processor in the US. In our view, all these arguments help to explain why big data has not yet been as impactful in fixed income as it has been in equities. Having said that, big data has arrived in fixed income markets, too, and will likely keep gaining mind and wallet share relatively fast. One accelerator could be that government statistics itself will rely more on big data over time to improve accuracy. It therefore behooves fixed income investors to get ready!

Whether big data is coming earlier for EM fixed income or DM fixed income is less clear. Some EM are woefully behind in online and sensor penetration, which makes the generation of big data more difficult. But some EM leapfrog the classic offline infrastructure and go straight to an online setup. And some countries have natural advantages in terms of the generation of big data. China not only has 1.4 billion people; it also has far fewer constraints in terms of privacy laws, which makes it much easier to harness big data. At the same time, given the fact that Chinese government data is notoriously unreliable, even more so than is the case in the US, there is a higher likelihood that the market reacts to privately generated economic statistics – which is not necessarily true for the US. As such, traditional EM fixed-income managers are only half lucky. Yes, they have been more shielded than equity fund managers; but big data usage is accelerating in EM fixed income, and maybe even faster than in DM fixed income, at least for some countries.

So where should investors start? To our mind, there are two important investments that managers must make. First, investment managers have to acquire the data. The data acquisition can happen in house, for example, by creating a unit that engages in web scraping. Alternatively, the data can be bought from outside vendors, either in a form that has already been processed or in its original form. Unless the data has been already processed by the vendor, the next step for investment managers is then to process the data. The goal of this processing is to move from unstructured and/or big data to "small" data that can be fed into the existing models. Once that step has been accomplished, it is straightforward to analyse whether model performance improves thanks to the new data. Traditional investors who rely less on quantitative models will find it harder to ascertain whether there is value in the new data source. In determining whether to build or buy, there is an important trade-off. Building will almost certainly result in higher costs. On the other hand, if alpha is found through an in-house analysis, it will be a more significant and longer-lasting source of alpha, as the data will not be replicated as easily by competing investment managers.

One problem with this approach can be that new data sources may not necessarily have a long back history. That means it will take some time until a sufficiently long data series has been acquired to be able to trust the backtests when feeding the new data into the models. This is a very important problem, especially for pure quants who aim to add big-data-generated indicators to their models. In this sense, more fundamentally minded investors may actually have an edge, because they can be more open to implementing models even with data series that are too short for significant backtests as long as the new indicator is in line with solid fundamental principles.

So what indicators should EM investors focus on? We think the focus to acquire and process big data should obviously be where the money is. For EM fixed income, we think the key is to improve CPI estimates. The reason is that local rates are the EM asset class that is mostly driven by local factors, while FX and credit are much more globally driven. As such, the focus has to be on local rates when investigating which local data to focus on. With most central banks targeting (headline) inflation, the obvious number to spend resources on predicting is inflation. Luckily, forecasting inflation numbers with big data is also more promising than using big data for labour market or activity data, for example, because as more retailing activity moves online, web scraping is becoming a better way to understand price behaviours. Of course, the trick is to try to forecast the government inflation print, rather than the true behaviour of inflation. This requires some institutional knowledge about how statistical agencies process the data in the various countries. At Citi, we had some success improving CPI forecasts for Mexico with web-scraped data.[1]

Outside of the CPI space, the most important indicator that would be extremely useful is alternative data regarding Chinese activity. The reason is, of course, that Chinese growth has very significant implications for global macro and therefore also impacts the more globally driven EM asset classes, i.e. EMFX and credit, not just Chinese rates. Given how much the Chinese government seems to smooth at least the GDP statistics, we think that in the case of China, it is more relevant to try to model "the truth" rather than try to forecast the relevant government statistics. To the extent that we are mostly interested in the spillover from Chinese growth to other EM, a focus on trade will be helpful. Promising approaches relate to tracking data of cargo ships using satellite data, for example. Finally, we also note that data to measure sentiment based on polls can also be helpful. While such polls are clearly small data rather than big data, the fact that polls have become more efficient to administer through technology makes them part of the new data landscape.

For investment managers who plan to outsource data acquisition, there is a mushrooming industry catering to big data and its applications. For a list of providers,

---

[1]See also Willer et al. (2019d).

TABLE 11.1   What Investors Want in the Big Data World.

Category	Interest level
Consumer transactions	12%
Geolocation	12%
Business insights	11%
Pricing	11%
Reviews and ratings	7%
Web-crawled data	7%
Data aggregators	6%
App usage and web traffic	6%
Consumer insights	6%
Public sector	4%
Online search	4%
Store locations	3%
Social media	3%
Sentiment	3%
Employment	3%
Advertising	3%
Trade	1%
Open data	1%
Satellite and weather	1%
B2B datasets	1%

Source: Citi, Eagle Alpha.

see Montagu et al. (2017). In this piece, the authors also highlight an interesting chart from Eagle Alpha, an aggregator of AI and big data services, which highlights the level of customer interest. We replicate the information in Table 11.1. The highest interest was in customer transactions and geolocation, while the lowest was in satellite/weather as well as B2B datasets. The table illustrates that equity investors are likely heavier users of big data than fixed income clients, as the top categories are more geared toward equity investing. But pricing data also scores highly, and that is, as we have outlined, very relevant for fixed-income investing. Interestingly, social media and sentiment are not in the top group, even though there must be some promise in measuring and trading sentiment. Employment is also not overly popular: from a fixed income point of view, it is hard to measure on a national level; and from a corporate point of view, it is not as good an indicator for revenues or profits as pricing. Satellite data also does not score highly. We feel that satellite data must be important in getting the all-important trade flows to and from China right. While processing satellite data is very complex, we see big room for improvement here, especially for fixed income.

While the new data sources that are likely to develop are very exciting, exploring and using such data is unlikely to be revolutionary. All that will happen is that combing through big data sources will create new small data sources, which will then be fed into trading models. Early movers will benefit from such new small data sources until they are broadly adopted, after which the alpha will disappear. But as mentioned earlier, if anything this means investment managers should aim to be early movers, as sitting it out will not be feasible.

11.2   MACHINE LEARNING: SUPERVISION IS NEEDED FOR SUPERVISED LEARNING

ML is the other concept that the investment management industry has to incorporate in its business models. Of course, ML as a technique is really not that different from the old regression models. The main difference is that a lot more regressions can be fit very efficiently, including allowing for quadratic and higher moments. This clearly raises the potential for overfitting, which brings with it high risks of a sharp deterioration of performance out of sample. This suggests to us that the best use cases for ML are when researchers have truly big data for the machines to learn from, in order to avoid overfitting. This is very rare in financial markets unless investors care about intraday data. On our time horizon, we mostly care about daily data; and for a collection of daily data to qualify as big data is extremely rare in financial markets. Furthermore, time series data in general are not well suited for ML, given the auto-correlation in the data. It is therefore not too surprising that the big successes of ML are in cross-sectional data (like Netflix video recommendations) rather than in financial markets. And in a cross-sectional context, sovereign fixed income is not an obvious place to apply ML, as there are only a few dozen tradable countries. Equities are a better bet, given the number of equities that are traded is much higher, though even there the data may not qualify as big data. While the Eureka ML index suggests good performance, it is difficult to know what is driving this. Our guess is that the most successful strategies use intraday strategies and are more biased to equities rather than fixed income. The main public ML fund, AIEQ, uses IBM's Watson with the goal of outperforming the SPX, but its performance has so far been relatively weak.

Having said that, one way to use ML is to stick with techniques that allow researchers to observe which features are the main drivers for the relevant outcomes (which most deep neural networks do not allow investors to do). If the features that are observed as significant make fundamental sense to the researchers, they add those features to their existing models. Without a fundamental justification for why something should matter, they will not add that factor. This is again an example where fundamental researchers may have an edge over pure quants who are less interested in using ML this way. This is similar to the idea that a human with a chess computer beats a chess computer: human supervision is necessary for supervised ML. And again, it requires a tremendous amount of data to be available in order for ML to add much to an existing investment process. Eventually, it is of course plausible that the fundamental knowledge of the human expert can be added to the ML code, making human intervention superfluous: i.e. there could be code that tells the machine when to listen to its results and when not to. This is indeed likely to happen, and the only question is how quickly we generate sufficient data to make this a feasible proposition.

Having warned about the dangers of overfitting, we are of course as keen to test out ML models as the next financial market participant. Here we offer some early results of

TABLE 11.2   An AI Horse Race.

Method	IR	Parameters
Mean of trading signals	1.04	ESI for EM, BRL, and EUR, MA signals 4,10, 20 wk
Random forest (RF)	1.24	No. of trees = 10
Logistic regression (LR)	0.54	Default
SVM classifier	0.91	Linear kernel
Gradient boosting (GB)	1.2	Default
K nearest neighbours (KNN)	1.04	Default
Voting classifier	1.26	RF, LR, SVM, GB, and KNN

Source: Bloomberg, authors' calculations.

a horse race of the various ML techniques. We focus on EMFX as an asset class where we have the longest history and where humans may benefit the most from the help of AI, given how difficult it is to generate alpha in FX. To the extent that regime changes happen more often in EM than in DM, researchers must be even more careful about interpreting results in EM than in DM. But then again, it is far from obvious that mushy (human) brains do well with regime switches, either.

We run several popular ML learning/classification algorithms and stick to supervised learning models. We then feed the outcomes of various classifiers into a voting classifier to see if the combination of ML algorithms improves the IR ratio. This approach is similar to the one described in Banga and Brorsen (2019), where the authors demonstrate some success in trading JPY using ML approaches on both a daily and monthly horizon. To be precise, here we aim to predict the weekly performance of the BRL. We take three economic surprise indices and three technical indicators to generate a trading signal from each. Trading signals are either long or short. We run various ML classifiers to predict whether the subsequent week's return is positive or negative. Table 11.2 presents the results.

The table shows that the IRs of RF and GB are higher than a simple equal weighted allocation to the underlying signals. The voting classifier also performs better than a simple equal weighted allocation to the various ML signals. We think that for a fundamental EM manager, using classifiers to combine fundamental driven views/signals with technical/quant signals may work well. This approach has the potential to outperform smart beta strategies. More work is needed; in particular, data logging will be required for some time before ML is able to run on a combination of fundamental signal and systematic signals.

11.3   NO DISAPPEARING ACT FOR EMERGING MARKETS

There is also a more pedestrian topic to address when thinking about the future of emerging market trading. And that is whether one day, all the EM will become DM. In theory, there should be a way for EM to "graduate" to developed market status. After all, the US, for example, was at some stage in its history a developing country. As such, there must be a development path to reach developed market status. More specifically, in a rates context, for example, there is a path to, over time, lower the positive correlation between VIX and EM interest rates, which characterizes true EM. With rising wealth and increasing formalization of the economy, the service sector usually expands, both as a percentage of a country's GDP and as a fraction of the consumption basket for which inflation is calculated. This leads to lower FX inflation pass-through over time, which eventually should also impact the psychology of linking inflation to the exchange rate. The reduction of debt denominated in foreign currencies is also a typical development as EM increase the size of their local financial systems over time, creating a natural demand for local currency-denominated assets. Therefore, we would expect local currency bonds in EM to trade less with the exchange rate (which is the transmission mechanism from risk aversion to rates) and behave more like developed market rates.

Some of this has already happened. In the 1997–1998 Asian financial crisis, not a single country was able to cut interest rates before FX stabilized, despite very deep recessions. This is because inflation shot up due to large currency devaluations (which were exaggerated by several countries coming off FX pegs). Central banks were forced to stand idly by or even hike rates into a recession. A decade later, during the 2008 global financial crisis, most EM were able to cut interest rates before the worst was over in terms of FX depreciation, as can be seen in Figure 11.1. The key reason was that pass-through from FX to inflation seemed to have come down for many EM since the late 1990s. Consequently, investment managers made large profits in the aftermath of the 2008 crisis by betting on lower emerging market rates. *Ex post*, that seems like a very obvious trade. However, it is worthwhile to remember that at the time, it took

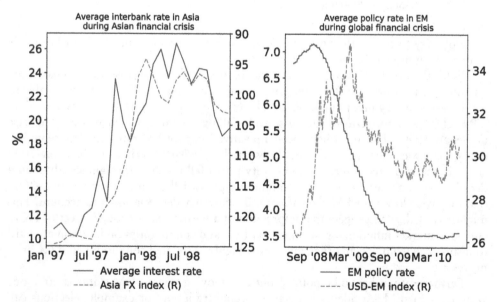

FIGURE 11.1 EM Rates Decouple Earlier from FX Than in the 1990s.
Source: Bloomberg.

TABLE 11.3 Commodity Prices Were Much More Deflationary in 2008 Than in 1998–1999.

| | Energy prices (Bloomberg Energy Index) | |
	1997–1998	2008–2009
MYR	−20%	−73%
KRW	34%	−64%
MYR	3%	−70%
PHP	−4%	−71%
SGD	−11%	−70%
TWD	−6%	−70%
THB	20%	−71%
IDR	193%	−65%

| | Food prices (Bloomberg AG index) | |
	1997–1998	2008–2009
MYR	1%	−43%
KRW	70%	−24%
MYR	31%	−36%
PHP	22%	−38%
SGD	13%	−36%
TWD	19%	−36%
THB	52%	−39%
IDR	272%	−27%

Source: Bloomberg, EIA, FAO.

some bravery to bet on the unknown, given that EM central banks had not been able to implement monetary stimulus early in the previous crisis.

From the point of view of policy makers, the 2008–2009 episode is a heartening outcome, as it shows that EM have come a long way since the 1990s and were able to use a G3-like policy mix to fight potential recessions. But there are some caveats. First, 2008–2009 was an environment of sharply falling US rates, which was not the case in the late 1990s. This must have been a positive force for EM rates. But, more importantly, there was one major difference between the 1997–1998 crisis and the 2008–2009 crisis: in the more recent crisis, commodity prices fell much more significantly than a decade earlier, as per Table 11.3. Commodity prices fell so drastically in 2008–2009 that they were lower for EM even after taking currency depreciation into account. This might have led to an exaggerated impression of a weaker pass-through effect of FX to emerging market inflation, as the impacts of FX and commodities on inflation are hard to distinguish from one an other, given how highly correlated commodity and FX price moves are.

Furthermore, it has to be pointed out that moving toward DM status is not a one way street for EM. Accidents happen on a country level. For example, elections can have consequences and can throw countries back on their development trajectory. Just because this has rarely happened in the last 10 years does not mean it won't happen

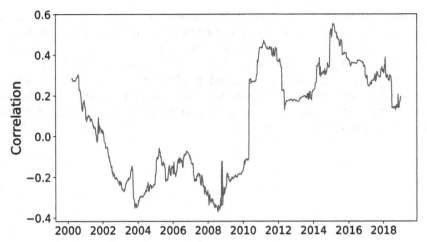

FIGURE 11.2 Progress Toward G10 Status is Not a One-Way Street.
Note: Two-year rolling correlation between Greece 10-year bond yield and VIX.
Source: Bloomberg.

more frequently going forward. The most recent example is Greece, where bonds traded like an almost risk-free G3 asset until the 2008 crisis. Since then, the correlation between rates and risk aversion has steadily risen and was strongly positive in late 2018, as illustrated in Figure 11.2. Chile also comes to mind, as the protests that began in late 2019 may undermine Chile's status as the Switzerland of Latin America for years to come.

More generally, whenever the global business cycle turns down and the world goes into a recession, it usually reverberates to EM and often results in severe setbacks to some countries' development plans. Just as the gods punished Sisyphus by having the boulder he was pushing continually roll back down the hill, global recessions tend to push EM back to the foot of the mountain. Unlike the case of Sisyphus, the task for EM is difficult but not hopeless. The key for EM is to "arrive" at the peak before the global climate turns hostile again. A few countries have made it so far. Many of those that reached developed market status did so with strong institutional support from the developed world, for example, as part of the European Union. Overwhelming institutional support can keep the boulder at the top of the mountain. While we are very optimistic about the long-run development potential for many EM we also believe that we will be left with enough true EM to enjoy trading them for some time to come.

11.4 SUMMARY

We finished the book with a discussion of the future of the asset class. Big data will move more and more from equity markets to fixed income markets, including EM. The arms race has, of course, already started. We advise focusing on CPI estimates for various countries and tracking Chinese activity. Early movers will generate alpha for a time. When it comes to AI, the scarcity of price data for financial instruments that we are trying to forecast, and the resulting high likelihood of overfitting is an important hurdle. However, we find promise in random forest and gradient boosting models for trading EMFX. This area will remain an important part of the research agenda going forward. We also addressed the question of whether we could run out of EM. We doubt that this is likely. Even if some countries succeed in achieving developed market status, new countries will make it from the frontier into the main benchmarks. As such, we look forward to many more decades of happy EM trading, AI enhanced or with a mushy brain at the controls. Thanks for reading!

Basic Concepts

Breakevens: Short for break-even inflation. The market expectation for inflation that can be inferred from the difference between nominal and real rates that are traded in the market. Using those two legs, breakevens are actively traded in many market.

Carry: Return obtained from holding an asset if prices remain constant. In FX space, the carry is the implied yield of the FX forward, minus Libor. In bonds, carry is the yield on offer minus the funding cost. If the bond can be repoed, the funding cost is the repo rate. If it is cash financed and FX hedged, the funding cost is the implied yield in the forward market.

Credit default swap (CDS): A financial derivative or contract that allows investors to *swap* or offset their credit risk with respect to an issuer. The buyer of the swap buys protection and makes payments to the swap's seller until the maturity date of a contract. The sellers of protection agree that they will pay the buyer the security value in case the issuer defaults. CDS spreads are quoted over Libor and can be used to calculate default probabilities under the assumption of risk neutrality.

Duration: An approximate measure of a bond price's sensitivity to changes in interest rates.

DV01: The dollar variation in a bond's value for a change of the yield by 1 bp (1/100 of 1%). A DV01-neutral flattener is a flattener where when the front-end and back-end yields move both lower by 1 bp and the USD P&L of the trade is flat.

ESG: Using environmental, social, and governance factors to evaluate companies and countries regarding how far they have advanced with sustainability.

Flattener: A position that benefits from the interest rate curve getting flatter, either by the front end moving higher in yield (bear flattening) or the back end moving lower (bull flattening). Usually done DV01 neutral, which means that the notional of the position in the front end is much larger than in the back to make sure a 1 bp move in both the front and back ends in the same direction has no P&L impact.

Information ratio (IR): Measurement of how successful a strategy is. The IR return is calculated as the average return of a strategy divided by the standard deviation. Comparing IRs of returns makes it possible to identify which strategy is superior, as often, strategies can be levered up to the same volatility, making it clearer which strategy is the most promising. When funding costs are meaningful, Sharpe ratios are better for the comparison across strategies.

Linkers: Bonds that pay a certain real rate and inflation on top of this rate. Because the inflation that will be paid is not known *ex ante*, linkers can be used to infer inflation expectations from the market. Investors prefer linkers over nominal bonds when they think inflation will be higher than this inferred, break-even rate, and vice versa.

Payers: Positions in the interest rate swap market that benefit if interest rates rise. Payers pay a fixed longer-term interest rate and receive the floating short term interest rate.

Principal components analysis (PCA): A technique used to identify a small number of uncorrelated variables known as principal components from a larger set of data. The factor loadings are the correlation coefficients between the variables and factors.

Real rate: Nominal rates minus inflation, where different inflation measures can be used. Real rates are also traded in some countries directly in the linker markets.

Receivers: Positions in the interest rate swap market that benefit if interest rates fall. Receivers receive a fixed longer-term interest rate and pay the floating short term interest rate. This results in a P&L stream similar to buying a bond and hedging the FX (where the implieds in the FX forward are the equivalent of the floating rate). The IRS is unfunded, though, creating leverage.

Risk parity: An approach to investment portfolio management that focuses on allocation of risk, usually defined as volatility, rather than allocation of capital. One example is to determine sizing such that a one standard deviation move in each asset leads to the same USD loss or gain in the portfolio.

Sharpe ratio: Measurement of how successful a strategy is. The Sharpe ratio adjusts the IR for the risk-free return (Libor) and is calculated as average return minus risk-free rate, divided by the standard deviation of returns.

Steepener: A position that benefits from the interest rate curve getting steeper, either by the front end moving lower in yield (bull-steepening) or the back end moving higher (bear steepening). Usually done DV01 neutral, which means the notional position in the front end is much larger than in the back to make sure a 1 bp move in both the front and back ends in the same direction has no P&L impact.

Term premium: The excess yield that investors require to commit to holding a long-term bond instead of a series of shorter-term bonds, i.e. a risk premium for owning longer-maturity bonds.

Z-score: The number of standard deviations a variable is from its mean. Levels of more than 2.0 typically suggest extended variable readings, as 95% of readings lie between a z-score of -2 and a z-score of 2. However, this assumes a normal distribution, which is often not the true underlying distribution. When a 10 standard deviation event is claimed to have taken place, typically the model is misspecified.

Bibliography

Adrian, T., Crump, R., and Moench, E. (Oct 2013). Pricing the term structure with linear regressions. *Journal of Financial Economics* **110** (1).

Banga, J.S. and Brorsen, B.W. (2019). Profitability of alternative methods of combining the signals from technical trading systems. *Intelligent Systems in Accounting, Finance and Management* **26** (1): 32–45.

Bernanke, B. (2015). The Taylor rule: A benchmark for monetary policy? Brookings.

Borensztein, E. and Panizza, U. (2008). The costs of sovereign default. IMF working paper 238.

Brunnermeier, M., Nagel, S., and Pedersen, L. (2008). Carry trades and currency crashes. *NBER Macroeconomics Annual* **23** (1): 313–348.

Burnside, C., Eichenbaum, M., and Rebelo, S. (May 2007). The returns to currency speculation in emerging markets. *American Economic Review* **97** (2): 333–338.

Carrière-Swallow, Y., Gruss, B., Magud, N., and Valencia, F. (2016). Monetary policy credibility and exchange rate pass-through. IMF working paper 240.

Cashin, P., Céspedes, L.F., and Sahay, R. (2004). Commodity currencies and the real exchange rate. *Journal of Development Economics* **75** (1): 239–268.

Çatık, A., Helmi, M., Ali, F., and Akdeniz, C. (2018). Monetary policy rules in emerging countries: Is there an augmented nonlinear Taylor rule? DIW discussion paper 1588.

Chen, S. and Kang, J.S. (2018). Credit booms – is China different? IMF working paper 1802.

Chua, J. and Kim, J-W. (2019). Asia economic view: Assessing spillovers from the US-China "tariff war" – part 2. Citi Research.

Costa, L. and Vicol, D. (2018). CEEMEA multi-asset strategy focus: Navigating through the capital control universe. Citi Research.

Cruces, J. and Trebesch, C. (2013). Sovereign defaults: The price of haircuts. *American Economic Journal: Macroeconomics* **5** (3).

Coudert, V., Couharde, C., Mignon, V. et al. (2008). Do terms of trade drive real exchange rates? Comparing oil and commodity currencies. Centre d'Etudes Prospectives et d'Informations Internationales (CEPII).

Dalio, R. (2018). *Principles for Navigating Big Debt Crises*. Bridgewater.

de Prado, M.L. (2016). Building diversified portfolios that outperform out of sample. *The Journal of Portfolio Management* **42** (4): 59–69.

Dingman, S. and Gill, E. (2018). In focus: Trading momentum in FX flows revisited. CitiFX Quant Focus.

Domac, I. and Isiklar, G. (Oct 2014). Turkey Marco View. Should we get excited about lower oil prices? Citi Research.

Donnelly, B. (2019). *The Art of Currency Trading: A Professional's Guide to the Foreign Exchange Market*. Wiley.

Egbers, T. and Swinkels, L. (2015). Can implied volatility predict returns on the currency carry trade? *Journal of Banking & Finance* **59**: 14–26.

Eichengreen, B., Hausmann, R., and Panizza, U. (2007). Currency mismatches, debt intolerance, and the original sin: Why they are not the same and why it matters. In: *Capital*

Controls and Capital Flows in Emerging Economies: Policies, Practices, and Consequences (ed. S. Edwards), 121–170. University of Chicago Press.

Frankel, J. and Rose, A. (1996). Currency crashes in emerging markets: An empirical treatment. *Journal of International Economics* **41** (3–4): 351–366.

Fratzscher, M., Gloede, O., Menkhoff, L. et al. (2017). When is foreign exchange intervention effective? Evidence from 33 countries. CEPR discussion paper DP12510.

Gill, E. (2018). In focus: Trading EM assets using EM macro risk. CitiFX Quant Focus.

Gill, E. and Dingman, S. (2019). In focus: FX mean reversion strategies. CitiFX Quant Focus.

Gilmore, S. and Hayashi, F. (October 2011). Emerging market currency excess returns. *American Economic Journal: Macroeconomics* **3** (4): 85–111.

Gunnar, F., Busch, T., and Rassen, A. (2013). ESG and financial performance: Aggregated evidence from more than 2000 studies. *Journal of Sustainable Finance and Investment* **5** (4): 210–233.

Harberger, A. (2004). The real exchange rate: Issues of concept and measurement. Paper prepared for a conference in honor of Michael Mussa.

Heath, A., Galati, G., and McGuire, P. (2007). Evidence of carry trade activity. *BIS Quarterly Review*.

Kahnemann, D. (2011). *Thinking Fast and Slow*. Farrar, Straus, and Giroux.

Kasikov, K. (2018). In focus: Economic surprises and data change index cross-sectional ranking strategies. CitiFX Quant Focus.

Kiguel, A. and Willer, D. (2018). Is there enough term premia in EM rates? Citi Research.

Kiguel, A. and Willer, D. (2019). Quantitative EM strategy focus: How to use EM term premia. Citi Research.

Lam, K. and Willer, D. (2017). Latam emerging markets strategy weekly: Disinflation is here to stay in Latam. Citi Research.

Lam, K. and Willer, D. (2018). EM multi strategy focus. How to cross over in EM. Citi Research.

Liao, T., Yuen, A., Layton, M. et al. (2019). China commodities focus. Citi Research.

Lubin, D. (2018). Dance of the trillions: Developing countries and global finance. Brookings.

Lubin, D., Willer, D., Chua, J. et al. (2019). Emerging markets economic outlook and strategy: The "new" China and its consequences. Citi Research.

McCauley, R. and Scatigna, M. (2011). Foreign exchange trading in emerging currencies: More financial, more offshore. *BIS Quarterly Review* (March).

Menkhoff, L., Sarno, L., Schmeling, M., and Schrimpf, A. (2012). Carry trades and global foreign exchange volatility. *The Journal of Finance* **67** (2): 681–718.

Mohanty, M.S. (2013). Market volatility and foreign exchange intervention in EMES: What has changed? *BIS Papers* 73.

Moldaschl, M., Hale, J., Bishop, G., and Amin, A. (2017). Global macro strategy focus: Commodities and portfolio diversification – now the time is ripe. Citi Research.

Montagu, C., Krause, H., Murray, J. et al. (2017). Searching for alpha: Big data. Citi Research.

Moreira, A. and Muir, T. (2017). Volatility-managed portfolios. *The Journal of Finance* **72** (4): 1611–1644.

Mulder, A. and Tims, B. (2018). Conditioning carry trades: Less risk, more return. *Journal of International Money and Finance* **85**: 1–19.

Netto, V. (2019). *The Mechanism*. Penguin Books.

Noual, P. (2015). In focus: Trading FX with signals from economic surprise and data change indices. CitiFX Quant Focus.

Nozaki, M. (2010). Do currency fundamentals matter for currency speculators? International Monetary Fund.

Orsagh, M., Allen, J., Sloggett, J. et al. (2018). Guidance and case studies for ESG integration: Equities and fixed income. CFA Institute.

Panizza, U., Sturzenegger, F., and Zettelmeyer, J. (2009). Sovereign and debt and default. *Journal of Economic Literature XLVII.*

Revilla, E., Willer, D., Bladinieres, J. et al. (2019). Latin America economic outlook and strategy: Collateral damage: The impact of the trade war in Latam. Citi Research.

Rink, R., Miller, A., Whitten, Z., and McKinnon, E. (2019). The rise of AI in ESG evaluation – exploring AI-led ESG vendors. Citi Research.

Sachs, J.D. and Warner, A.M. (1995). Natural resource abundance and economic growth. Technical report. National Bureau of Economic Research.

Schatzker, E. and Burton, K. (2018). Stan Druckenmiller says algos are robbing markets of trade signals. Bloomberg.

Serban, A.F. (2010). Combining mean reversion and momentum trading strategies in foreign exchange markets. *Journal of Banking & Finance* **34** (11): 2720–2727.

Stephens, T. (2016). In focus: CTOT momentum strategy looking Sharpe. CitiFX Quant Focus.

Sun, L. and Mathur, S. (2017). China FX & rates focus: China bond market map – what drives system liquidity? Citi Research.

Sun, L., Garg, G., and Peng, J. (2019). China multi-asset view: Panda hugs global indices – when, how and implications from China's bond and equity market inclusions. Citi Research.

Swift. (2019). Beyond borders: China opens up to the world. Report.

Willer, D. (2019). Emerging markets credit strategy focus: How to trade credit ratings changes. Citi Research.

Willer, D. and Dabholkar, S. (2019a). How to trade relative value in EMFX. Citi Research.

Willer, D. and Dabholkar, S. (2019b). Quantitative EM strategy focus: EM funds are long – should we care? Citi Research.

Willer, D. and Guarino, D. (2018). Emerging markets credit strategy focus: How to trade IMF programs and the case of Argentina. Citi Research.

Willer, D. and Guarino, D. (2019). Emerging market credit focus: 50 cents and Argentina. Citi Research.

Willer, D., Costa, L., and Garg, G. (2018). EM strategy weekly: Just positioning. Citi Research.

Willer, D., Costa, L., Guarino, D., and Mittra, A. (2019a). Emerging markets credit strategy focus: EM credit according to Ray Dalio. Citi Research.

Willer, D., Guarino, D., and Mittra, A. (2019b). Quantitative EM strategy focus: How to beat the benchmark. Citi Research.

Willer, D., Lam, K., Costa, L., et al. (2020). Global EM bond portfolio strategy: EM rates as risky assets. Citi Research.

Willer, D., Lam, K., and Kiguel, A. (2019c). Re-inventing ESG for emerging markets. Citi Research.

Willer, D., Revilla, E., Lam, K., and Dabholkar, S. (2019d). Quantitative EM strategy focus: Predicting the Mexican CPI using web-scraped data. Citi Research.